Notes & Apologies

Subscriptions to *The Believer* are $48 for a year—that's five perfect-bound issues, including one themed double issue. Each edition of the magazine features essays, reviews, journalism, many two-toned illustrations, writers talking to other writers, filmmakers talking to musicians, and, as was recently the case, the occasional musician talking to themselves. Subscribe online at believermag.com.

Submissions to the 2021 Believer Book Awards are now closed. Submissions to the 2022 Book Awards will open again in the spring. The awards—which are given in the categories of fiction, nonfiction, poetry, and graphic narrative—honor the best and most underappreciated books of the year. The 2021 longlists will be announced in January 2022 on the Logger, and the winners will be announced in March 2022. On a mostly unrelated note, the writing of this post constitutes the first time we have written out the year 2022. It has a nice look to it, we think, with all those twos.

This issue features a series of microessays by Jude Stewart on pages 30, 34, 38, 45, 49, and 112. Each microessay explores the history of a particular smell. Stewart says the following about why she became interested in smell:

> I began writing about smell for several reasons. For one thing, it's largely unmediated by technology—you can't smell anything on the internet or your phone. For another, most great smells don't cost anything: they're as freely available as air. Above all, I like how smells are invisible but undeniably real. I also like how a too-avid interest in smell seems awkward. "Follow the awkwardness" is something of a mantra for me as a writer. I was already working on a book about smell when the pandemic hit. Millions of COVID-19 survivors worldwide became newly aware of how important smell is to their quality of life. Suddenly my private interest in smell was no longer private at all. And yet now I wonder: How quickly will we all forget again?
>
> In choosing which smells to write about, I thought of Proust's famous tea-soaked madeleine, in whose smell and taste he found his entire childhood folded like an impossibly detailed origami. Similarly, I wanted to discover how many stories one smell could contain; the smells I chose were the ones that unspooled the most surprising and layered stories.
>
> Learning to become a better smeller has made me more mindful than any traditional meditation ever has. Smelling returns you to your body; it pins you to the here and now. Sniffing alongside other people gives you a surprisingly intimate shared moment. I wanted to feel less expert, more vulnerable, and more alive—and smell has given me all of those things.

Illustration by Samar Haddad

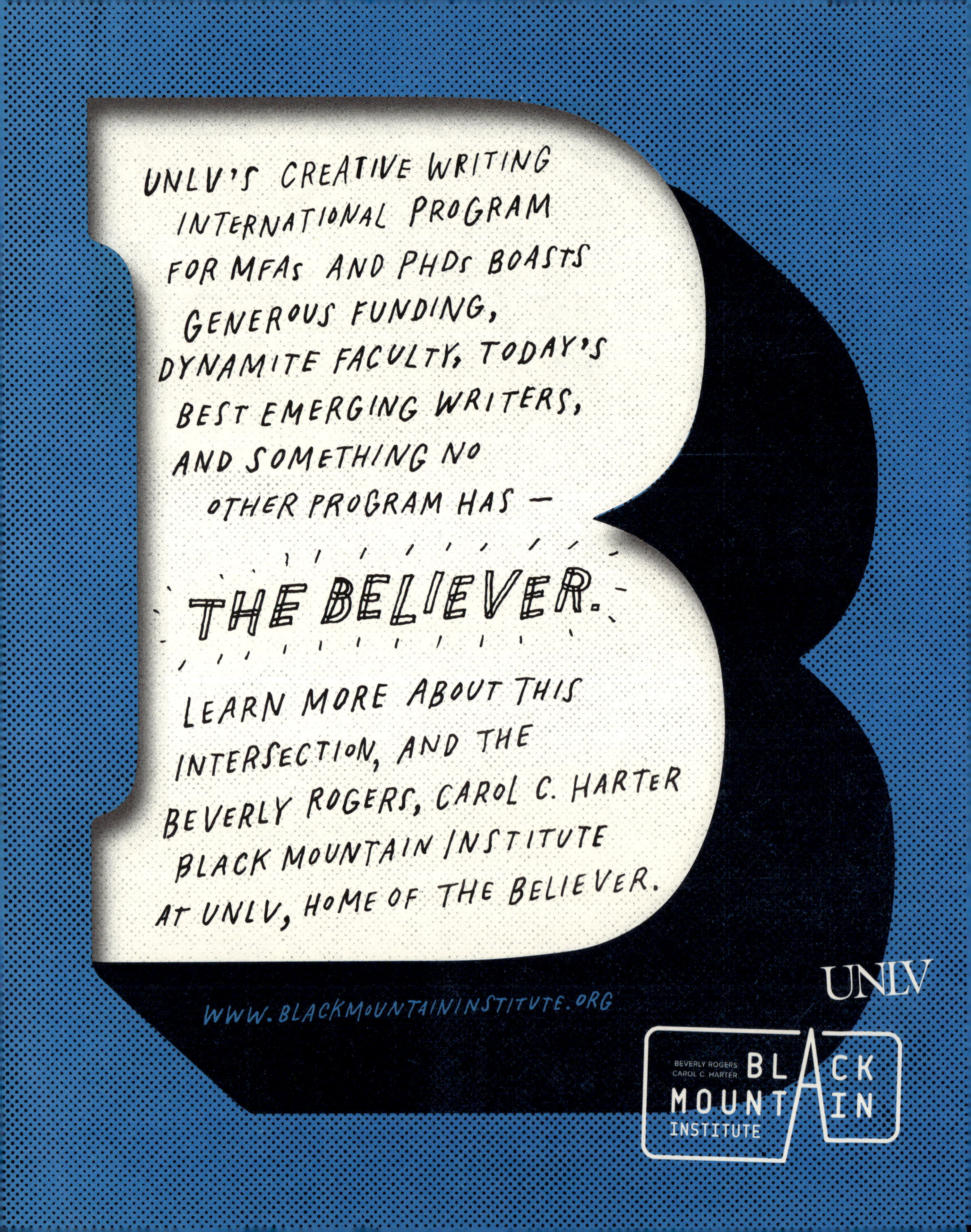
UNLV'S CREATIVE WRITING INTERNATIONAL PROGRAM FOR MFAS AND PHDS BOASTS GENEROUS FUNDING, DYNAMITE FACULTY, TODAY'S BEST EMERGING WRITERS, AND SOMETHING NO OTHER PROGRAM HAS —
THE BELIEVER.
LEARN MORE ABOUT THIS INTERSECTION, AND THE BEVERLY ROGERS, CAROL C. HARTER BLACK MOUNTAIN INSTITUTE AT UNLV, HOME OF THE BELIEVER.
WWW.BLACKMOUNTAININSTITUTE.ORG
UNLV
BEVERLY ROGERS CAROL C. HARTER BLACK MOUNTAIN INSTITUTE

FEATURED ARTIST: JON AYE

INSIDE THIS ISSUE'S INCIDENTAL ILLUSTRATION SERIES: PRACTICE

"Michel de Certeau's *The Practice of Everyday Life* is a book that has inspired my thinking for a long time, and I returned to it for this series. Specifically, I'm interested in his analysis of the various ways we are able to reclaim a sense of autonomy and individuality within a landscape shaped by commerce, politics, and culture. In addition to drawing some common examples of practice—basketball, skateboarding—I drew activities we might not immediately consider, but which also require practice—thinking, navigating, walking in the city. The series aims to capture individuals engaged in small, private pursuits that can become significant as expressions of individuality."

Conversations with Contributors

*This issue's question:
If you could give your younger self advice about embarking on a writing career, what would you say?*

Anelise Chen

YESTERDAY, I CALLED Connecticut's "weeds specialist" to get a briefing on the state's latest counter-bindweed tactics. What intel did he have that I hadn't already gleaned from the internet? Bindweed smothers everything in the garden, crawls all over the vegetables and flowers and consumes them in dense, twisting tendrils. Was it true about dish soap? Epsom salt? Bindweed mites? Marigold beds? It sounded like he was absentmindedly clicking through a PDF in the background. Sensing his waning attention, I said we were prepared to get extreme about it. As in, we were prepared to spray Roundup, then torch, then mulch, then pour scalding water all over the beds if he thought that would work. Surely, he must know of a more efficient method than crouching in the dirt for hours, digging and sifting through bundles of fat spaghetti roots.

"You can try everything, but I'm afraid you will be disappointed no matter what you try," he said. "Try to live with it."

There is no fast answer, no shortcut technology that will make writing any easier. I wish I had known this before I started writing. Writing takes time and sweat, makes your muscles taut and sore, and its rewards have little to do with results. Most of the time, the results are so far in the future, you can't really see them, like when Henry Kissinger asked Zhou Enlai about the impacts of the French Revolution. It's always too early to tell.

I think one way to train myself out of my instant-gratification frame of mind would be to plant a tree somewhere in my vicinity. I believe that is the proper time frame for art-making. In Ross Gay's *Book of Delights*, there's an essayette in which he's planting hickory trees with a friend in their community garden. "How long until the hickories start making their fruit?" Gay asks. "Oh, they'll be in full production in about 200 to 250 years," his friend responds.

I like to remind myself that besides having patience, nothing I try will ever get to perfection. Adopting a different attitude might allow me to better savor the pleasures of the present.

During the height of the pandemic, my dad texted to update us on his lawn mower situation. He couldn't get a blade replacement, but he wasn't peeved. I saved this screenshot from him:

> It won't cut very perfect with such a long weed condition, but I don't care. It is perfect for me and my Fuzzy philosophy.
> And I sweat a lot when pushing it.

Kameelah Janan Rasheed

I GREW UP in East Palo Alto, California. When I was in elementary school, we had a publishing center. This publishing center was a trailer, where an older woman with a typewriter, an assortment of paper, and a comb binding machine enthusiastically awaited students, who would come there to make books. By age seven, I'd published at least half a dozen, five of which my mother managed to save. They ranged from a

Illustrations throughout by Kristen Radtke

science-fiction story about a planet that steals resources from another planet, to a revenge tale that ends in a utopic sharing of resources, to a pop-up book describing what was then my favorite dinosaur, the Ankylosaurus. I also published a poem in our school anthology about an anthropomorphized waterfall. Young Kameelah had range! The advice I would give myself is not to abandon the spirit of younger Kameelah. She wrote with curiosity and confidence. Write about whatever you want. Experiment with content and form. As I navigate back to a more writerly life, I am excited to finish a poem on animal countersurveillance and a short story about a cult that spreads through one sheet of magenta paper. I am eager to approach writing with the energetic curiosity of second-grade Kameelah.

Stephen Kearse

WHEN I WAS younger, I had a blog. WordPress. I'd update it on a whim, cranking out a post in response to current cultural debates or fixations. I launched my blog during the early SEO era, a time when rosy terms like *the commons* and *public square* were in vogue. Writers and publishers hadn't yet gotten wise to the grift of search engines, so everyone was convinced that boosting web traffic would save the world and the industry. In practice, this meant that every thought—no matter how undeveloped or unsolicited or, frankly, wrong—was legit as long as it drew a sizable audience. No one would say this outright, of course, but the gold rush was on.

I was a wee prospector with no particular goals, so I wrote about everything: my summer job at a Brooklyn bakery, NPR interns liking Drake more than Public Enemy, X-Men comics. This churn was great for habituating myself to regular writing and reading, but it did nothing to make me a better writer. Though I received some feedback in the form of comments and traffic stats, I lacked direction and self-awareness. I never rewrote and I certainly never thought, Maybe I shouldn't publish this. I thought I was independent; actually, I was rudderless.

Capable editors showed me the light. I dealt mostly with yes-men early in my career, so if they thought I was a great writer, they left my writing alone. I thought that indifference was a compliment until I met editors whose comments emphasized the reader rather than me: "Whom is this for?" "You should unpack this more." "Weird word choice here." "Let's streamline this." Until I encountered actual editing, I had never thought about my readers. My writing was structurally sound but rarely inviting, welcoming, conversational. Put differently, my audience was me.

I deleted my blog a few years ago. I'd never done the legwork to grow its readership, plus I'd grown tired of knee-jerk writing. I still write for myself, and I always will, but I now know that I write for you too. ✶

A few words with our cover artist

Jesse Zhang

Who: I'm an artist born, raised, and still stubbornly rooted in Brooklyn, New York. I always feel awkward talking about myself, which I suppose is telling you something about myself.

What: The cover illustration is a personal piece about mindscapes. I'm constantly off in my own universe, which tends to be a double-edged sword. I find my imagination safe but also suffocating.

When: I tend to draw from early evening late into the night. I like that I don't have to respond to anyone, since it's considered "off-hours" for most people. It allows me to focus solely on drawing.

Why: I've been thinking a lot about isolation. There's a comfort in engulfing myself in ideas and creative work, but at the same time, it's lonely. I'm finding the way in which I navigate my mind to be more important than what's in it. ✶

The Field

TIMELY AND TARDY
DISPATCHES FROM
THE CULTURE

Everything under the sun

The exhibition began, like the fall of mankind did, with an apple. Or rather, it began with a glut of photographs of apples: red apples, green apples, yellow apples, sliced apples, bushels of apples, an apple with the word "Google" carved into it. These images were pinned to a wall and clustered around a label featuring a single, simple noun: "apple."

This was *From 'Apple' to 'Anomaly,'* on display at the Barbican Centre in London in 2020. For the project, the American artist Trevor Paglen culled around thirty thousand images from the online database ImageNet, printed out small-scale versions, and pinned them to a lengthy curved wall, categorized by noun: "soil," "valley," "syringe," "pizza," "mascot." The result was breathtakingly expansive: seen from a distance of a few feet, it resembled a shimmering mirage of animals, plants, minerals, and people.

The near-infinite visual library was possible because ImageNet is one of the largest publicly available libraries of images. It is also the pioneering dataset for much of the world's image-recognition technology. Everything from Facebook's self-tagging feature to self-driving cars to drones is trained to see the world using massive datasets like ImageNet. It was amassed over the course of nearly a decade, largely by workers who, for pennies, matched images to associated words on the task website Amazon Mechanical Turk. The result was a dataset of more than fourteen million images, cataloged and labeled so machines could learn to match an image of a rose to the word "rose." Paglen made visible this wild, freewheeling taxonomy of everything under the sun, including the sun itself.

In 1668, an English clergyman and natural philosopher named John Wilkins unveiled a similarly vast project: he renamed the world. In his masterwork, "An Essay towards a Real Character, and a Philosophical Language," which ran to almost seven hundred pages, Wilkins laid out a template for a universal language, one that would be so perfect in its powers of expression that it would bring humans closer to God and "not signifie *words*, but *things* and *notions*."

Wilkins was writing against the backdrop of the English Civil War and the loss of Latin as a common Christian language. He was also grappling with an enduring human problem—the gap between words and their meanings. In an essay about Wilkins and his language, Jorge Luis Borges wrote, "Apart from the composed words and the derivations, all the languages in the world… are equally inexpressive." Words bear no inherent relation, after all, to the things they name. Or, as the poet Robert Hass later wrote, "All the new thinking is about loss / In this it resembles all the old thinking" in its insistence on the notion that "because there is in this world no one thing / to which the bramble of *blackberry* corresponds, / a word is elegy to what it signifies."

Wilkins's solution to this problem seemed fairly straightforward. First, he would separate the world into forty categories, or genuses. Then he would subdivide these categories into "differences," and from there, divide everything further into "species." Each genus, difference, and species would be assigned a monosyllable, which would then be strung together to form new, more perfect words. A curious young reader could then sound out not only a word, but also something of its meaning.

So it fell to Wilkins to break the world into its component parts. In the late seventeenth century, systems of taxonomy and classification were flourishing in the natural sciences,

Illustrations throughout by Kristen Radtke

particularly at the Royal Society, of which Wilkins was a founding member. There was still not much established order of things. When it came to animals, for instance, most early ecologists used the divisions provided by Genesis—water, air, and land. Warm-blooded and cold-blooded animals were often separated. Beyond that, animals could be arranged by size, rarity, symbolic meaning, or simple alphabetical order. (Neither did everyone agree about which animals needed to be classified: early encyclopedias were still divided over whether griffins and centaurs were found in nature; Wilkins thought not.)

Wilkins's forty genuses of things and notions range from "Transcendental" to "Elements" to "Space." Underneath these umbrella categories is a set of "differences" and "species" that get increasingly specific, and which he charts in the next part of the essay. Under animals, we come to the section "Of fish," in which Wilkins divides fish into the categories "viviparous" and "oviparous." Then he denotes "viviparous oblong fish," which are subdivided further by characteristics like "rows of very sharp teeth" (sharke, glaucus) and "thorns on their backs" (thornback dog, hog-fish). There are also viviparous cartilaginous fish, oviparous fish whose back fins are soft and flexible, oviparous fish having two fins on the back, oviparous fish having one fin on the back, oviparous fish of an oblong figure, fishes of a hard crustaceous skin, squamous river fishes, and so on. Wilkins's named world unspools, paradoxically, toward organization and classification.

Taxonomy is essential to image-recognition technology; machines must break the world into human concepts and categories in order to perform any kind of "recognition." Algorithms must be taught quite literally to tell apples from oranges (and green apples from red apples, and mandarins from tangerines). But this requires answering a deceptively simple question: What makes an apple an apple?

In *From 'Apple to 'Anomaly'*, Paglen acknowledged this predicament with a wink to the French surrealist René Magritte. Near the entrance to the exhibition, Paglen included a reproduction of Magritte's *Ceci n'est pas une pomme*, a painting of an apple beneath the phrase "This is not an apple." Magritte was toying with the distinction between an object and its representation, the distance between a painted apple and an edible Granny Smith. In Paglen's updated version, Magritte's painting was overlaid with an algorithmic tag that identified it: "red and green apple." The machine had declared, with no ambiguity, that "ceci est une pomme," after all.

Philosophical questions about representation and reality get flattened by algorithms. The ambition of ImageNet is to make all things knowable by splitting them into groups. This leads to some absurdity, which Paglen illustrates. From "apple," we move to "apple tree" and "apple orchard," which are simple enough. Then there are "valley" and "soil," the general realm of the pastoral. And then there is "laborer." Here we see men at work, bent over in rice paddies and irrigated fields. Notably, almost all are Black or brown. Soon, traveling along the curved gallery wall, we arrive at "investor," a group composed almost entirely of white men in suits and ties, pointing at whiteboards or hunched over laptops. We begin, perhaps, to see the cracks in the foundation of this labeled visual universe. We recognize stereotypes about race, class, and gender, as spat back to us by machines.

As we continued through the gallery, the nouns Paglen had selected trended increasingly toward the abstract, and the labeling became increasingly chaotic. The word "segregator" was attached to images of both Barack Obama and George W. Bush. Photos associated with "wine drinker" and "alcoholic" bled together on the wall but were subtly different: a man sniffing wine was a wine drinker, while a woman with a large margarita with a salted rim was an alcoholic. Paglen visualized the consequences of a taxonomy based on collective human biases, which are then replicated exponentially by machines. He also showed how difficult it is for machines to make sense of any kind of abstraction, and for us to try to teach them what a "segregator" would look like. We begin to wonder: Is it possible to label the universe like this, after all? And even if it were possible, would we want that?

In one of the most poignant parts of his essay, amid his classification of animals, Wilkins briefly digresses. "He that looks upon the Starrs, as they are confusedly scattered up and down in the Firmament, will think them to be (as they are sometimes stiled) innumerable, of so vast a multitude, as not to be determined to any set number:

but when all these Starrs are distinctly reduced into particular constellations, and described by their several places, magnitudes and names, it appears, that of those that are visible to the naked eye, there are but few more then [sic] a thousand in the whole Firmament." The same is true, he argues, of many other things, including animals; there are fewer than we might imagine, and it is possible to number and name them all.

Wilkins then sets out to rebuff the doubters—specifically, the atheists who have argued that all the world's animals could not possibly have fit into Noah's ark, given the dimensions described in Genesis (three hundred cubits in length, fifty in breadth, and thirty in height). In the ensuing passage "A Digression Concerning Noah's Ark," Wilkins aims to prove the Bible right. In a table and a diagram, he denotes the number of each kind of animal on the ark, their proportions, the size of their stall, and their food requirements (hay for the herbivores; sheep for the carnivores). In a series of calculations—including a careful consideration of shipbuilding practices—he determines that there would have been ample space. "In this enumeration I do not mention the Mule, because 'tis a mungrel production, and not to be rekoned as a distinct species," he writes. "As for the *Morse, Seale, Turtle,* or *Sea-Tortoise, Crocodile, Senembi,* [sic] These are usually described to be such kind of *Animals* as can abide in the water, and therefore I have not taken them into the Ark, tho if that were necessary, there would be room enough for them." Rodents would not be assigned specific stalls, but there would certainly be space for them underfoot. Thus, the ark was literally possible, the atheists were wrong, and the Bible was true.

It becomes clear, reading this section, that Wilkins has verged into a mode of rationalism so extreme as to become absurd. It may be technically possible to squeeze the animal kingdom into an ark of specific proportions. But, paradoxically, it feels as if this mathematical endeavor takes us away from the bright candle of belief, religious or otherwise, that animates the mysteries of the universe. In insisting that it is possible to count and name the stars, Wilkins has achieved a certain proximity to them, but he is in another sense farther than ever from truly perceiving them as stars—infinite, boundless, and beyond our reach.

There is quite a bit of beauty in *From 'Apple' to 'Anomaly'.* The side-by-side repetition of photos of fried eggs and sunsets has surprising visual resonance. Even the glitches can be serendipitous, as when a cheetah is mistakenly classified as a "honeycomb." The project of ImageNet is awe-inspiring in its dimensions; after all, we are in the presence of a contemporary attempt to make a catalog of the physical world, the vast and expansive fields of human and non-human experience. But Paglen shows us how this attempt devolves, and we see not just the troubling and darker aspects of bias in machine learning, but also a more foundational absurdity—the idea that we can break the universe down into clearly defined categories in the first place.

Wilkins's project represents an earlier failure, a more individual one, to get closer to God through classification. And yet it is also breathtaking to leaf through his tables and lists. Wilkins's wrongheadedness is beautiful because it so clearly illustrates something fundamentally human: the quest to make everything knowable and legible, and to give it a name.

"Obviously there is no classification of the universe that isn't arbitrary and subjective; the reason is simple: we do not know what the universe is," Borges writes. We do know, however, watching Wilkins flail, something about the nature of being a person who perceives the universe—how badly we want to know what is, and to decode what Borges calls "God's secret dictionary." Reading Wilkins, we can also recognize how much he did with the language he already had at his command. He conjures for us not only a fish, but a viviparous oblong fish with rows of very sharp teeth (sharke).

One of God's first instructions to Adam in Genesis was to name the animals. One of the first things we learn to do is name things. As we come out of the disorientation of babyhood and into the clearer fog of toddlerhood, we learn to say: "This is a flower"; "This is a dog"; "This is a tall girl." The act of putting language to our experience of the world we encounter, thereby dividing it into parts and categories, becomes our basis for understanding it. Looking out the window at blooming white flowers on a tree on my street, my first though is: Are those dogwoods or magnolias? I ask because I am moved, on a cold spring day in the northeastern corner of the United States, by these blossoming flowers. I sense that I would be somehow closer to them if I knew their names.

And yet. This desire to know and name can quickly become perverse, an act that has to do less with love and more with a kind of conquest. This is especially true in an age when I can easily download an app that will label and tag these flowers with their Latin names. (One such app, Pl@ntNet, was partly trained using ImageNet.) I could demystify the world beyond Wilkins's wildest dreams, and I would get no closer to God or to anything sacred. What I have learned from Wilkins, inadvertently, is to stand still and marvel at a universe that is impossible to contain within categories, and that is ultimately numberless and nameless.

—*Sophie Haigney*

Forget-me-nots

There's a phrase from a Borges poem that I can't get out of my head. It's short, just four spare words, less than a line, scavenged from its original place in the poem and repurposed as the title of a now-famous Colombian memoir: *El olvido que seremos*. I remember the words not for themselves but because my father and I once had an impassioned disagreement about their potential translation, and by extension their meaning. I thought the English version had to be something like "the forgetting we become": the inevitability that our lives and everything we create inside them—all we deposit into the world, the love we dish out and accept back and plead for hopelessly—will be forgotten by anyone who might've once been around to remember us. Memory is a frail casing; one day, finally, we'll be gone. But my father had a different opinion. He believed the phrase could be translated like this: "We become what we forget." El olvido que seremos: how the many things that jump the ship of our memory come to haunt and define us, long after (either by choice or by neglect) we've forgotten them.

I wish I could ask Francisco Goldman—or his doppelgänger protagonist, Francisco Goldberg—about the Borges phrase. I'm sure both men, in whatever real or imagined world, would have some scrupulous, incandescent thing to say about its meaning. Both have read Borges and likely know about his many idiosyncrasies, his fear of mirrors, his blindness, his claim that languages aren't essentially synonymous, his avowal that he was constantly in love. Both, I suspect, would understand all the vast and unconquerable distances at play: between one language and another, between any two distinct readings of the world, between any one father and his son.

Goldman's *Monkey Boy*—his fifth novel, alongside a book of investigative journalism and a chronicle of Mexico City—is a book something like that Borges phrase: closely examined, it might come to mean the very opposite of what you first believed it to mean, until its true meaning, untranslatable, seems composed of the very act of self-diversion, an accumulation of disparate and irreconcilable meanings. First it is a story about an older man visiting home. Then it's a love story. Then it's a story about war. Then it's a story about familial violence. Before, during, and after, in the novel's many wanderings and creases, it's a story about all we cannot know about one another and our own selves in the past, and the lengths we go to pursue inaccessible truths.

Francisco Goldberg is born in suburban Boston to a Guatemalan mother and a Russian Jewish father. Like Goldman did, he spends part of his early childhood in Guatemala, then moves back to the US after being diagnosed at three with tuberculosis. Home again, he is the object of many corresponding cruelties: his father's abuse, rampant bullying at school and racialized taunting (from which the book gets its title), the confoundments of early love. Later he will become a novelist and a journalist, as Goldman himself did, covering the Central American wars in the 1980s, living far away from his family as a seminomad, more or less incapable of maintaining long-term love. When he's made aware of a threat to his life as a consequence of his politically incisive journalism, he is forced back home, from Mexico City to New York City, and then to New England on a weekend trip to visit his mamita and a cast of other women from his past.

The entire book takes place over the five days of that trip, beginning on the Amtrak train from New York to Boston, and is divided into sections labeled: "Thursday," "Friday," "Saturday," and "Sunday." But it is also true to say that the novel spans decades and generations—from the stories of his parents' respective childhoods, to vivid recollections of his own childhood and early adult life, to his failed romances of years past, to his current obsessive love interest, Lulú López. Francisco's heart is moored to Lulú, but we meet her only through a series of ambiguous text messages, or else in the past tense. "Nothing happens only when it happens," writes the poet Ross Gay. In *Monkey Boy*, nothing is happening when it happens: the action-ridden scenes of the book—the teenage first kiss, the sex, the near-death childhood beatings, the war times and funerals—are never depicted but instead are recalled from the safe distance of years away. This form allows us to encounter a mind in the throes of retrospection, but it comes at the cost of some narrative heat, the feeling of really living inside scenes as they take place. I believe it is an inevitable and ultimately worthwhile trade-off, though—proximity and distance having their respective, interminable capacities and blind spots (like two drawings of the same jacaranda tree, one sketched from one hundred feet away, the other while looking up from the shade under its branches, neither more necessarily true or beautiful, and each the evidence of the other's limitations). Inside Goldman's enveloping language, we move frenetically between the present and the past, with the mimicked arbitrariness of memory. By the end of the book, the day-section demarcations feel almost like a joke.

"Five days a week and sometimes on Saturdays, too, my father used to get up at 5:45 a.m. to go to work at the Potashnik Tooth Corporation." This is the beginning of *Monkey Boy*, the very first line. It reminds me, instantly and almost uncannily, of the beautiful Robert Hayden poem "Those Winter Sundays": "Sundays too my father got up early / and put his clothes on in the blueblack cold." The similarity of the subject, plus that identical hanging "too"—the lines feel like cousins. Whether or not the allusion is intended, perhaps the poem and the sentence can be read together as a prophecy of the book's journeying and deepest aims. Over the course of the long weekend, Francisco visits his mother, two of his childhood nannies, his high school unrequited love, and is headed to see his sister as the novel ends. But all the while he is searching most desperately for his late father, the man whose oil-and-water mix of love and violence has colored his life in bruise-tones. Goldman's prose—its dexterity, its twin grace and force—is put to full use in his writing about a son struggling to recollect his father, to both remember him and make him a coherent figure in his mind, all the while perpetually stuck in his orbit—ever propelled by him, unable to get a good, stilled look. I hear one of the last lines of that Hayden poem in Goldman's book, too, repeating like a breath or a pulse: "What did I know, what did I know..."

I must confess I find it hard to critique a Francisco Goldman novel, since his work means so much to me; a few years ago, reading *Say Her Name* made me want to become a writer. It was the novel that showed how deep thinking can be a means of traveling toward our pain, and not—as it so often is—a form of protection from it. But I do believe rigorous love invites, even requires, critique. It's in that spirit that I've been thinking about Francisco's various love interests in the book. Each is decidedly singular, brought to us in high pixelation—and some of the most stunning lines arise from Francisco's elaborate thinking about his romantic sagas of the past and present. But I'm not sure if these women ever stop being artfully crafted instruments and become characters, if they ever stand on their own outside their utility to the plot or as mirrors or windows through which the protagonist gets to look. Perhaps we are crammed so tightly inside our protagonist's mind that it is the work of the novel to encounter the world not only through his various insights but also through his delusions. I wonder if his romantic partners could have been given more room to breathe in the story, and where that might have led the book's questions.

In one remembered scene, Francisco visits the corpse of a torture victim in a Guatemalan morgue, then immediately afterward goes out for quiche with his colleague. It sets him wondering how those two experiences could possibly "fit coherently together inside the same hour—or even inside the same life?" It is a question that returns to us again and again across the pages of *Monkey Boy*. How can a father wage both love and brutality against his children? How does a childhood full of bullying and shame fit together with an entirely distinct adult life of writing, traveling, romance, and spurts of measured loneliness? Goldman has given us a protagonist made in his image—Goldberg—half-white and half-Guatemalan, half-Jewish and half-Catholic, as incoherent as our families and our nations. Goldberg can't turn his mind off or look away from the stitching artificially holding disparate things together. The result is the kind of thoroughly contemplated, self-aware beauty in ideas that thrums a novel into life.

I don't know what either Francisco would say about that Borges quote, if they would decide it was I or my father who had a better translation. After recounting a childhood memory in Guatemala of passing a toy truck through the bars of a window to strangers on the other side, another boy and his mother, Francisco wonders if memory is "like the broken-off half of a mysterious amulet that can only be made whole if that now-grown little boy remembers it, too, and we can somehow meet and put our pieces together." This is one example of the kind of high-wattage thinking found again and again in Goldman's work, often accompanied by some line or reference to a piece of literature; it's an idea weighty and textured enough to hold in our hands. Memory is piecemeal, and complete memory is irretrievable. Maybe forgetting, like memory, the Franciscos would tell me, is just as necessary and incomplete. We both remember and forget to go on living. Goldman is a master writer—of personal and national myths, adorned like colonial-era costumes or false teeth. In *Monkey Boy*, he leaves nothing at bay, attending to the most important questions facing our nation and the most gentle questions turning in our hearts. It is a book, like any journey across vast distances, that we cannot help but commit to imperfect, passionate memory.

—Ricardo Frasso Jaramillo

Seen and blurred

When a police officer kills a Black person and a camera happens to capture the encounter, I think of *Cops*, Fox's infamous reality show that followed law enforcement as they patrolled US streets. The grainy footage, the blurred faces and license plates, the strangely rigorous time stamps in the corner of the screen—everything felt coated in a hazy, drowsy skim. Before it was canceled, in 2020, and syndicated throughout the aughts, *Cops* came on late, wedged between dramas and sitcoms and the local news. That time slot and the show's distinct lack of narrative and continuity seemed to signal a shift from fiction and entertainment to something more perverse and gawking. As a young viewer in the 1990s, I did not typically complete episodes; whenever I did, I felt duped. The theme song, which seemed mixed to maximum loudness, invoked "bad boys" and imminent danger ("What you gonna do when they come for you?"), but *Cops* was essentially a variety show. The policework was directionless and random, guided by whim rather than probable cause—an improvised fox hunt. And the "stars," the hawkish beat cops whose perspectives we followed, despite their noirish narration and canned charisma, seemed indistinguishable from security guards or traffic cops. They were sentient stop signs, essentially: sophisticated traffic lights. Whether they were chasing someone down or having a conversation with a suspect that wasn't bleeped into incoherence, I couldn't discern how one encounter differed from another, why one person was pursued and beaten, while another was cuffed, warned, and let go.

The one thing I could count on in any given episode was that law enforcement would be the aperture through which I saw crime. This is the core premise of the show: to see the public through the eyes of the police. Thanks to the internet and the efforts of countless activists, victims, and bystanders, that premise has grown increasingly untenable. We know that the menacing, chaotic public that *Cops* insists must be handled with force is a gross fiction generated through standard reality show tricks. (We also now know that the show's producers coerced suspects into signing consent forms and granted participating police departments editorial approval.) But even with the knowledge that police work is less dangerous than landscaping, roofing, logging, and garbage collection, it remains difficult to watch dash-cam and cell phone footage and not *see* like a cop. Scrutinizing body language, assessing tone of voice, monitoring hands—the cop gaze directs us even when we watch videos that expose its biases. For this reason, I don't watch such footage anymore. It's too limited in scope, too brined in paranoia and power.

The cop perspective isn't limited to viral videos of police killings, though. It also permeates fiction, especially films. Whereas reality TV shows like *Cops* present themselves as virtual ride-alongs, films about policing and crime tend to follow cops outside the cruiser, into their lives, into their career cases. I call them "live-alongs." Both genres traffic in authority, insisting that how cops see is infallible, and that what they see is true. In different ways, the films *Queen & Slim* (2019) and *Empty Metal* (2018) target that authority. Both movies insist that looking is an act, not a passive experience—we choose what to see and what not to see. This approach allows the films to probe what and how cops see when they look at the world. Rather than positing a single, coherent perspective whose stability audiences can take for granted, these films explode with perspectives, using the aesthetics of music videos, portraiture, and surveillance footage to bend familiar ways of looking into strange shapes. Both films are flawed, but their visual experiments highlight the creation embedded in sight: vision's capacity to produce as well as to observe. In the worlds of these films, to see is to act, and to see like a cop is to enact violence.

Directed by Melina Matsoukas, *Queen & Slim* begins with an awkward Tinder date in a grungy diner. The Black-owned diner is harshly lit and spare. Slim discusses the Black proprietors with pride, smirking at Queen, a defense attorney, like he's let her in on a family secret. His charm is ineffective: Queen has no appetite and little interest in the date or the restaurant. Earlier that day, the state of Ohio decided to execute one of her clients, and that loss is haunting her. The day worsens.

They exit the diner into a chilly Cleveland night and are stopped by a police officer, who removes Slim from the car and coerces him into allowing a search of his trunk. Slim is annoyed—by the cold, by the inconvenience—and doesn't do a good job of hiding it, which the cop takes as an insult. Queen steps out of the vehicle to defend Slim, using her legal expertise, and things escalate until Slim ends up shooting the officer dead in self-defense. Queen insists they flee, a plea that has the weight of counsel. A few hours into their escape, they encounter clipped dash-cam footage of their experience, and Queen's foresight proves to have been wise. In the clip, shown on a cell phone, the scene has a ready-made narrative: routine traffic stop, officer dead, armed suspects. The availability of that summary feels tied to the dash cam as a device: It's not designed to capture the anxiety of driving while Black, to disclose the racist assumptions that fuel random stops, to probe the absurdity of armed patrolmen enforcing traffic laws. The dash cam produces evidence, full stop, and Queen and Slim look guilty—like criminals, like cop killers rather than survivors.

The footage spreads quickly, turning Queen and Slim from strangers into coconspirators. It's an awkward fit. They have no destination or plan at first, scrambling between waypoints and struggling to tolerate each other. They are not a couple, or even friends, and their worldviews are disparate. Slim is open and trusting, Queen elusive and suspicious. Matsoukas depicts their journey with dreamlike whimsy: confined to the car, they begin to exchange yearning looks; evocative music plays as they zip down verdant country roads devoid of traffic and potholes. The sky is bright and blue, and the sunlight is constant yet soft, giving Queen's and Slim's skin a youthful glow. They are on the run, yet it feels like they are in a hip car commercial. They grow close.

As the duo comes to grips with their new circumstances, they resist the images of themselves that circulate. They do not view themselves as heroes, as the son of a mechanic they hire believes them to be; nor do they identify as crusaders against cops, as they inform a white couple that reluctantly stows them away. Their most spirited defense is against the mechanic who charges them extra to repair their car. He upsells his service because he recognizes them and disagrees with their flight. Queen and Slim insist they didn't have a choice, an argument he scoffs at. They capitulate and pay the upcharge.

The one image of themselves they don't contest is a photograph they take at the mechanic's shop after their car is repaired. The portrait is suave and theatrical, the kind of too-cool picture intended to sell an exceptional day or night as an MO: *This is how we do*. Dressed in a studly tracksuit, Slim leans back against a sleek 1973 Pontiac Catalina and tosses the camera a stony gaze, while Queen, perched atop the vehicle in a form-fitting animal-print dress, admires Slim with longing and awe. This is their memorial to themselves, their self-written legacy. Slim says the photo will be "proof we were here," a statement that gives the coolness of the photo an air of correction. If the dash-cam footage is the official record of their lives, the photo is the revisionist version. They do not keep the photo.

Where *Queen & Slim* seeks to humanize reluctant criminals, directors Adam Khalil and Bayley Sweitzer's *Empty Metal* aims to criminalize the police state. The plot revolves around three blurred photos that are laid across a coffee table like evidence during a police interrogation. The three figures in the photos are George Zimmerman, Daniel Pantaleo, and Darren Wilson, and the obscuration is likely a function of libel law, but the overall effect is that the men are rendered faceless. The film's main characters, members of a rudderless noise band, are out to assassinate this trio as part of a scheme to battle the surveillance state, and the viewer, like the band, must learn to look at the targets differently.

The band is radicalized by an underground network of militant psychics. The psychics—a Rastafarian hacker, a Native activist, and a white sovereign individual—are more symbols than characters, but they have a sense of purpose that the band lacks. They've fought the state through computer hacking, civil disobedience, and protesting, and have come to believe that their enemy is too powerful to confront head on. Their solution is guerrilla warfare, and their secret weapon is something on the fringes of a drone's crosshairs: regular people. Enter the band, who commit themselves to becoming "empty metal," human weapons in the psychics' invisible insurrection.

Sweitzer and Khalil portray the band's radicalization through experimental montages that overflow with hacked, offbeat imagery, of which the photos of Wilson, Pantaleo, and Zimmerman are just a small part. The directors re-create infamous police murders as trippy animations that look like tutorials in a video game. The faceless cops and victims that populate the animations seem homogenous and stiff, as if they were acting out predetermined roles.

These sequences appear alongside images of unarmed Native protesters shot in profile contra armed cops in formation and slow-motion images of boiling soup. Deadpan voiceovers and droning ambient music link these scenes to the simmering rage of the band, giving the film a sense of hallucinogenic dissociation. To see themselves differently, the band must view the world anew as well.

It works. "If anyone could know all this—" one band member says, referring to Pantaleo's documented choking of Eric Garner, "Why the fuck is he still alive?" another finishes. The exchange is clearly directed at the audience. Despite these scenes and perpetrators of police brutality being warped and distorted, they remain identifiable, which feels intentional. Letting killer cops and their proxies go free is an American tradition, a collective choice. We recognize these episodes because our inaction made them possible. This is a sweeping provocation, but it feels more actionable than the dignified martyrdom of *Queen & Slim*. After all, the conflict in that film boils down to a contest between the dash-cam footage that initiates Queen and Slim's flight and their enduring likeness, seen on a mural at the film's end, that proves they were more than fugitives: a wrong image versus a right image.

As far as character arcs go, *Empty Metal* has a lot in common with *Cops* in that there are no arcs or characters at all. But ultimately its provocations are instructive. While *Cops* presents its leering, disciplinary perspective as objective, and *Queen & Slim* settles for prettied respectability, *Empty Metal* posits that that vision is tenuous. There is no Goliath-toppling kill shot in *Empty Metal*, no final showdown, no everlasting justice. Instead, there are sight lines, and they are always changing, always treacherous. I find that view to be as hopeful as it is grim. The crosshairs may catch us, but they will never contain us.

—*Stephen Kearse*

CASTING CALL

A poem by Keith Leonard

Hospital patient
to die on-screen.
Must be able to stay dead
for money. Must stay dead
for several takes.
Must not flinch
when the protagonist's tears
make a lake
of your mouth.
Must not swallow.
Craft services provided.
Must be able to pronounce
the words perseverance
and dream and soon.
Part has no lines.
Part requires only your lack
of breath. Part requires
the prolonged feeling
of someone's knee
on your diaphragm.
3 to 5 years' experience needed.
Must stay dead for reshoots.
Must stay dead for money.
By "money" we mean exposure.
By "money" we mean a thin
gold chain that comes away
green in your wet hands.
You're going to make it, kid.
We all are.

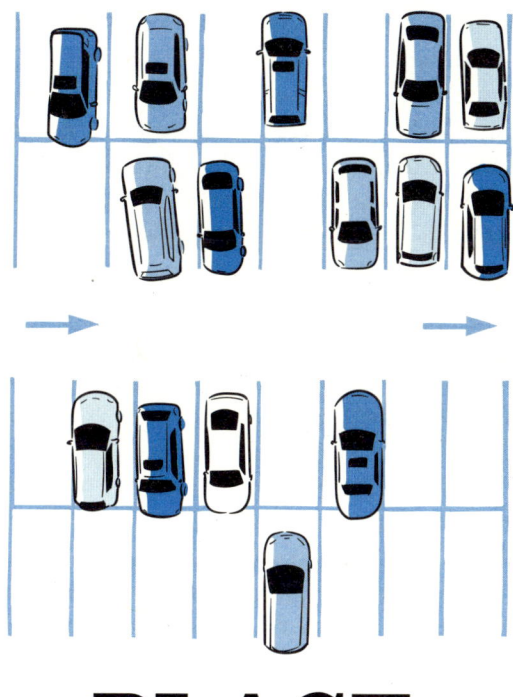

PLACE

IKEA PARKING LOT

FEATURES:
- ✭ Taco trucks
- ✭ Sycamores
- ✭ Supportive birds
- ✭ Freakish weeds

During the early weeks of the pandemic, I found myself pacing in parking lots. After teaching my classes some afternoons, I would just wander out in a kind of daze. I live on a street that borders Wooster Square, a small municipal park in New Haven, Connecticut, that people use to walk their dogs or jog loops around. This would have been a convenient place to pace, but in those days I wanted to avoid people at all costs, so I wandered farther, to where there were fewer people. It was like osmosis happening. Density sought emptiness; something yearned for nothing. Eventually I found my way to a huge IKEA parking lot.

The parking lot for the international housewares store is wedged between a messy tangle of several freeway exchanges (I-95, I-91, the notorious Oak Street Connector), the Metro-North rail yard, a post office, a sprawling office complex, and a stretch of garbage-strewn urban coastline touching Long Island Sound. On foggy days the air smells like brine and seaweed; on dry days, like bright metallic fumes and burned rubber; on humid days, there's a chemical vapor, oddly sweet, which is perhaps off-gassing from the oil storage tanks across the harbor. Usually there are taco trucks parked on Long Wharf Drive, but when things shut down, they evaporated, too, along with the construction guys and long-haul truckers who had stopped there for lunch.

For me, extended time in parking lots has always signified an emergency, precise moments of narrative dissolution: one version of the good life has come apart irretrievably, and you must, humbly, construct another. Outside hospitals and motels, breakups and break*downs*. I paced because pacing feels like the good, primal thing to do when a body is penned in. It's what lions and tigers do in their zoo enclosures. Back and forth, up and around, prowl, prowl, repeat. I organized my movements by row: up and down the parking rows toward the now-dim signs for exchanges, returns, exit, enter. The circularity of the movements, plus the weird, abstract commands, felt cosmic. I was in an undetermined space of pure matter, performing a ritual of eternal reincarnation, living many lives.

The functions of things were all floating above. I wanted to affix them but I couldn't. Questions unspooled. What was "IKEA" if not a place to buy disposable furniture; what were "citizens" if not the purchasers or returners of these products; what was "parking lot" if not a place to temporarily store one's car as one entered yet another temple of modern life? We were unmoored from purpose. What did it mean to be a body in space, a body that didn't buy or sell, or go to the grocery store, or see friends, or go to school, or travel from *A* to *B*, or perform routine life as we had always imagined? This body was made of nothing if not limitations.

One day, while pacing, I noticed a few acrobatic brown birds swooping into my path and scampering alongside me. With what looked like concerned, pitying expressions, they seemed to pause and peer back at me once in a while, as though waiting for me to catch up, before rushing ahead. I had the feeling they were cheering me on. *Come on! You can do it!* Like in a marathon. They had black-and-white

Illustration by Kristen Radtke

stripes on their chests, as if they were wearing high-contrast bibs. What were those birds? Oh, killdeer! The internet said they were a kind of plover, and they loved fields, airports, and yes, parking lots next to water. They weren't here for me; they were enacting their migration and living the way they had always lived. But I'd never noticed them before.

Spring went on, and greens, pinks, whites, and yellows started popping up everywhere. There were trees planted on the margins of the lot. Swollen, reddish-chartreuse nipples—buds—appeared on the branches. Later, I learned the trees were sycamores. Their bark was white and mottled, like skewbald horses. What were those sounds above me? A soaring shadow; a cinematic, nature-show-worthy shriek. Red-tailed hawk? I saw a lot of seagulls and I became curious about identifying them too. Herring gull. Ring-billed gull. Without any human food to scavenge from the taco trucks, the gulls reverted to their gull ways and began hunting. They picked up shellfish—clams, mussels, oysters—and dropped them from great heights. They experimented with the cracking power of many different surfaces. The concrete promenade next to the Canal Dock Boathouse worked best. Soon this area was strewn with a shattered mosaic of sparkling shells.

Each day, as each new word entered my vocabulary, the world seemed to refill. What had previously been a nonplace, without identity or history or relation, was slowly transforming into a place. It was getting harder to pace, because there was so much to look at. Pacing was too fast a speed for these investigations. Every other step: Wait, look down. What are those miniature hyacinth things poking out of the cracks? They look like upside-down bunches of grapes. My sister had pointed them out to me during one of our walks. Grape hyacinth. Apt name.

Summer arrived, and because the municipal crews weren't mowing, the weeds were allowed to flourish. The weeds, overnight, burst upward with the freakish speed of an unregulated condo development. The median strip between the road and the sidewalk became a vibrant weed city, densely green. From one seething afternoon to the next, the bees, wasps, and flies arrived in droves, weaving in and out of the wildflowers. Clover, aster, dandelion. The leaves of the tall mugwort in particular were like love motels for breeding lady beetles. Each leaf was a cool room, shading them in privacy.

I thought about the mugwort on the nights I couldn't sleep, of which there were many. Mugwort: a plant long connected with magic and healing, an herb to put under your pillow to grant vision dreams. "She helps you to find the truth of a cycle," one blog helpfully explained. The mugwort was gendered female. "We are never still. If we are not changing, we are dead." I stayed up late reading. Demonstrations were continuing all over the country, and we seemed to be on the precipice. I crushed some leaves in my palm and placed them in a tiny jar, not wanting to dirty my pillow. Put my head down next to the jar. Closed my eyes. You enter a trash-blown wasteland, seeing nothing but the white lines zebra-ing up into view. There are limits and borders, structures and instructions. But when you open your eyes, you will see, if only for a fleeting minute, that in the process of shedding old functions, new functions arrive. New exigencies, new forms of life.

—Anelise Chen

Piano lessons

by Teresa Wong

When I was seven years old, my parents' friends offered to sell us their piano for cheap.

"If we buy it, you have to promise to play it," my dad said.

I agreed, not really understanding what that promise would mean.

So I took lessons

...

for the next ten years.

Even when my mother said she couldn't drive me across town to the conservatory anymore,

"They switched me to the evening shift, so you'll have to take the bus."

I never considered stopping.

"Here are the bus schedules for each route. Remember, you'll need to transfer twice, so hang on to your transfer slip."

"Ok."

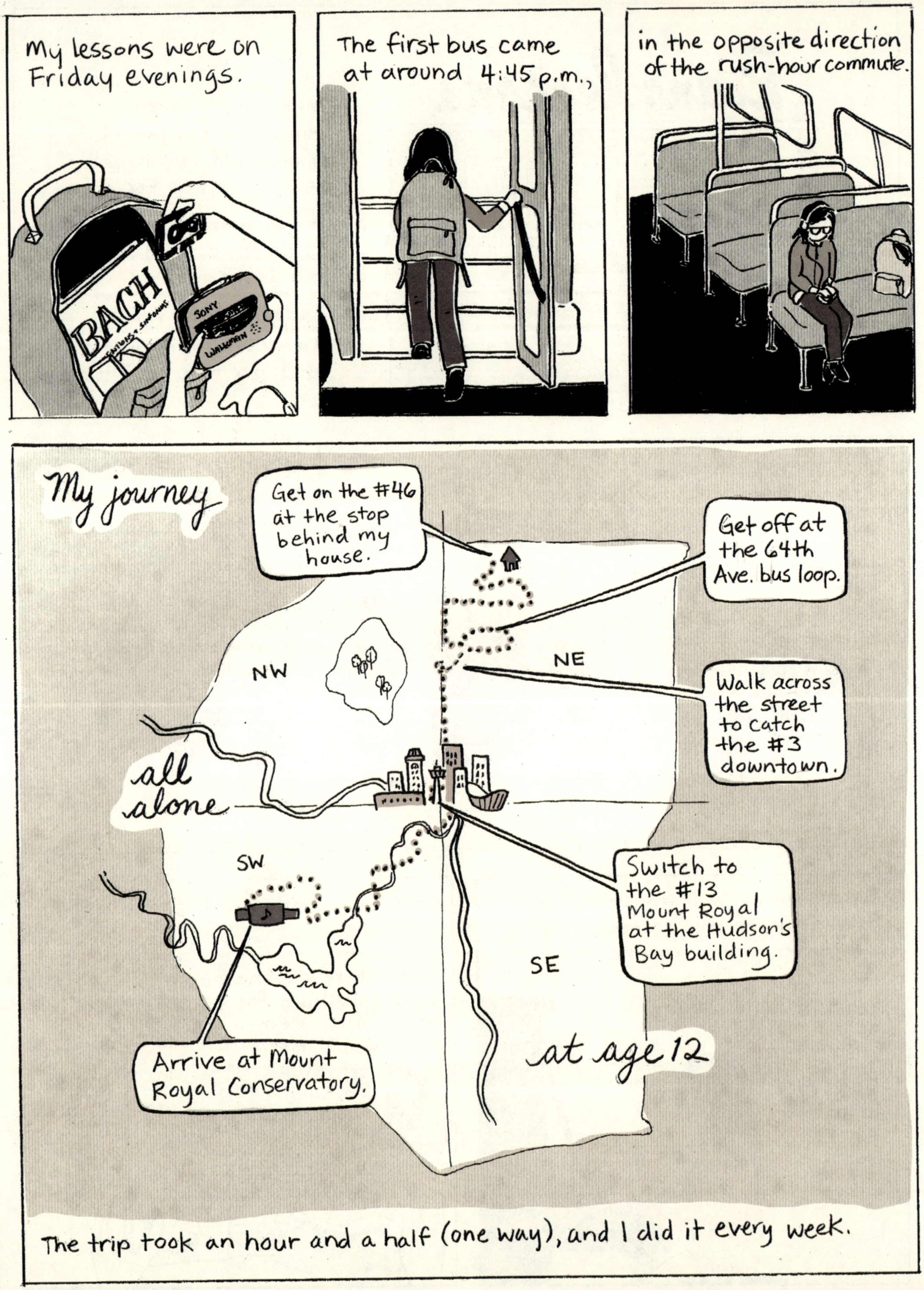
My lessons were on Friday evenings.
BACH
SONY
WALKMAN
The first bus came at around 4:45 p.m.,
in the opposite direction of the rush-hour commute.
My journey
Get on the #46 at the stop behind my house.
Get off at the 64th Ave. bus loop.
NW
NE
Walk across the street to catch the #3 downtown.
all alone
SW
Switch to the #13 Mount Royal at the Hudson's Bay building.
SE
Arrive at Mount Royal Conservatory.
at age 12
The trip took an hour and a half (one way), and I did it every week.

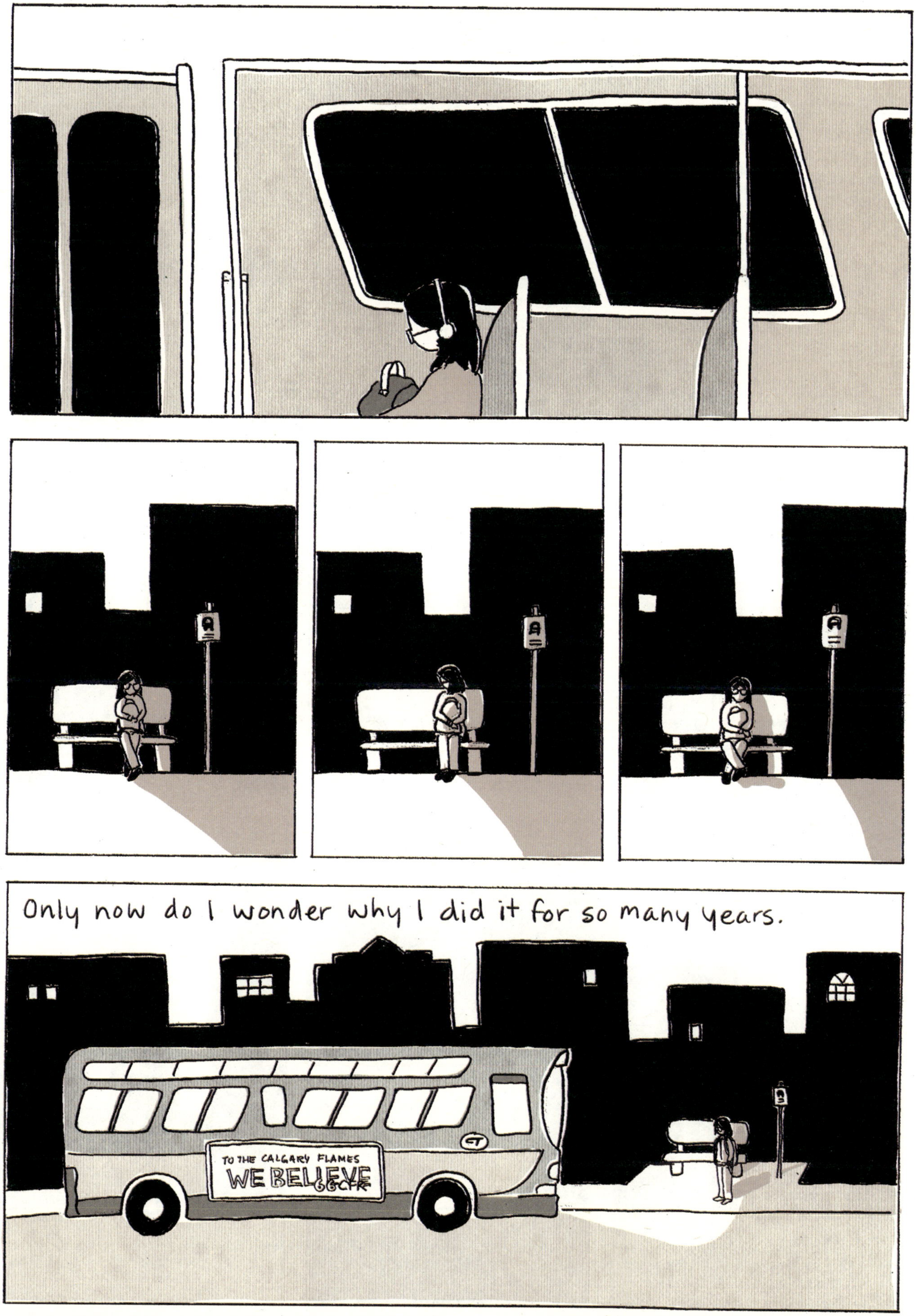
Only now do I wonder why I did it for so many years.
TO THE CALGARY FLAMES
WE BELIEVE
66CFR
CT

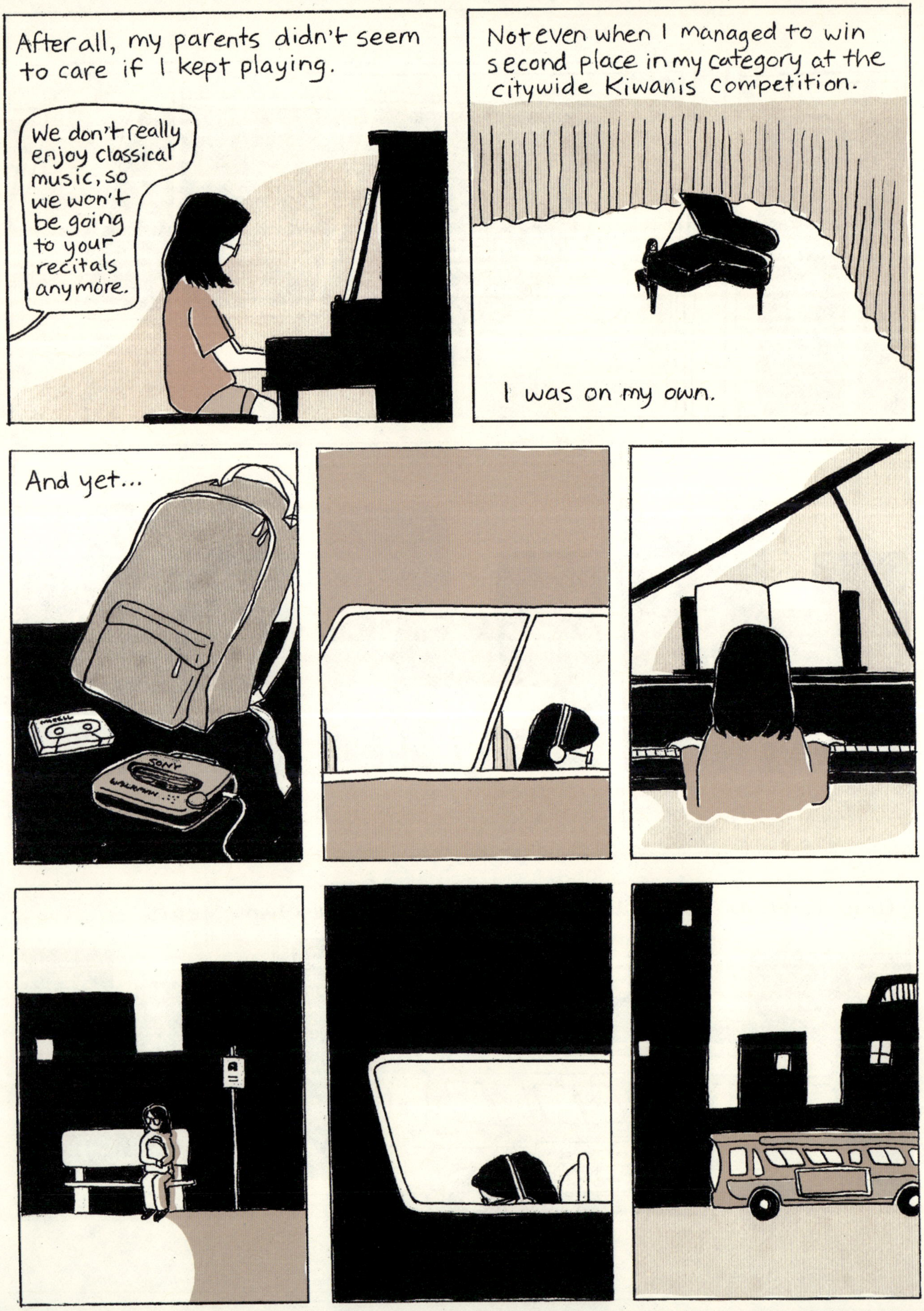
After all, my parents didn't seem to care if I kept playing.
We don't really enjoy classical music, so we won't be going to your recitals anymore.
Not even when I managed to win second place in my category at the citywide Kiwanis competition.
I was on my own.
And yet...
SONY
WALKMAN

Learning how to play the piano meant something to me.

When I played, it felt like I went away somewhere.

Or maybe like everything else had fallen away...

I don't know.

I was still just some kid, growing up in a random city in the middle of nowhere, but I could access the same music heard in the courts of Europe hundreds of years before.

It made my world feel bigger.

Just walking through the Conservatory gave me a view into a different life.

Elegant

Refined

Orderly

I always wanted to be more than I was.

What began as a promise to my parents became a commitment to myself.

Many people think classical music is only for the old, white, or wealthy — but that's not how music works.

You can still claim it, even if it was not written for you.

And it can still take you places.

HOW TO BECOME AN OBJECT

Most women aren't very good at pretending to be sex dolls. Scrolling through videos titled "Real Doll" on Pornhub, I can usually tell from the thumbnails whether they contain a product or a fantasy. This is not a complaint. A few years ago, while working on a poetry book, I became briefly obsessed with the RealDoll brand of life-size sex dolls. The book's keywords might have been *Asian*, *sex*, and *robot*, and doing what I called "research" often left me feeling like I'd been torn into slimy quarters and thrown into a well. It was on one of these nights, trawling those depths, that I found the video.

She had blue hair: anime hair. Like most dolls, she had enormous tits and a sweet, placid face. I was impressed by the timing of her blinks. Then I doubted: Was she real? Something about her seemed different from the other dolls, but how could a person lie so still while *this* was happening—as if the body were cut off from the head? It had to be a machine. Was it? Was she?

Ten minutes of this. Then she gagged—a tiny gag, so subtle it couldn't have been programmed—and I had my answer.

I wore a blue wig once in my freshman year of college, for a notoriously raunchy annual party. I'd just seen *Closer* and was in love with the idea of disappearing into sex. With the wig and my Asian face and what I perceived to be the enormity of my school's student body, I was ready to be anyone. Specifically, an anyone who would grind her body against strangers, who was open to offers, a stupid, slutty, gawkable thing. And when I detached myself from a boy's mouth and left the party, when I walked out alone into the October night, my hope was that I could take off the wig and take her off too—the thing of me.

Of course, it didn't work that way. Not only did thingness follow me around, but I panicked every time I saw the boy I'd wrapped myself around that night—or a boy I thought was him. The blue wig and dirt-cheap vodka, it turned out, had anonymized the world to me rather than the other way around. Unlike a doll, I couldn't stop feeling.

I watched the video of the woman with the blue hair over and over, talked about it to everyone I knew. It's maybe the queerest thing about me, or the most Korean thing—to love being torn up by an image. All the more so if the image is a monstrous version of what's supposed to be me, by which I mean an Asian lady, by which I mean submissive, inhuman, calculated, kink, estranged from language, spookily competent, and on and on. These were stories I'd heard my whole life, stories that had been broken into me with hands and jokes and long glances. To see her there, my thingness—the rumor that had been following me around since I was a child—lit me on a kind of sticky fire. I watched again and again, trying to catch the first signs of her breaking. Is it a problem that I could interpret the force of this meeting only as arousal? Or is this what arousal is: horror, mixed with recognition, mixed with a need to see more?

"Have you ever heard the term *Asian persuasion*?" said the blond boy I met one summer in high school. I hadn't. Years later, he would fail to persuade me to have sex, though my refusal didn't matter much to him. It happened as if I hadn't said anything at all, as if I had just been lying still, flushed and blinking.

For years, I forgot about that night with the blond boy, the night he scrubbed my words out of the air between us. Then one day I remembered. I remembered it, and remembered it

Illustration by Kristen Radtke

again, and each time there was nothing: no sadness or pain or anger, no feeling at all, just a story. First; then; finally. I wondered whether I was broken or brave. I wondered if it counted as assault if the memory didn't hurt.

Why would anyone want to become a thing? The answer to that question is about as long—and as fraught—as the history of feminist thought. The question makes me nervous, considering that the objectification of women like me has consequences I carry around like a stone—like a well where my heart should be.

And yet it's hard to imagine wanting to be a person *all the time*. How exhausting—all that chattering and burping and remembering and clock-checking, the constant gagging on one's failures. All the grief of being a tool of empire and capitalism, the grief of the things men do with their hands. Still, all I want is to live to spend another day walking into rooms and saying, *I, I*. What a racket.

So, like everyone, I depend on my technologies of disappearing: blue wig, rabbit hole, Bota Box. Like everyone else, I shatter my self through orgasm and sweat, or scroll it away. I hang up my personhood to try to save it from wear, and in the meantime, I become the room, the phone, the smooth repetitions of my knitting needles. To become an object, I mean, is both life-annihilating and life-saving. This is my tiny, secret pleasure—a few extra doors to slip out through.

Sara Ahmed, writing about Heidegger, says, "When the hammer is working, it disappears from view. When something stops working or cannot be used, it intrudes into consciousness." Pablo Neruda writes, "If you ask where I come from I have to start talking with / broken objects."

Maybe what I felt when I watched the woman trying to become a doll wasn't arousal but love. That is, I admired her for being a better object than I could ever be; I loved her for refusing, ultimately, to be one. For staying so still, for severing her smile from the horrors happening below, for being so useful, so perfectly useful—and then for failing. In gagging—that tiniest, unprogrammable gag—she failed, finally, to disappear into the smooth gears of all that makes us into objects. She broke, and I blinked. And somewhere between *I* and *I*, a door swung open.

—*Franny Choi*

STUFF I'VE BEEN READING

A REGULAR COLUMN

by Nick Hornby

BOOKS READ:
★ *Prince and the Purple Rain Era Studio Sessions: 1983 and 1984*—Duane Tudahl
★ *Last Chance Texaco: Chronicles of an American Troubadour*—Rickie Lee Jones
★ *What White People Can Do Next: From Allyship to Coalition*—Emma Dabiri

BOOKS BOUGHT:
★ *Wayward Lives, Beautiful Experiments: Intimate Histories of Riotous Black Girls, Troublesome Women, and Queer Radicals*—Saidiya Hartman
★ *The Mere Wife*—Maria Dahvana Headley
★ *Beowulf: A New Translation*—Maria Dahvana Headley
★ *London War Notes: 1939–1945*—Mollie Panter-Downes
★ *Prince: The Man and His Music*—Matt Thorne

"I slipped through school with a B average in spite of not being able to read very well," says Rickie Lee Jones in *Last Chance Texaco*, her gripping, lovely memoir. "I could read but I could not concentrate." It's a confession one suspects crops up in a million autobiographies by people who work in entertainment. Ozzy Osbourne probably wasn't a focused reader in school, and it's hard to imagine Elvis sitting in a well-lit corner flogging himself through *Huckleberry Finn*. What is remarkable, however, is that this admission occurs on page 167 of a 350-page book about a life that began in the mid-1950s and a career that began in the late 1970s. I know what you're thinking. You're thinking, You must be joking. I love Rickie Lee Jones, but I'm not reading seven volumes about her. But it's not like that. The pages leading up to her assessment of her high school career are thrilling, funny, scary, sad, packed full of life and extraordinary characters. It becomes very clear that these moments and these people are responsible for her career, her lyrics, even her sound, and you don't really need to know what mics she used, or what the record company did wrong with the promotion of the ninth album. She describes the genesis and success of her first two albums in detail and with fresh excitement, but they are the culmination of something, not the beginning.

Her grandfather was Peg Leg Jones, a vaudeville entertainer who could do a flip from a standing start, despite his eponymous disability; her mother was brought up in an orphanage; her father had gone off to seek his permanently elusive fortune when he was just shy of fourteen, and fought in World War II. He was sixty-three when he died—"younger than I am now but older than anyone in his family had ever been," a heartbreakingly simple description of life on the American margins. Rickie Lee's sister Janet was a handful who ended up in a home for wayward teenagers, and her brother, like her grandfather and also her uncle, lost his leg in an accident. Her mother and father fought, made up, moved, moved again. "What were they running from? Well, they ran from cities, houses, and eventually themselves, but they never got away from their difficult childhoods or their love for each other." (I wonder, by the way, what the geography of England has done to our artists? The English have bad luck and grinding poverty and explosive marriages, too, of course, but we don't have anywhere to run, really. I mean, you can keep moving and moving, but you can never move very far, and you can never escape the weather, or the architecture, or the culture. You have to move in your mind rather than in your pickup truck.) Trouble was heading for Rickie Lee. There was just too much heartbreak, poverty, chaos, and impermanence to avoid it. Rather than sit around and wait for it to arrive, Rickie Lee went out to head it off at the pass.

In 1970, she hitchhiked up to Big Sur from Long Beach, California, where her family was trying and exhausting their luck. She lived in a cave for a while with a bunch of hippies, but then she and a new friend decided to go and see Jimi Hendrix at the Ventura County Fairgrounds. Mind duly blown, she returned to the cave, only to find that the cave dwellers were moving on. They vowed to reconvene in a little town in Canada for July 4. Rickie got there, but only one of the cave crowd had bothered. She decided to travel back to the US with a guy who was crossing the border to buy pot. She was arrested and jailed, initially with adult criminals who were "howling like banshees." This happened when she was fifteen years old. All this takes up the tenth chapter of her book; it would occupy seven hundred pages of mine. Such are the terrifying twists and turns of the drama, and the immediacy and detail of the scenes, that one can occasionally be tricked into thinking one is reading a novel, and into making guesses about the eventual outcome of this young woman's life. I didn't have much hope for her celebrating her sixteenth birthday, let alone her sixtieth.

Studded throughout the book, like gleaming clues to a happy ending, are references to music, in particular the music that provided the singular jazz-folk-Broadway-rock-soul stew of her first album. She sees *West Side Story* at the movie theater as a little kid and is thunderstruck. She teaches herself Bob Dylan's "House of the Risin' Sun" and Barbra Streisand's "People" ("Musically, I was 'Barbra Dylan,' a collage of all I had heard"). She hears and is spooked by Dr. John while high during her Canadian adventure. And, perhaps most importantly, she comes across Laura Nyro, "not like anything else evolving out of the 1960s, as if the singer of the Shangri-Las had been raised by Leonard Bernstein." She had found her person, the one most creative people need to complete a metamorphosis. "Somehow, the moment I fell in love with Laura I loved myself just a little more. I believe an invisible cord came out of me and attached itself to Laura Nyro that summer. Or vice versa." As a portrait of the artist as a young woman, this book could not be any more enthralling or fun to read. Her troubles are not behind her, of course, once she has found her calling: the account of her breakup with Tom Waits, who walked away when he found out she was using heroin, is particularly piercing. You feel it, presumably because the author still does. Her first little album of covers was titled *Girl at Her Volcano*, a lovely way of describing influence. But many volcanoes have the capacity to blister the skin.

I don't know what Rickie Lee Jones means to you. She means a lot to me. Those two first albums are perfect, I think, and sound even better to me now—as if they were somehow newly minted, but the ambition, the voice, the arrangements, and the songwriting seem like greater achievements, after the forty years I've spent listening to things that aren't quite as good. I was in my early twenties when I first heard them, and I thought great albums would come along every few weeks. Rickie Lee was a pretty cool role model for me too. If I am not the worst man in the world—and I can think of at least seven off the top of my head whom I'd like to think I'm better than—then she is one of the women who helped drop me down the list. Jones spends some time describing the terror and the joy of being on *Saturday Night Live*, her first TV appearance, right when her first record came out. You can watch a grainy, hissy video of it on YouTube, and I recommend you do: she's note-perfect, rocking her trademark beret, happy, apparently full of confidence, and ready to burn down the world. The band swings and the audience adores her. It's impossible not to be moved by it, once you've spent a couple hundred pages discovering how she got there. I loved this as much as I loved Dylan's *Chronicles* and Patti Smith's *Just Kids*.

What white person wouldn't want to read a book called *What White People Can Do Next*, in the current climate? I am being flippant, regretfully. Both you and I can think of a ton of white people who wouldn't want to read it and aren't going to, and even those who follow the smart young academic Emma Dabiri on Twitter became unhappy when they heard about her book. "Before the book was even written, I had 'white' people tweeting me to tell me how offensive the title is." (We'll get to the quote marks around the word *white*.) Dabiri is not, as you may have guessed, a "white" person, and although the idea that a disastrously well-meaning "white" person might have written a book called *What White People Can Do Next* is comical, it's not entirely beyond the realm of possibility, judging from some of the encounters Dabiri describes in the book. After she took part in a public discussion on Afrofuturism, the blues, trap music, and ancestral veneration, a woman approached her to express her disappointment that there had been no mention of "allyship"; in other words, what's the point of Black people if they're not prepared to talk about white liberals and their willingness to help?

There is so much in these 150 pages that I found useful. In the chapter titled "Interrogate Whiteness," Dabiri asks us to let go of the whole notion of "whiteness." White people, as she points out, are "a relatively modern invention." What does Tucker Carlson really have in common with a Caucasian man in Flint, Michigan, who hasn't worked for ten years, or with a fisherman in England whose livelihood has been destroyed by the unintended but calamitous results of Brexit? They really have very little white privilege to check. Those of you who have seen *Judas and the Black Messiah* will recall Black Panther Fred Hampton's smart, successful attempts to form a "rainbow coalition" among impoverished and aggrieved residents of all races. As the poet and cultural theorist Fred Moten said, "This shit is killing you, too." And Dabiri is withering in her critique of the tendency of well-meaning whites to slip into the white savior lane: "Black people do not need charity, benevolence or indeed guilt…. As such, allyship appeals to a desire to help a 'victim,' constituting a reification of the power imbalance." There is so much I want to quote; maybe you should just read it. If you need any further persuasion, Dabiri calls the anthropologist Margaret Mead a "Karen," and provides a toe-curlingly unreflective Mead quote to prove her point.

I separated *Last Chance Texaco* from *Prince and the Purple Rain Era Studio Sessions* because I wanted to give the impression that I am a rounded individual and not just a relentless music nerd. Fuck it, I am a rounded individual, when it comes to reading, at least, but a Rickie Lee book *and* a Prince book? Come on. What's a rounded individual supposed to do, apart from raise his hands in surrender and promise to read more nineteenth-century fiction in the near future? I would recommend *Last Chance Texaco* even if you have never heard the author's music, but I don't think Duane Tudahl would really mind if I told you that if you don't love Prince, then this isn't the book for you. Tudahl's book is a day-by-day account of Prince's work in the studio between the beginning of January 1983 and the end of December 1984, during which period he became a global superstar. There are a ton of interviews with some of the people who were there with him—band members, the long-suffering and fascinating engineer Susan Rogers (now—and you probably saw this coming—a professor, after earning a doctorate in music cognition and psychoacoustics). Prince being Prince, Stakhanovite hard work, imagination, and lubriciousness are never very far away: the recording made on December 31, 1983, and January 1, 1984 (Happy New Year, Susan Rogers!), involved both the oud and the riq, an Arabic tambourine. The song was called "We Can Fuck," and it featured the sound of Prince's friend Jill Jones in the throes of orgasm. That's a lot of the oeuvre in a nutshell.

Those of you who checked out the expanded *Purple Rain* a few years back already know that he recorded much more than he needed for the album. But he was also making albums at the same time for Vanity 6 (who were replaced by Apollonia 6), the Time, Jill Jones, Sheila E. and the Family, and occasional tracks for Sheena Easton. His creativity and output were staggering. Oh, and "making albums" means writing them, producing them, and playing most of the instruments for them. This could lead to friction, especially with the Time, who in the movie were the big-shot band that the Prince character was trying to surpass. In real life, and even though the Time was a proper band rather than a collection of Prince sock puppets, Prince took over and sacked a few of the band members who he felt were ill-disciplined. The truth was, as becomes clear in Tudahl's book, he was more talented than everyone he played with. He was a better drummer, guitarist, keyboard player, and singer than anyone who might find themselves in the studio with him. That kind of talent is always going to spell trouble.

This isn't a gossipy book, nor does it try to decode Prince or tell us what he means. It is an attempt to discover his art through the truth of its creation, and that makes it invaluable and unique, certainly in the field of music writing, and rare in all arts writing. Tudahl intends to write books about the next few albums in this golden run, and I'll be there waiting for them.

I read a novel this month, too, a good one, and it isn't about music. It is about love and marriage and adulthood and all the things I am *just as interested in as music*. But I seem to have run out of space, and I will have to write about it next time. ✭

THE ACT OF SMELLING: THE NOSE
BY JUDE STEWART

IF ALL OUR genius lies in our nostrils, as Nietzsche remarked, the nose is an untrained genius, brilliant but erratic. The human nose can detect a dizzying array of smells, with a theoretical upper limit of one trillion smells—yet many of us are incapable of describing these smells in words more precise than *smelly* and *fragrant*.

Our auditory and visual receptors offer little mystery—they were mapped and explained by scientists many decades ago—but human olfactory receptors were discovered only in 1991. This might be an indication of the massive complexity of smelling: the human body has only four visual receptors, compared with more than four hundred olfactory receptors. Or perhaps it's a matter of cultural priority: smells are so often thought of as unwanted intrusions.

Smell begins when odorous molecules—often called "odorants"—are whisked through the air into the nose. The air bumps through the nasal passages, where it is warmed and filtered, and arrives at the olfactory epithelium, a mucous-lined layer of the nasal cavity where olfactory neurons nestle like carrots in earth. These neurons detect the smells, but it's the olfactory receptor proteins that actually bind to odorants. These receptors, in turn, fire an electrical signal to the olfactory bulbs, two buds that hang from a bundle of nerves connecting to the brain, and which are located at the bridge of the nose, roughly where your eyeglasses would rest.

The olfactory bulbs are thought to be the brain's primary processing center for smell.[1] The bulbs take in information from the olfactory receptors, encode it into a unique odor signal, and then pass this signal to the olfactory center in the brain's cortex. Olfactory neurons regenerate every four to eight weeks; over time, they respond to whatever smells they encounter most often. That means you can train your nose to smell more effectively just by practicing.

How a receptor detects a smell remains a deep riddle to scientists. The odorant's shape appears to determine which olfactory receptors it binds to; beyond that, we have no idea why molecules smell as they do. Take the example of benzaldehyde, which smells like bitter almonds, and which can be found in maraschino cherries and marzipan. Add a double-bond of oxygen to its tail and the smell shifts to cinnamon. But throw on another five-carbon atom chain and the smell shifts again to a generic floral. There's no pattern at the molecular level that scientists can discern—yet.

Olfactory receptors are concentrated in your nose but exist throughout the body. Your kidneys, for example, have olfactory receptors—they can "smell" signals from your gut bacteria after meals and moderate your blood pressure in response. (Like taste, smell is a chemical sense; what the kidney receptors are really doing is detecting chemical changes.) Sperm, too, are guided by smell: swimming blindly in a silent void, they are drawn by the egg. Your lungs, blood vessels, muscles: they're all constantly smelling.

Smells can be detected by technology. Electronic noses monitor food factories for spoilage and nuclear reactors for leaks. But we won't transmit smells on the internet anytime soon—an electronic exchange of smells is impossible. Attempts to do so—like Cyrano, the 2016 "digital smell speaker," or its 2014 predecessor by the same inventor, oNotes[2]—are basically cons. What's transmitted is not the smell itself but an electronic signal that releases a prepared vial of scent on the receiving end. Smells can be digitized and recorded, but they can't be mediated by telecommunications. You are the smeller, and you can smell things only in person. ✭

---

[1] I say "thought to be" because this basic relay of signals has recently been thrown into doubt by a controversial study of certain left-handed women who apparently lack olfactory bulbs but can still smell everything normally.

[2] oNotes allowed an iPhone user to snap a photo and tag it with smell descriptors in a companion app called oSnap. The user could then send this message—the oNote—to another oSnap user whose phone was connected to a receiving device, the oPhone DUO. This device would then emit a preloaded smell that best matched the transmitted descriptors. (When oPhone DUO couldn't find a match in its preloaded scents, which was often, the receiving phone's mobile app would just offer a vivid description of the smell.)

Spiritualism's theories of supernatural communication, the afterlife as media, and how technological hauntings live on in film

Enter Ghost

By John Menick

Illustration by Xavier Lissillour

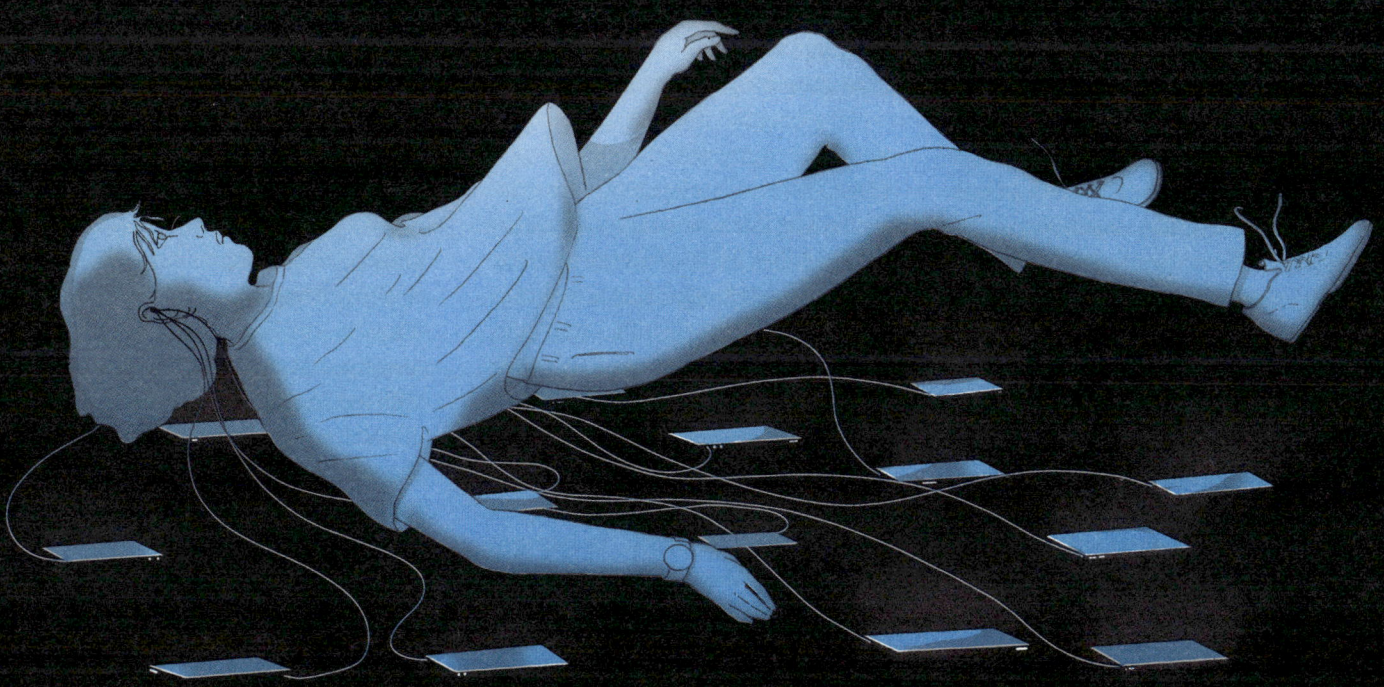

DISCUSSED: *Hollywood Prophecies, Zoom Calls, Pulse, Ghost Infestations, Disillusioned Protestants, Spiritual Telegraphs, The Spirit-Postmaster, Willie Lincoln, Automatic Writing, Electrical Noise, The Haunted Telephone, "Dial F for Frankenstein," Tim Berners-Lee, Goethe's Larynx, Psychometry, A Mise en Abyme of Solitary Looking*

1.

There is a kind of cinematic prophecy, a big-screen dreamworld that eerily anticipates the real. An event erupts into our attention—a natural disaster, a political movement, a war, a celebrity scandal—and we feel we've seen it already in a film, with worse writing and better-looking actors. How this happens is anyone's guess. These are prophecies without a prophet, the result of no supernatural power. They are just a strange by-product of Hollywood narratives engineered to fill seats. How many times did movie terrorists attack Manhattan before 9/11? How many viral outbreaks did we endure before the coronavirus pandemic? As governments scrambled to contain the current virus, their actions recalled the plots of pandemic films like *Contagion* (2011) and *Outbreak* (1995). The US government may not have been prepared for a global catastrophe, but Hollywood had already prepped our imaginations, giving the events of 2020, not for the first or last time, an unwanted familiarity.

So we went inside, where screens colonized what was left of our time. In only a few weeks, friends, family, coworkers, political candidates, and celebrities were reduced to grids of faces in glitchy chiaroscuro. Online video conferencing had an unexpected leveling effect, in which celebrity-packed theater productions and family birthdays were nearly indistinguishable in their format and awkwardness. People we once saw in person every day now appeared on our computer screens, competing with emails and Netflix. Digitized, encoded, flattened, and backlit, other people became digital ghosts, neither fully present nor completely unreal. These digital ghosts proliferated, in homes and outside of them—ghosts that were no longer just weird or eerie but also melancholic and bored. The melancholy was paradoxical: one missed one's friends and family, even though one could see them all the time. See them, but not be with them. Presence, rarefied, was now reduced to a field of pixels.

For two decades, horror movie producers have been grinding out films in which ghosts travel over digital connections, terrorizing teenagers in chat rooms and inconveniently intruding into video calls. Sporting tech-titles like *Unfriended* (2014), *Friend Request* (2016), and *Cam* (2018), these films are released, it seems, as frequently as app upgrades. They feature formulaic plots in which an online suicide or disappearance or rumor is not what it appears to be. Ghosts, demons—even Satan himself—are lurking in the network. The purer examples of the genre are shot entirely on webcams (or professional cameras imitating webcams) and use grid formats identical to those of a video conferencing app. It's all very silly, with the expected exploitational admixture of hot-button issues (teen suicide, cyberbullying) and freak-out entertainment (*The ghost is right behind you!*).

The haunted internet genre began with the upmarket template *Pulse* (2001), directed by Japan's horror master Kiyoshi Kurosawa. *Pulse* is the *Rosemary's Baby* (1968) of internet horror, a one-of-a-kind masterpiece that triggered countless rip-offs, spin-offs, remakes, and sequels, none of which re-create the movie's singular poetry.[1] *Pulse* is an enlarging spiral of terror whose starting point is a hacker's suicide and whose outer curves contain a Tokyo emptied of people. In between is a plot involving an afterlife that has run out of room for the dead. With nowhere else to go, ghosts are downloading themselves into present-day Tokyo via a website featuring videos of wraith-like people in darkened homes. After a character discovers the website, ghosts begin appearing, the character commits suicide, and their apartment is declared "forbidden." Meanwhile, other characters receive phone calls from the dead, and images of darkened rooms proliferate across more computer screens. Room by room, almost the whole of Tokyo disappears into the afterlife. *Pulse* then shifts genres, becoming a post-apocalyptic film, with the few unlucky survivors wandering through a depopulated Tokyo, eventually trying to escape by boat to South America.

Pulse doesn't make any sense, but it doesn't have to. The film elevates mood over logic, free association over cause-and-effect, somehow giving lines like "Instead, they'll try to make people immortal by quietly trapping them in their own loneliness" an explanatory power. *Pulse* conceptualizes the internet as a necrotic space that warehouses ghosts, but also as a finite space, prone to overflowing into ours. *Pulse* is a film whose every frame is infected with a loneliness that spreads like a virus. And with that loneliness comes the lonely act of watching: people watching people on screens watching people on screens, with the film's audience, of course, the last link in the chain. In one instance, a character looks at a screen on which they can see themselves, from behind, looking at that same screen, opening up a mise en abyme of solitary looking.

Today, it's hard not to find Kurosawa's film premonitory. People isolating themselves indoors, their apartments filled with clutter. Solitary, unwitnessed deaths. Long hours spent in front of computer screens looking at other lonely people. Television reports of dead strangers, each absolutely ordinary in their smiling headshot. Depopulated cities, quieted by a viral outbreak,

---

[1] In 2006, a US remake of *Pulse* was released as part of a wave of Western productions based on Japanese horror films. It was largely faithful to the original, but much of the original film's poetry was lost to cheap scares. Two straight-to-DVD sequels followed.

the remaining pedestrians transformed into the last people on earth.

2.

Every communication network addresses an absence: someone has left the room, the house, the country, this life, and we want them back. Our networks will only ever bring back a piece of that person—a voice, an image—but sometimes a piece is enough. It is not hard to see how a technology that traffics in these pieces might be confused with the ghostly, and how in our imaginations, our communication networks might be confused with the afterlife. Ghosts have been infesting communication networks long before Kurosawa's film, starting with the very first telegraph transmissions in America. The invention of the electric telegraph was synchronous with the rise of spiritualism in America. Both came out of a desire for communication—one with the living, the other with the dead—and both were optimistic gambles on the country's future.

Spiritualism—having emerged from the same wild cluster of New York counties that gave the nation Mormonism, Adventism, and Millerism—was a socially progressive movement. Not all abolitionists, feminists, or socialists were spiritualists, but most spiritualists were all three. Spiritualism drew its members mostly from the white middle and upper classes, educated men and women who were disillusioned with Protestantism's conservatism and patriarchy. They were determined to abolish slavery and give women the right to vote. (The house in Rochester that hosted some of the earliest séances was also a stop on the Underground Railroad.) Some Black political radicals gravitated toward the movement, including Sojourner Truth, who lived for a decade in Harmonia, a utopian spiritualist community. Spiritualism was one of the few women-led movements in nineteenth-century America, and more of its writers, artists, and mediums—the last, famous, highly paid, and sought after—were female than male. Historian Ann Braude has shown that spiritualism's stages and séance tables were among the few places women could have a voice in America at the time. (Though, paradoxically, not always with their own voices, as trance mediums were often said to be channeling the voices of dead men.)

At the time, death was everywhere: children died often and young; slavery destroyed countless Black lives and would lead to civil war; and families were lost to what would become preventable diseases. First Lady Mary Todd Lincoln organized séances in the Red Room of the White House, some of which were attended by the president. Mrs. Lincoln was not alone: by 1890, forty-five thousand Americans were formally associated with a spiritualist society, though the number of believers was probably much higher.

Meanwhile, these same Americans were sending telegrams and learning to make phone calls, two technologies that, even to the educated, appeared to border on the supernatural. For the first time, the world was communicating with itself across great distances, nearly instantaneously, and spiritualism was right there to ride the wire. The "spiritual telegraph" became the movement's prime technological metaphor, though it was frequently literalized when some mediums offered their services for intercontinental communications. Scholar Anthony Enns writes of the medium James V. Mansfield, a.k.a. "the spirit-postmaster," whose arm would spasm during séances as if charged by "an electro-magnetic circuit, enabling [the spirits] to approach and influence the nerve-center of his motor system." This "human telegraph" would then tap out the letters with his finger, in a manner that was "business-like, orderly, and straight."

Spiritualism lacked a foundational book, and it had no real theology. The movement was many things, but it was also a theory of communication—a wild, pseudoscientific one, but a theory all the same. Its message was simple: there was an afterlife, and we could speak with it. By the turn of the century, spiritualism was a clearinghouse of supernatural communication technologies: table rappings, talking boards, automatic writing, spirit slates, trances, even fanciful machines. Some of these technologies, such as automatic writing, were far older than the United States itself, while others were as new as the telephone. Spiritualist publications

> **Every communication network addresses an absence: someone has left the room, the house, the country, this life, and we want them back.**

freely sampled from the current scientific discourses on electricity and chemistry, and much of the movement's theorizing was done by scientists operating on the margins of their professions. Spiritualism designated its members as "investigators" rather than believers, encouraging a kind of light skepticism. Rarely, an investigator ranked among America's new scientific elite, as in the case of Thomas Watson, an assistant to Alexander Graham Bell.

Every Sunday in 1875, Watson convened a "spirit circle" with his childhood friend George Phillips. With Phillips leading, the table they sat around tipped and rapped in response to their questions—the efforts of a "disembodied spirit," according to Watson. Soon John Raymond, the future mayor of Salem, Massachusetts, joined them, and the three men graduated from rappings to ventriloquizing the dead. In one session, Raymond started convulsing and, perhaps in preparation for his political career, declaimed a thirty-minute speech from a dead orator.

For Watson, his parallel activities—the invention of the telephone and the séances—produced a paradoxical confusion between electricity and the spirit world. As he would later write of the séances: "I was now working with that occult force, electricity, and here was a possible chance to make some discoveries. I felt sure spirits could not scare an electrician, and they might be of use to him in his work." Notice the reversal: electricity was the true occult science, one that might explain the spirits away while also assisting the electrician in his scientific work.

Late at night, Watson spent hours "listening to the many strange noises in the telephone and speculating as to their cause." He heard snaps, grating sounds, a twirling like the chirping of a bird. He was the first to hear these sounds, and with scientific theories of electrical interference yet to arise, he speculated that they came from another planet. As Avital Ronell writes in *The Telephone Book: Technology, Schizophrenia, Electric Speech*, Watson "opened an altogether original channel of receptivity… [he was] the first convinced person actually *to listen to noise*."

By "noise," Ronell means electrical noise, static. Long before forward-thinking electronic-music composers made static a subject of serious listening, Thomas Watson was concentrating his ears on it, hearing what he thought might be interplanetary voices. Voices, music, soundscapes, the ghostly—the next century would search for signals

THE ACT OF SMELLING: PETRICHOR
BY JUDE STEWART

IN THE INDIAN city of Kannauj, perfumers have been making a scent called mitti attar for centuries. From April through May, workers pry blocks of parched clay from the ground. The blocks are baked into disks in ovens, which are then warmed over water distillers. When the clay reaches the right temperature, steam slowly releases the earth's smell. That steam is captured and distilled into vats of sandalwood oil, the perfume's base. The smell that's released is petrichor, the scent of dry earth after rain, a bright mineral tang edged with a hint of sourness. In Kannauj, this is the scent of the precise day when months of dry heat give way to monsoons.

The Greek word *petrichor*, meaning "blood of stones," was coined in 1964 by two Australian scientists, Isabel "Joy" Bear and Richard Thomas, who were researching this substance and its purpose. As part of their work, the scientists extracted a golden oil from a variety of soil types: sand, dirt, clay. They learned that plants secrete these fatty acids, mostly palmitic and stearic acids, into the soil, and that those secretions become concentrated between rainfalls. After a drought ends, plants often have a surge of growth, and so Bear and Thomas suspected that petrichor was a fertilizer. It turns out, however, that it's a defense. Plants secrete the fatty acids to slow the growth of nearby plants, reducing competition when water is scarce.

Petrichor emanates from millions of raindrops falling all at once, giving this smell a stereoscopic quality. In 2015, a team of MIT scientists determined how petrichor reaches our noses. Using high-speed cameras, they observed that when a raindrop hits a porous surface, it traps tiny air bubbles at the point of contact. In a slow-motion video, you can see a raindrop hitting a surface. The drop briefly assumes a doughnut shape, then flattens into a disk. Infinitesimal droplets rise from the disk like fireflies buzzing over a lake. Those droplets lift petrichor from the soil, infusing the air.

Petrichor reminds you of the idea that smell is what happens when a substance becomes airborne. In the case of petrichor, that substance is a golden oil, secreted into the soil by rivalrous plants. Smells ride on air and impart personality to it.

Petrichor also reminds us that air is three-dimensional. The air's stillness after a rain shower is monumental, pungent, and temporary. (Picture petrichor as a golden cube of air above the ground, trembling like amber-scented Jell-O.) As you smell, you're observing a change happening *here* and *now*. With petrichor, it's particularly noticeable. Each smell pins a moment in space and time, with you, the smeller, as its witness. ★

where there were none, sometimes as a prank, more often in search of meaning.

The telephone would become the next century's great interrupter. Globally, the phone network fragmented attention. Dinners, quiet nights at home, intimate conversations, and reading time would rarely be free from intrusion by distant voices. Intimacy was rewired, near and far scrambled. Voices from the past, ex-lovers, bill collectors, family members looking for money—the phone suddenly produced anyone and anything we'd tried to forget. And why not the dead? Starting in the nineteenth century and running well into the twentieth, one could read of haunted phones and phone-switching stations, of calls from dead relatives and murdered lovers. In 1878, *The New York Sun* reported that calls coming from a telephone installed in a cemetery's office were waking a Catholic bookseller in the middle of the night. When it was found that no one had accessed the cemetery phone, and that the bell was mechanically operated, the cemetery owner locked and secured the room holding the phone. The calls continued, and everyone involved suspected a spirit was at work. On September 24, 1907, the *Alexandria Gazette* reported that a new phone exchange had been built in Wellesley, Massachusetts, because phone operators believed the old one was haunted. (A night operator had been found dead there two years earlier.) In the January 1933 issue of *The Telephone and Telegraph Journal*, a subscriber complained that after a repairman fixed their supposedly haunted phone, a rumor spread in the town that the house itself was haunted.

It took longer for the haunted telephone to cross from news into fiction, with Elliott O'Donnell's 1934 story "The Haunted Telephone" being one of the earliest known examples. It tells of a country doctor who, after answering a telephone call, finds that his identity becomes blurred with that of his disappeared predecessor. The story is also one of the earliest in which telecommunication causes confusion between the past and present. The plot of Nigel Kneale's now-lost 1954 BBC radio play *You Must Listen* sounds very much like the urban legends circulating in the margins of the press: After a phone is installed in a solicitor's office, the staff hears a woman's sexual monologue on the line. (No voice ever responds.) The voice, they learn, is that of a mistress whose lover is refusing to leave his wife. She commits suicide and her voice haunts the line. Mario Bava's three-part film *Black Sabbath* (1963) features an episode in which the voice of a supposedly dead ex-boyfriend haunts a woman's phone. Around the same time, Richard Matheson adapted his short story "Long Distance Call" for a 1964 *Twilight Zone* episode ("Night Call"), in which a lonely elderly woman receives calls from her deceased husband. In the TV version, before she hears her husband's voice, the woman hears static on the other end of the line.

3.

In Arthur C. Clarke's 1965 short story "Dial F for Frankenstein," the phone network does not transmit the dead but becomes its own living being. Clarke's story is set in 1975, then the near future, on a day when all the world's phones ring in unison as a kind of planetary prank call. Everyone who answers the phone hears not a voice, not a recording, but "a sound, which to many seemed like the roaring of the sea; to others, like the vibrations of harp strings in the wind." But it is the sea sound that predominates, the rush one hears when listening to a conch shell, that "secret sound of childhood."

In London, at a café across from the Post Office Research Station, a group of engineers debate what caused the call. Was it a power surge? Or was it the recent satellite launch, intended to connect all the world's telephone networks? The group's amateur sci-fi author has an idea: Since Alexander Graham Bell, he says, the telephone system has been thought of as a giant brain, with each switch acting as a neuron. What if, after the satellite launch, the switches in the phone network reached a critical mass of connectivity? And what if, like a newborn, the network is now awake and looking for food?

As they talk, the lights flicker. A jet flies unusually low over the building. Later, a fire alarm rings. After that, a bank receipt shows an employee with almost one billion pounds in the bank. One of the engineers opens a newspaper, and although the layout has the normal columns of type and photographs, the text is scrambled into "a sea of gibberish." What is happening? The engineers guess that the new "supermind" is like a newborn baby: it's looking for food—electricity—while extending its reach and causing havoc. A BBC report confirms that across the globe there have been industrial failures, the launch of guided missiles, airplane groundings, the shutdown of stock exchanges. The communications satellites have cut themselves off from central control—there is no way of shutting them down. Then the BBC signal goes silent, leaving the engineers to consider whether humanity itself has reached its end.

When the story was published, none of Clarke's readers would have expected a fire alarm to connect to the same system that lays out a newspaper. There wasn't yet an internet, and telecommunication networks were a specialized topic. Tim Berners-Lee, inventor of the World Wide Web, later claimed he read Clarke's story as a child and that it had inspired the Web's creation. Though, considering that the story ends in an apocalypse, it's hard to see why anyone might want to emulate it.

Predating *Pulse* by a few decades, "Dial F for Frankenstein" imagines a network that expands beyond its confines, laying waste to its makers. There is no ghost—for the first time, it is the network itself that is alive. Unable to speak, it prank-calls the world. And when the world answers, there is no spirit on the other end of the line ready to announce its arrival. What's calling is the line itself. Without a voice, without a soul.

The German media theorist Friedrich Kittler was a collector of these kinds of calls, calls that said nothing, came from nowhere, sounded like the ocean or like a conch shell's roar. In his book *Gramophone, Film, Typewriter*, he writes about a dream of Franz Kafka's in which the writer finds two telephone receivers, or Hörmuschel ("listening shells"), on the parapet of a bridge. Kafka picks up both receivers and asks for news of someone named Pontus (the name of an ancient sea god). On the other end of the line he hears "a sad, mighty, wordless song and the roar of the sea. Although well aware that it was impossible for human voices to penetrate these sounds, I didn't give in, and didn't go away."

Kittler traces that static-like sea sound through early modern literature, from Kafka to a little-known 1907 short story by Maurice Renard. In it, a composer and his friend, grief-stricken by the loss of several of their dinner club members, alternate between listening to a recording of their dead friends and putting their ear to a seashell. One asks: "What if this ear-shaped snail stored the sounds it heard at some critical moment—the agony of mollusks, maybe? And what if the rosy lips of its shell were to pass it on like a graphophone?"

Later, Kittler discusses another lost short story, this one by Salomo Friedlaender, a.k.a. Mynona: "Goethe Speaks into the Phonograph." The story's conceit is that sound waves and voices never fade: "These [air] vibrations encounter obstacles and are reflected, resulting in a to and fro which becomes weaker in the passage of time but which does not actually cease." Build the correct machine, the story's professor protagonist believes, and you can snatch the sounds back from the past—in a way, resurrecting anyone you wish. His first test subject? The father of German literature, Goethe himself.

After a visit to the writer's tomb, the professor hooks up a microphone and phonograph to an anatomically correct re-creation of Goethe's larynx. He brings the contraption to the writer's study, placing the larynx on a tripod not far from where Goethe's mouth might have been. There, the professor and his audience listen to the writer speak with poet Johann Peter Eckermann about Newton's theory of color.

Kittler stresses that with the invention of voice recording, one could, for the first time, capture not just the sign of a thing but its physical residue, emanating waves frozen in wax. (The same could be said for photography, which captures the light bounced off bodies.) This fact changed how we thought about our media, its powers as well as its possibilities. Kittler does not seem very interested in spiritualism, though he would have found it offered a playground of strange media ideas. In particular, he could have discovered a cluster of theories that proposed that no image or sound is ever lost. Like in our own digital age of cloud storage and Time Machine backups, this is a dream of a past in which everything is recoverable. The dead come back if you know where to look—all you need is the right sensitivity or ingenious machine. An artificial larynx and a phonograph, maybe, or a supernatural talent allowing a person to miraculously repossess the past.

> **By midcentury, the dead were no longer up for a telephonic chat: they pestered, sabotaged, interrupted, and terrorized. In a word, they haunted.**

4.

Annie Denton Cridge claimed to be just such a person. Little is known about Cridge today. What survives comes from her spiritualist publication, *The Vanguard*; her stream-of-consciousness books, including *My Soul's Thraldom and Its Deliverance*; and the few traces researchers have found in archives. She was born in England in 1825. In the 1840s, along with her brother, the geologist William Denton, she immigrated to the United States. By age twenty-three, she was a writer, a memoirist, and a socialist. She was also a grieving mother who had seen her infant child's spirit rise from its body to be greeted by its deceased grandparents. From that moment, Cridge was an ardent spiritualist and claimed the ability to see ghosts.

According to her brother, Cridge was also a "psychometrist," a person who, by laying hands on an object, can glean information about the object's past. The term was coined by Joseph Rodes Buchanan, a physician and her brother's employer. In a journal he published, Buchanan wrote that psychometry, from the Greek for "soul measuring," was a gift available to certain people, who, just by touching an object, could learn something about its effects (if it was a medicine) or its previous owners (if it was a personal item). In experiments he describes at exhaustive length, Buchanan claims to have shown that individuals with "acute sensibility" could read the contents of a sealed letter by holding it to their head (thus anticipating Johnny Carson's Carnac the Magnificent by more than one hundred years). Others, when presented with a written autograph, could produce a "mental daguerreotype" of the autograph's owner. Buchanan's crackpot science could, he claimed, revolutionize human communication, medicine, archeology, and history. It might even lead, Buchanan wrote in a fit of the manic optimism that colors much of his writing, to the reconstruction of all of human creation.

Buchanan does not mention Annie Cridge in his 1885 *Manual of Psychometry: The Dawn of a New Civilization*, but her brother devotes space to her in his own 1863 book, *Nature's Secrets: Or, Psychometric Researches*. For several chapters, Annie and her sister-in-law, Elizabeth, are William Denton's star subjects. When presented with a host of rocks and fossils, first Annie and then Elizabeth narrates the objects' origins with novelistic vividness. After Annie is presented with a piece of limestone from near the Missouri River, she sees a hill by a river. When Elizabeth is presented with tufa from near Vesuvius, she has a vision of a violent eruption.

Psychometry's trigger is touch, but vision is its real operative sense. The women are presented as seers. "I see…" begins most of the testimonies. Though the telegraph might have been the medium's preferred metaphorical machine, for the psychometer, the world-governing metaphor was the daguerreotype. Like most of the pseudo-scientific writing on spiritualism, William's book begins with a reasonable premise: we retain memories that we unconsciously repress and bring back involuntarily at a later point. Denton then expands his theories to argue that objects retain unconscious impressions of what takes place around them, like a daguerreotype. Here he makes the leap: "In the world around us radiant forces are passing from all objects to all objects in their vicinity, and during every moment of the day and night are daguerreotyping the appearances of each upon the other." Enter Annie and Elizabeth, whose brains are "sufficiently sensitive to perceive [these radiant forces] when [their brains are] brought into proximity to the objects on which they are impressed."

In Denton's writings, history—the deep history of geology, or the more recent history of one's life—operates like a photograph, or, more accurately, a film strip. What is of interest in Denton's writings is not their scientific accuracy but his anticipation, almost by accident, of the cinematic apparatus. The first film cameras would be invented at the close of the century, but here is an idea that the world retains not just a single image of itself but a succession of images. When Cridge and Elizabeth narrate their visions, they are static—they are describing paintings, really—but on occasion their language suggests motion, as when Vesuvian lava flows into a boiling ocean. What Denton describes is a kind of cinema avant la lettre, history as a phantasmagoria, "the history of its time passed before the gaze of the seer." Far before Orwell and the Stasi and the National Security Agency, the world becomes a giant recording device, aimed in all directions, with total information awareness.

Nigel Kneale, the writer of the lost telephone radio play mentioned above, used these ideas in his cult TV show *The Stone Tape*, a bizarre 1972 BBC Christmas special in which a ghost is projected from the stone wall of an ancient house. (A ghost of a woman appears, falling from the same staircase over and over again, as if looped on a tape. The "tape," a group of scientists learn, is the stone itself.) Denton's ideas took a century to find their ideal home: on a TV show (among the first to be shot entirely on video) about ghosts who are trapped like images caught on video tape. This is the afterlife as media, as a space in which one's image is predestined to play in infinite reruns.

Likewise, spiritualism's afterlife is found in the movies, where it is doomed to repeat, perhaps forever, the same gestures and plotlines. In narrative films like *The Uninvited* (1944), *The Changeling* (1980), and *Hereditary* (2018), one can watch the familiar séances and psychometric visions; child ghosts who return to grieving mothers; and chalkboards writing their own messages. On occasion, one gets a complex evocation of the movement, as in Olivier Assayas's *Personal Shopper* (2016). But more usually Hollywood depoliticizes spiritualism, stigmatizing its ideas and transforming its mediums into eccentric crones. Christianized, the lesson of Hollywood spiritualism is that one shouldn't play with Ouija boards and that Satan lurks in every basement.

There is, though, in films like *Pulse*, a residue of the movement's weird theories of mass communication, however dark this vision may have turned. The happy miracles of the "spiritual telegraph" have become the nightmares of the haunted internet genre. As scholar Jeffrey Sconce has written, spiritualism's optimism concerning communication technologies was greatly tempered, if not completely reversed, during the twentieth century. By midcentury, the dead were no longer up for a telephonic chat: they pestered, sabotaged, interrupted, and terrorized. In a word, they haunted. Now, with cloud storage and 24-7 connectivity, the past, it seems, is always recoverable. But it is impossible for us to believe that cell phones and Zoom calls will deliver this past free from worry and fear. The problem is not how to bring back the past, but how the dead can, once and for all, stay that way. ✶

THE ACT OF SMELLING: SKIN
BY JUDE STEWART

BODY ODOR EXISTS on three levels. At the uppermost level is what's known as BO, which is battled (or not) with deodorants, showers, and fragrances. The midlevel smell is determined by cultural factors like diet, occupation, and hygiene. Beneath these scented layers of sweat, lotions, and last night's meal, you'll find a person's baseline smell. This note is subtle, enveloping, and unchanging beneath the daily fluctuations. Unlike synthetic fragrances, which are designed to be noticed, this baseline scent is amplified only by body heat. To observe it at all requires drawing close.

Among other tangled human reasons, we choose mates whose bodies smell good to us, partners whose major histocompatibility complex (MHC) genes differ robustly from our own.

Mating by smell is complex. For example, smell preferences can get scrambled in women who take oral contraceptives. As their bodies are chemically tricked into believing they're pregnant, these women prefer the smell of partners—male or female—whose MHC profiles resemble their own. (Imagine the chaos of going off the pill, and off your partner's scent: How much is smell implicated in divorce?) Mating isn't always centered on baby-making, either. When asked to sniff T-shirts worn by gay or straight men, gay men can identify—and prefer—the smell of other gay men.

Many diseases announce themselves with a shift in bodily odor. Typhus makes the body smell of freshly baked brown bread, tuberculosis of stale beer, yellow fever of the butcher's shop, plague of overripe apples. Diagnosis by smell is both quaintly outmoded—how recognizable is measles today by its smell of plucked feathers?—and newly relevant. Trained doctors and dogs can detect the smells of Parkinson's disease, malaria, multiple sclerosis, COVID-19, and cancers of many kinds.

Your baseline smell is unique to you, more so than a thumbprint. The digital chemical sensors used at TSA checkpoints could theoretically be updated to differentiate you from your identical twin or match you to a database of individual smells. (You can't willfully stop emitting your baseline smell.) Bodily smell also reveals our thoughts, or at least the heated pendulum of our moods. Apocrine glands work overtime during stressful situations, giving emotional sweating a more pungent tang than heat-reduction sweating. Humans can detect joy, fear, frustration, and sadness by smell alone. Each person's smell forms a nimbus or halo around their body.

I've been inhaling my partner's scent for a quarter century, but if asked, I would have trouble describing its particulars. It's warm, well balanced. However, I can describe what it registers inside me. Burying my face in his neck is an action I've repeated thousands—maybe millions—of times. His smell is a particular and deep kind of home. I feel still, encircled, known. My blood pressure plummets and my stress hormones evaporate. (Your lover smells this way to you too.) To me this smells like relief, like a concentrated jet of grace. ✶

"OUR ART KNOWS MORE THAN WE DO."

MAGGIE NELSON
[WRITER]

Over the last decade, Maggie Nelson's writing has become one of the guiding intellectual lights for artists of all disciplines. Her books on aesthetics, gender, violence, and, most recently, freedom, allow for the kind of open, generative quality of thought that suits the artistic temperament. In this way, she has not established herself with a series of spicy opinions or fixed positions, but through a celebration of the endless challenge of uncertainty.

Nelson began her career writing poetry and published three collections while living in New York City in the '90s and early aughts. These received little attention at the time of publication but have recently been reissued in response to her growing readership. In the mid-2000s Nelson began focusing on variants of nonfiction that could contain her poetic impulses and document patterns of culture more explicitly.

Each of Nelson's books seems to consider the relationship between memoir and critical thought through a new set of concerns. In The Argonauts, a deeply personal work about her experience starting a family, Nelson coined the term autotheory as a riff on writer Paul Preciado's term self-theory. Bluets, *one of her early expansions into prose, is a collage of microessays on the color blue and her experiences of melancholia. According to Nelson, her career has been an ongoing vacillation between introspective and critical projects. This is her way of maintaining balance in her life and work.*

Her newest book, On Freedom: Four Songs of Care and Constraint, *falls toward the critical end of that spectrum. Like much of her writing, the book is a document of Nelson's love of reading, and it brims with fascinating morsels of knowledge gathered from across disciplines, especially philosophy and contemporary art. Nelson taught for years at CalArts' School of Critical Studies, but recently she has begun teaching in the writing program at the University of Southern California, where one of her courses is called Wild Theory. She continues to teach, in part, to avoid relying on the publishing cycle for income, and to remain a sovereign thinker.*

I spoke to Nelson in April via video chat, though we quickly realized we live in the same neighborhood and grew up not far from each other. She called from a cottage she rents to maintain a distance from family life while writing. During our conversation, she often responded to my questions in fragments, twisting through quotations and subject matter with the kind of elegant segues that have long characterized her writing. Afterward, she edited her answers twice and recommended a good local acupuncturist.

— Ross Simonini

I. THE BOILING CAULDRON

THE BELIEVER: Did you feel your childhood was characterized by a lack of agency?

MAGGIE NELSON: It's funny that I've written this book about freedom, because it's not as if a saga of feeling imprisoned has been the principal drama of my psychic life. I mean, my childhood was marred by traumas of various kinds, and those stand out more as the markers of my psychic life.

BLVR: As a parent, do you think about the agency of your child?

MN: Well, it's a bad year to talk about freedom, because, as you know, our children have been on house arrest. My son went back to school this week, first time in over a year, and it seems to have awakened something in him. He told me this morning, "I'm in revolt." And I was like, Oh Lord. But, yes, being a child is a series of injustices based on curtailed liberty. On the other hand, children don't tend to feel cared for if they have a feeling of boundless freedom. There's the rub.

BLVR: Do you think about parenting with the kind of critical mind you bring to your writing?

MN: I explicitly didn't really use parenting as a fulcrum in this book [*On Freedom*]. But I will say that I teach a lot of autobiography as a professor, and I've read tons of autobiographical writing, and it seems very clear to me that no matter what parents do or what kind of childhood one has, the grievances remain. So it helps to remember that there's something structural about individuation, and hopefully the feeling that your parents did you wrong won't persist forever. I mean, I've yet to meet any student—except for maybe first-generation students who are rehearsing an understandable script of gratitude toward the opportunities they've had—who wasn't sitting atop some avowed or disavowed boiling cauldron of feeling that their parents did them wrong.

BLVR: Right. The larger structures of revolution in society are playing out internally as well, for all of us. Children go through their own personal little revolts, as yours is now. And that's natural.

MN: The youth tend to be interested in moments of liberation, and older people tend to be more alert to ongoing practices of freedom. And I do feel that's clearly true in my own life, in terms of what my attention is called toward. As I say in the book, moments of liberation are utterly crucial, as radical change rarely happens without them. But their aftermath can create a certain amount of suffering. There's a lot of letdown if and when moments of liberation aren't followed by ongoing practices of freedom. It can become a source of anger and disappointment for a person growing up to feel that nothing's changing, that nothing's going to change. So I do think the message is that the work is ongoing. And it's never too soon to deliver that message.

BLVR: You've talked about the radical freedom of teaching art at CalArts. And now you've moved to USC, which is a more traditional format. Do you find that within the disciplines of art and literature there are different senses of freedom?

MN: In *The Art of Cruelty*, I talk about the writer Brian Evenson, who once taught at Brigham Young University, where a student complained that she felt poisoned by reading his violent fiction. I get that. But to me, books provide so much more space in terms of how you can interact with them than other forms of art provide. I have always found movies and live performances, and some forms of visual art, much bossier than reading, because usually when you experience them you are in a venue that is more difficult to get out of. Like, if you're not in the mood for one second, you've got to push past everybody in the dark and it's a big deal that you left your seat. I feel this a lot when I watch movies with my son, when he tells me he doesn't want to see anything too scary. Sometimes, even if I'm sitting right by the computer, Voldemort appears too quickly. And without that fucking nose. And I can't get it off the screen fast enough. And he's like, "I saw it, I saw it!" But books aren't like that.

BLVR: Do you think your work is bossy to readers in that way?

MN: I mean, I've received some hate mail. But I don't really want to know how people receive it. I'm on a need-to-know basis with that.

BLVR: You don't read reviews?

MN: It depends. I mean, if you write a poetry book, you might get one review in ten years. So I'll read that. But with *The Argonauts*, at some point I stopped reading reviews and didn't feel like I needed to read any more.

BLVR: Do you ever purposely reach for transgression in your work?

MN: I think a lot of the things people think are transgressive for transgression's sake are actually just people speaking their truths to people who aren't familiar with those truths, or with their demographics. I just wrote an introduction to a book I love by Hervé Guibert, and I've noticed, reading around, that a lot of people write about Guibert as if he were *trying* to get a rise out of the bourgeoisie or something. But he was just writing about his sex life. And if it doesn't resemble something you've heard about or lived, then you're going to be like, *This is so shocking!* But it's not shocking to him. I don't think he is sitting around thinking, How am I going to get a rise out of someone? So I think a lot of transgression just depends on where you're coming from.

BLVR: In *On Freedom*, you discuss artists who feel they should have total freedom to make whatever they like, regardless of how the work may be received. But you seem almost ambivalent to reception.

> **There's a lot of letdown if and when moments of liberation aren't followed by ongoing practices of freedom.**

MN: I think different people have different ways they try to protect their capacity to create, and for some people that might be ravenously reading all the reviews and then collapsing into self-hatred, then getting over it. For somebody else, it might be a studied avoidance. But I don't think anybody could participate in the worst elements of contemporary discourse and take on the most draconian ideas of responsibility for the feelings of others and continue to preserve their practice. I just don't see it. But I think people solve that in different ways.

BLVR: And your way is…

MN: Well, I guess I don't really feel like I'm even making art sometimes. So I don't even know if I put myself in this category. I'm really grateful for coming up in poetry, where audience was just not a big consideration. And I feel like that's pretty solid within me, you know?

BLVR: Right, and it's probably related to why you don't use social media.

MN: I don't. I live in horror of my first thought being broadcast. Because a lot of thought is tone. Tone is where a symptom occurs, you know? So if your symptom is anger or reactivity, or defensiveness, or repression, that will come out in the tone. So I have to work on a book and hear its tonal issues long enough to see where my symptoms and obstacles are and what I'm struggling with.

BLVR: You're not a "first thought, best thought" kind of writer.

MN: I came up loving "first thought, best thought" poetry. But I've also always been really interested in the illusion of immediacy, the construction of immediacy. I want to have the feeling of immediacy of speech but with thought that I feel like I can stand behind, even if just for the moment, even if I change my mind later.

BLVR: It's interesting that you make the distinction between art and not-art, because your writing doesn't seem to make that distinction.

MN: I do think it's all part of one flow. And to me, how personal it is and what form it takes on the page are just a Bob Creeley, "form follows content" kind of a thing. But at the same time, I'm alert to what different genres can do. And I think if someone calls *Bluets* a novel, I'm like, OK, that's fine. To me, it's within the realm of experimental speculative nonfiction. Someone could say *The Art of Cruelty* is a series of essays, but it was not conceived as a series of essays. It was conceived as an ongoing thought that had episodic rings of action. *On Freedom* is weird because it's four long chapters, which are each, like, seventy-five pages in manuscript. This was not a particularly elegant form to me. There was no real experimenting with the accretion of fragments, like I've done before. And then that became a kind of formal question to me, like: How can things this long hang together? I like to come up with subtitles, like "a reckoning" or "a murder" or things that kind of name something about the form. And I always thought of these sections of *On Freedom* as long songs. That was my idea about them. Songs can be quite long and still hang together, and they are less boring than chapters.

II. REENCHANTMENT

BLVR: Your work always complicates genres and structures, and I feel like this is what you do with subjects as well. The subject appears more complex to me by the end of a book. You dissolve binaries. You make it hard to think easily about something.

MN: Henry James has this phrase that I love about how his novels have to have the right degree of bewilderment. There's a broad degree of bewilderment where you just feel like someone's led you further into murk and you don't feel any enjoyment; you don't feel any clarity. So I think I aim for a kind of complexity that feels clarifying. I have these weird images about writing. I don't know if they make any sense to anybody else, but for me it's a complexity that has *shine*. It's not murkier.

BLVR: For a lot of nonfiction, I think people pick up a book on a subject and hope that what starts as a broad survey ends up as a focused and clear resolution. Then they can walk away feeling certain. But your work seems to open up so many forking paths. And at the end of *On Freedom* you say you have a new relationship with anxiety after writing the book. Is that related to this opening up?

MN: I don't say that I had anxiety after writing the book; I say that a reckoning with freedom brought me into a reckoning with anxiety. You know, if you're open to indeterminacy and all of what we don't know—we know we were born and that we'll die, but that's about it—that's a very anxious situation. And if you're not gonna try and end indeterminacy, which is of course a fool's errand, then you have to find another way.

I think this brings us back to the "art versus non-art" thing. Some books pose questions that have answers. If I wrote those kinds of books, you might ask of, say, *The Art of Cruelty*: Does seeing violent works of art make us crueler? Open this book and you'll find out! For *On Freedom*, it could be: Should we keep the concept of freedom central to our hearts and politics, or has it in some ways run its course? I mean, there are plenty of books out there like that, which offer strong theories about those kinds of things, and I've read many of them. And if you publish more mainstream books, then you hit more mainstream expectations. But I'm not doing that. On the other hand, just saying, "Whoa, man, life's complicated"—that's not rigorous.

> If you're open to indeterminacy and all of what we don't know—we know we were born and that we'll die, but that's about it—that's a very anxious situation.

BLVR: There's an undercurrent of Buddhist ideas in *On Freedom*, which feels like a good expression of how to live with the complexity we are talking about.

MN: I think it's kind of an inevitable body of knowledge that you have to touch if you're interested in these ways of nonbinary thinking.

BLVR: Right. And you are also willing to talk about the "magic" of art, which is a hairy word for many people.

MN: I definitely don't think of myself as very witchy, but that paragraph about art and magic was one of the last things I wrote, and I think it felt like a limb I could finally stand on.

BLVR: Because of the mountain of research behind it?

MN: I spend a lot of time with artists. I love artists. I love teaching artists. And I do think that a lot of the way certain people's brains work makes mainstream discourse and expectations just deadening to them. There are people who want to go arrange twigs on a riverbank for thirty years, and there's not a Twitter discourse about how to deal with that. I got a chance to spend some time with Carolee Schneemann before she died. I wrote a profile of her and I titled it "The Reenchantment of Carolee Schneemann." And *enchantment* can be kind of a bad word in certain circles. But it was a word she used in talking about how to keep falling in love with life and art over and over again, and it moved me.

BLVR: I think enchantment is a very necessary counterpart to criticism. Otherwise, it doesn't really seem to invoke the nature of art.

MN: I mean, I know this'll sound tendentious to some, but in a recent statement about *Scaffold*[1] that Sam Durant put out, he talks about a moment when someone shouted at him during a lecture, "You should have known!" Without contesting the heckler, Durant also reminds us that artists "are not all-seeing, all-knowing beings with the capacity to grasp all ramifications

of their work." Now, I'm not saying anything about what he should or shouldn't have known about *Scaffold*, or that the costs of this particular not-knowing weren't extremely high, or that his not-knowing here wasn't related to his whiteness in disturbing and predictable ways. I'm just saying I'm interested in his reminder, as it asks us to remember that which we literally cannot remember, a.k.a. the unconscious.

BLVR: The unconscious is real.

MN: Yeah. And our art knows more than we do. It *does* different things than we do, or that we can bear admitting to. And sometimes that will come out and be amazing, and sometimes it will come out and people will be like, *How on earth…?* But to me, the fact that we don't know everything about ourselves or our expression is great news. It doesn't mean it's always comfortable or positive. It's just part of what makes being alive fascinating.

III. THE NEURODIVERSITY OF THE IMAGINATION

BLVR: In *On Freedom*, you write about Helen Molesworth, who says that the avant-garde is moving away from the sensationalism and shock of the past—Artaud, for example—and more toward "caring."

MN: Right. So professional curators and critics are kind of tasked with articulating, or prognosticating, trends. I don't say this in a

---

[1] *Scaffold* (2012) by Sam Durrant is a sculptural reconstruction of the gallows used in US state-sanctioned executions by hanging between 1859 and 2006. The sculpture's installation at the Walker Art Center in 2017 was protested, ultimately leading to its removal.

good or bad way. But I don't see myself in that business. And so I think in some ways Molesworth is not just noticing something but calling it into further being by noticing it. You want to call attention to certain artists and to curate shows that say, *This is what's happening now*. And then that *makes* it happen now, even more so. And then we look back in history and we say, *Oh, that was the era of caring or whatever*. I'm interested in all that, but I'm also interested in the fact that there's so much art happening at any given time, and a lot of artists are being subsumed under certain headings that they don't necessarily want to be subsumed under, and yet they also don't want to *not* be in a show, right? So there are all the people who want to say what's happening now and what this art means, and then there are all the weirdos making stuff who are saying, *Well, if you've got to put that in the press release, I guess I could say that's what it's all about*. I want to pay homage to the latter as much as to the former.

BLVR: And once someone says that art is part of a movement, it's also stamping an expiration date on it.

MN: Yeah, or you're also doing reclamatory work of some kind, and privileging certain terms. You go back and you say, Actually, this painter from the twenties was doing a form of this thing that we're valuing now. And that's fine. And that can be really interesting, but they're all just lenses that you put on people's work. They're not the truth about what that work was. I don't really traffic in the truth of what the work was. I'm more interested in—as I think my books make clear—how art changes in meaning over time. So it's never ontologically fixed.

BLVR: The kaleidoscopic quality of your writing feels that way, and you use so many quotes and points of reference to achieve this. While I'm reading your books, I'm often wondering if you have some kind of reading practice, some way of culling all this information.

MN: Reading is such a raw topic these days because the pandemic has just—especially for people with children—it's just demolished the time to read. So it's a little painful to talk about reading. On the other hand, I often have this ideal of reading for pleasure that's never been a reality for me. Like I think, One day I'll finally read in this way that everybody describes. I'll read a beach book, you know? And the fact of the matter is, I'm a writer who typically gets hot on an idea and then follows it. I track down names that were mentioned, hunt for sources. I read with a pen in my hand. And so it's a kind of carnivorous reading that's never really in line with this ideal I have of reading as recreation.

We have all our cheap paperbacks right by the door; it's like a very thin shelf with *Silas Marner* and other pocket paperbacks on it. In the Before Times, when I would be leaving for the airport—remember *the airport*?—sometimes I'd just grab a paperback on the way out. And that was, like, the only time when I would be like, Oh, shit, I forgot a book. I guess I'll just bring *Mrs. Dalloway*. That would be the only random reading I would ever do. But also, I mean, we read all day on our phones. I feel like I just spent a year standing in the kitchen, homeschooling, just scrolling through the bad news. But was I really reading?

BLVR: You write about the inherent limits of imagination. We assume imagination to be a space of total freedom, but it's limited by our experiences, just like everything else. Do you attempt to push against these constraints of your own imagination in your work?

MN: I would have thought that as I got older, and less concerned about worldly things, I would feel freer, but writing actually feels more constricted. This isn't to say it feels less possible or anything. I think I just have higher standards now than, say, writing a good sonnet. So in my twenties I might've been like, Wow, that's a really refreshing turn of phrase. I bet nobody's ever put those two words together before. I should try and get it published! Whereas now I'm onto other things.

I think I'm a little recalcitrant about my mind, and it's probably worked for me so far, but I actually turn down a lot of projects with the idea that *that's not how my mind works*. Collaborative projects, namely. Anything that involves speaking to other people in a room. There is a lot of this in LA. I don't do that. But, I don't know, maybe I'm selling my brain short. I'm not sure. I think probably some of that protectiveness I'm talking about around art is my own. I'm just describing my own protectiveness.

But neurodiversity in terms of our imaginative life is profoundly real. I mean, my partner's a sculptor, and he sees sculpture in his head. I'll be talking and I will ask, "Are you listening to me?" And he'll be like, "I'm sorry, I'm just seeing a sculpture." My mind doesn't work like that. And this is part of the degree-of-bewilderment thing I mentioned before. There should be a real respect of heterogeneity. So when we talk about what art is, where or what the imagination is, or what its limits are, we should also remember that everybody has a different relationship to these things and to their brain, and that brains don't all work the same way. Like, *at all*. So if someone is paranoically insistent on preserving a sense of imaginative largesse, this might be because otherwise they'd fall into a puddle of hell.

BLVR: Right. And in that way, thinking about audience could be more dangerous for some than others.

MN: I mean, my experience of writing—which is not the same as a lot of other people's—is that I've always written the book first and then tried to find a publisher for it later. Because I don't want anybody to expect anything about what the book is going to be. People who need to live on advances don't live that way, but, you know, that's why I have a day job. And also, the world's a mysterious place. I'm thinking about a book like *Bluets*, which was rejected by everybody and then published very small-ly and greatly by Wave Books. But now, thanks to the success of *The Argonauts*, I just did a whole week of press for the French version of *Bluets*, and it's like this literary event, almost twenty years after it was written. So, I mean, you have no idea what a book's second or third lives may be. Or if it'll ever have even one life. Or it may have a life a hundred years after you die. So it's all about accepting that indeterminacy. And, given all that, trying to make the book that you want would seem to be the only thing to strive for. I mean, that's all we've got. ✶

THE ACT OF SMELLING: PENCILS
BY JUDE STEWART

PENCIL WOOD USED to be much more fragrant. Pencils in the early nineteenth century were made of eastern red cedar from Florida, Georgia, and Tennessee. These pencils smelled of spicy black pepper and cinnamon and their shavings were colored pinkish-red. As recently as 1890, red cedar was so abundant that Southerners built barns and fences with it—until the production of millions of pencils thinned the wood supply and jacked up prices.

The US Forest Service recommended incense cedar as a replacement wood for pencils: it was cheap and functionally ideal. But manufacturers worried that pencils made with incense cedar—the pencils we have now—would be too pale and too weakly scented to fly with consumers. So around the year 1920, manufacturers dyed and perfumed incense cedar to simulate red cedar. History doesn't record when this practice stopped, but eventually, the smell of pencils dwindled.

As for what's inside the pencils, it turns out that pure graphite has no smell. But pencil manufacturing has progressed a long way from pure graphite. In their original form, pencils were made of a lead alloy wrapped in paper or string; then pure graphite slats were encased in red cedar wood; then graphite powder was purified and mixed with clay or wax to form a slat encased in wood. These additions helped stretch the limited supply of graphite in a way that was truly industrial and scalable. And it gave pencils variety as a consumer product. A mix containing more clay and wax yields a sharper, paler line, whereas a pencil containing more graphite writes darker and softer. The mechanical pencil inserts of today smell bright, clean, forward, and uncomplicatedly metallic. That smell isn't from the graphite, though—it's from the clay and wax additives. And yet the smell of modern graphite is worth pausing over. In a real sense, it's the smell of an early triumph of the Industrial Revolution.

The smell at the other end of a pencil, the eraser, isn't usually detectable: it's often too dried-out to smell like much of anything. But a block eraser's smell, on the other hand, is an indicator of its quality. An odorless eraser is a cheap and useless one, while aromatic erasers contain more natural rubber, the best material for erasing. Natural rubber erasers smell cheerful, ugly, forthright. Erasers smell most when they're being used. The act of erasing makes us hunch closer to the paper. To blow away the twisted rubber strings, you must first inhale and smell what you're doing. This is smell in action—a pencil's odors of incense cedar, clay, wax, and rubber emerge not while you are writing, but while you are sharpening and erasing, in the pauses between. ✶

THE COUNTRY OF LONE WOLVES

A poem by Fernando Valverde

For the strength of the Pack is the Wolf,
and the strength of the Wolf is the Pack.
—Rudyard Kipling

There is always a wolf in the night of the world
in the nightmares of the earth
under the light of the moon
the law
is a wolf
lonely
the law is old
and certain
like the night
or like the barking of dogs
Lee Harvey Oswald shows the camera his Italian-made rifle
in the yard of his house
on the outskirts
because the strength of the pack is the wolf
and because there will always be a lone wolf willing to do the country a favor
from a window
or a doorway
or at point-blank range
the important thing is not to devour it whole
you have to leave the skin
or the head
as they say the most elementary laws
James Earl Ray points his Remington rifle at the balcony of the Lorraine Motel in Memphis

a single bite will suffice
it is not advisable to lose control
or be too proud
because lone wolves travel for the pack
over the hills
or the snow
or in the desert
crossing through the nightmares of the earth
and its prayers
Sirhan Bishara Sirhan empties his .22-caliber revolver
because wolves are nomads that walk in circles
and when a deep sorrow invades them
they cry
and their lament crosses the plains and forests
where someone erases their tracks
while they lick themselves
from the tip of the nose to the paws
firm in their solitude
and their misfortune
because it is hunger that pushes them
and the appetite their motivation
Mark David Chapman shoots a special .38 caliber revolver
because the war is not over
and the wolves walk on the water
and their language is flesh
and their lair the world
and some escape by walking away
while others
stop,
safe, paralyzed,
not daring to run
sitting in a movie theater or in a doorway
waiting for the empire of men
and law.

Translated from the Spanish by Carolyn Forché

SIDE QUEST

A GUEST COLUMN
by Bijan Stephen

LIST OF GAMES MENTIONED:

★ Magic: The Gathering
★ *Fortnite*
★ *Valorant*
★ *Counter-Strike*

LIST OF '90S TRADING CARD MAGAZINES MENTIONED:
★ *The Duelist*

As you might imagine, I play a lot of video games. I grew up with the medium; I sometimes feel like I came of age as it did, though I think everyone who's lived alongside video games could probably say that. I grew up playing couch co-op and multiplayer games with my brother and our friends in unregimented, undocumented time. One of the more satisfying things I learned was how to modify my play in response to whomever I was matched up with—to attack more quickly against this person or wait out someone else. It wasn't until years later that I learned that this concept was called metagaming, a word that doesn't appear in many dictionaries and that describes the only way humans play with one another.

Every game has a metagame: even spades, even tag. The word comes from Nigel Howard, a game theorist of the Cold War, who coined the term in a 1971 book that attempted to solve a version of the prisoner's dilemma based on a "nonrational" approach—a version of the game that relied on a game that *might* exist if players chose their strategies with full knowledge of other players' decisions. How does a game become different, in other words, if you know what your opponent will do?

The definition that's most commonly used now, however, comes from Magic: The Gathering designer Richard Garfield, who wrote his theorization of the concept in the spring 1995 issue of *The Duelist*, a magazine put out by the venerable game publisher Wizards of the Coast. Garfield realized that his *relationships* to the other players at his table influenced the outcome of their games—that each game wasn't its own, independent event. Five years later he'd argue that "there is of course no game without a metagame… A game without a metagame is like an idealized object in physics. It may be a useful construct but it doesn't really exist." A game is a socially constructed thing.

In video games, where mechanics replace rules—because rules are socially accepted, and because it's hard to modify code on the fly—metagaming has colloquially come to imply all the externalities that surround games. That's everything from optimal strategy to the social codes that form around each particular game; everything from knowing what the best weapons in *Fortnite* are at any given time to knowing how to conduct yourself on its subreddit. "Before a videogame can ever be played—before software can be considered a game in the first place—there must be a metagame," Stephanie Boluk and Patrick LeMieux write in the introduction to their book *Metagaming: Playing, Competing, Spectating, Trading, Making, and Breaking Videogames*. The metagame, in other words, arises from the discontinuity between the experience of play and the mechanics of a video game.

When it comes to online multiplayer games, you have to be present; you have to be aware of and paying attention to the other players. Which is why I like Garfield's definition: the metagame here is just reading other players. A further expansion, I think, comes from a concept published by theorists Marcus Carter, Martin Gibbs, and Michael Arnold, about Thomas F. Gieryn's boundary-work theory. Gieryn's idea is a sociological one, used to explain how people distinguish science from nonscience. It can

Illustration by Kristen Radtke

be applied to video games, as Carter, Gibbs, and Arnold write, to explain how players figure out and enforce the unspoken social rules that every game has: "Players place recognition of the implicit rules of the game *above* recognition of the formal rules of the game."

Lately I've found myself playing a lot of *Valorant*. It's a tactical shooter, which means that it's part of the genre of games in which precision in positioning and strategy trumps raw aim a lot of the time. The point of the game is to win rounds by planting or defusing what's called a "spike" in game parlance—it's a bomb, really, much like the one you find in *Counter-Strike*—or by eliminating the enemy team. It's a race to win thirteen rounds (though you do have to win by two in competitive games).

It's also the first PC first-person shooter I've ever seriously played, which means that I'm at the bottom of a steep learning curve. It's hard to internalize recoil patterns and remember to clear every corner I see, because it's not something I've ever done in a video game.

But what's kept me going—and what's most satisfying about the experience—is the new group of people I regularly play with.

I could tell you that *Valorant*'s metagame has a lot to do with coordinating team plays using imprecise and improvised information—that you play the other team by figuring out their quirks as much as by lining up your shots. But what's more satisfying, I think, is feeling like I've somehow gotten back to those days on the couch, learning more about the people I've chosen to play with. Queueing up with a couple of friends and a couple of strangers to play *Valorant* over the internet isn't quite like having people over to game and shoot the shit—but it's not unlike it either. The point, in both situations, is to be with people. ★

THE ACT OF SMELLING: CAMPHOR
BY JUDE STEWART

CAMPHOR DEMANDS ATTENTION. It pierces the nose, spreading a frosty latticework over the face. After that first sharp hit, the smell recedes into a pleasing, wintergreen roundness. Sniffing camphor is rousing, like drifting through a current of cold water in a warm lake.

These intense qualities appealed to mathematician Francis Galton. His thought experiment in what he called "arithmetic by smell" was carried out with various smells, including camphor, which he documented in a quirky 1894 paper. "Arithmetic may be performed by the sole medium of imaginary smells, just as by imaginary figures or sounds," Galton wrote. "I taught myself to associate two whiffs of peppermint with one whiff of camphor; three of peppermint with one of carbolic acid, and so on . . ." Galton declared the experiment successful, adding and subtracting scents with giddy abandon, although he "did not attempt multiplication by smell."

Camphor activates what is called the trigeminal system of temperature, touch, and pain nerves in the face and nose. Like other trigeminal smells, such as eucalyptus, skunk spray, and habanero peppers, camphor provides an example of how our senses can blur, compound, amplify, and overlap each other. No sense operates in isolation from the others—if one is removed from the equation, it affects the whole. This explains why, for instance, it's difficult to balance on one leg while blindfolded. Other sense interactions are even more curious. A group of scientists recently found neural evidence in mice of "smounds," smells whose perception is directly affected by hearing a particular tone at the same time.

Camphor comes from the wood of Southeast Asian laurel trees. Its potency is by design: the smell repels insects and fights microbes. In humans, it reduces inflammation, numbs aches and pains, clears the nasal passageways, and calms a cough. The Chinese nickname for camphor, *ping-pien*, or "ice flakes," suggests its sensory[1] effect, while its other nickname, *lung-nao-hsiang*, or "dragon's brain perfume,"[2] evokes an otherworldly quality. Sanskrit poetry associates camphor with the moon. In the tenth-century poem "Saundaryalahari," camphor flakes falling from the lips of the goddess Devi cool the searing heat of three smoldering cities.

In Hindu temples, burning camphor is used to activate the third eye, stoke intention for prayer, and purify the mind. (The etymology of the word *smell* in most languages relates to the word for *smoke*.) Smells like camphor can demarcate a sacred space and time for deep contemplation. In its fragile intensity, a smell can be a pop-up mosque or chapel: a spiritual state you dwell in briefly, before it wafts invisibly off. ★

---

[1] As opposed to *sensuous*. There's a whole body of premodern literature in several cultures that considers camphor an anti-aphrodisiac.
[2] Also the title of a book by R. A. Donkin, *Dragon's Brain Perfume: An Historical Geography of Camphor*.

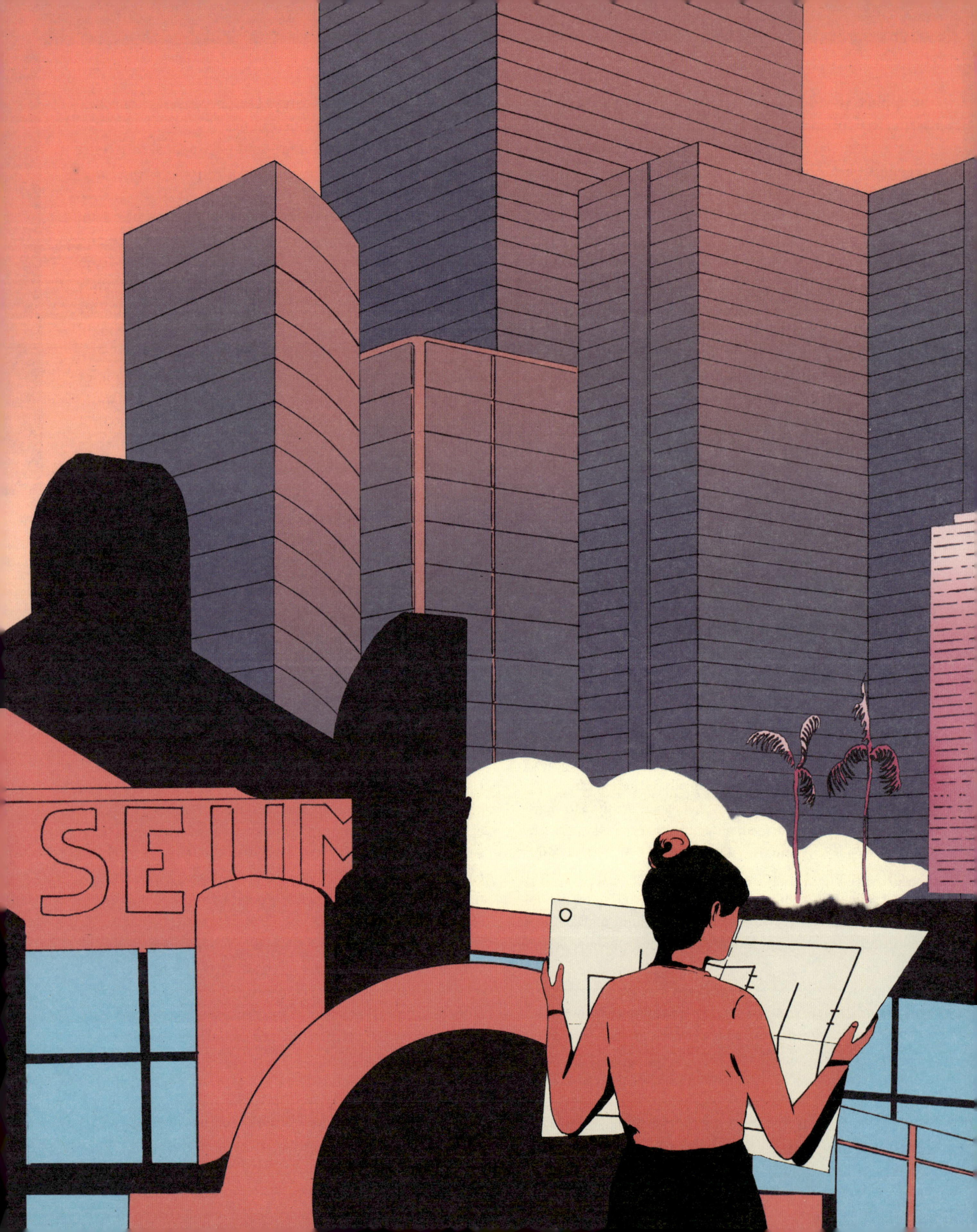
SEUM

FOR HER LAST MAJOR WORK, ARCHITECTURE'S GRANDE DAME DENISE SCOTT BROWN IS GOING SOLO.

ELIZABETH GREENSPAN

ART BY XAVIER LISSILLOUR

DISCUSSED: *An Enormous Spade; Photograph First, Think Later; "The Denise"; Main Streets; The World's First Postmodern Building; Ugly and Ordinary; Anti-Heroism in the Air; Both-And; A Tingling along Her Neck; Ayn Rand; Ducks and Decorated Sheds; A Prize Snub; Capital-A Artists; The Cult of the Expert; Learning from What You Don't Like; The Dernier Cri; A Whiskey Shower; The Ultimate Deadline*

It was the fall of 1966, as the Las Vegas Strip was just beginning to sparkle and sprawl, when a young architect and planning professor by the name of Denise Scott Brown invited her friend Robert Venturi on a weekend road trip to the desert. The pair rented a car in Los Angeles, where Scott Brown was teaching urban design at UCLA, and drove east toward Nevada. As the Strip's burgeoning silhouette came into view, Scott Brown, who carried a camera everywhere she went, had a sudden vision. Three structures jutted up from the landscape in the distance: the Dunes hotel and casino, all glass and crisp angles; the Dunes' enormous spade-shaped sign, almost as tall as the casino itself; and a lone, rugged-looking chimney. They pulled over alongside a gravelly, cactus-y patch of ground and Scott Brown styled a pair of photographs. She positioned Venturi, dressed in a boxy suit, with his back to the camera and to the right of the three structures. Click. Then she gave Venturi her camera and placed herself in the foreground of the same three structures, facing the lens, hands on hips and legs wide, smiling like a Cheshire cat.

Click.

She had already been to Vegas a few times by herself, drawn to its neon and billboards, guided by her instinct to pay attention to city spaces overlooked, and looked down on, by her peers. Scott Brown thought Vegas was fun—unlike a lot of modern design at that time—and she wanted to capture this sense of delight. So she played with distance and scale in the camera lens and styled Venturi to look like a fourth "tower" on the skyline, and herself like a triumphant skyline conqueror.

Scott Brown and Venturi married eight months after that road trip, at a ceremony on the front porch of Scott Brown's bungalow in Santa Monica. Five years after that, they copublished *Learning from Las Vegas*, one of the most influential design books of the twentieth century. Dense, theoretical, provocative, and funny, it established the simple yet profound idea that architecture communicates. A building is not merely "a machine for living in," as the Swiss French modernist architect Le Corbusier famously put it, but a canvas to interpret, a scene in a story. Translated into sixteen languages, and reprinted twenty-nine times to date, it remains a standard text across design and fine arts departments. Scott Brown both disagreed with and admired her early modernist predecessors, who had been obsessed with the question of architectural function, and had made an art of designing buildings to efficiently perform specific purposes, like housing a family or sheltering workers. *Learning from Las Vegas*'s essential insight was that communication was an architectural function too. Buildings convey meaning, which everyone reads—just as Scott Brown did on that festive, fecund desert journey, when she saw three faraway buildings and felt a sense of joy and play. She turned the Vegas skyline into a sentence in the unfolding story of her new romance.

Fifty-four years later, I sat in Scott Brown's dining room in Philadelphia, looking at these photos with her. It was sixteen months after Venturi had died at the age of ninety-three, and weeks before a global pandemic would quiet cities across the US. Scott Brown is one of architecture's rare grande dames: she turned ninety in October 2021. But her recognition has been belated; for decades, her partnership with Venturi wasn't acknowledged. Instead, Scott Brown witnessed, up close, what it meant to be seen as a capital-A Artist, the status afforded to Venturi, who was celebrated as one of his generation's most brilliant architectural minds, though she was denied such a standing herself. She told me that for "The Denise"—the image of her, and the pose, that quickly became iconic in design circles—she staged herself and told Venturi where to stand with the camera and he pressed the button. "So," she said, with both humor and edge, and not really asking, "whose picture is that?"

Today, Scott Brown is at work on her seventh book, the first to feature her vast archive of photographs, most of which have never been publicly displayed. It's titled *Wayward Eye*, the play on *eye* and *I* intentional. Rather than centering her famous partnership, the book tightens the spotlight on her vision, till now obscured by the attention paid to her husband. Being seen as an Artist is always the result of a fickle, fragile kind of elevation, but it matters, affecting what the market rewards, how other artists think, what powerful people argue for, maybe even how the rest of us decide we want to live. In the context of decades of creative collaboration and being passed over by the capital *A*, Scott Brown's solo album creates an opportunity to know her artistry—and, also, her transgressive way of seeing cities.

Scott Brown grew up in Zambia and South Africa in the 1930s and '40s, the daughter of Jewish immigrants from Latvia and Lithuania. Her mother, who had studied modernist architecture, encouraged her to pay attention to space and light and art. At the same time, Scott Brown was drawn to styles and compositions that pushed against the zeitgeist—a lifelong attraction. She saw neon on a childhood visit to an amusement park in Johannesburg and was enthralled. Some years later, she saw a canteen made from a repurposed Coca-Cola bottle, decorated with multicolored beads over and around the red logo's white script. She would remember it for the rest of her life. It was a local design: red beads conveyed one message, blue another. It also exemplified the art of taking an existing thing and adding ornamentation to create something new, one that says something, if you know how to read it.

She began taking pictures as a teen, guided by photographers like Cartier-Bresson, who advised never to question in the moment why something was prompting you to raise the lens to your eye, lest you lose it. Her mantra was to photograph first and "think later." In the '50s, when she moved to the UK to study architecture—including with Alison and Peter Smithson, famous for their gritty, everyday brutalist style—Scott Brown started photographing London's Main Streets, especially ordinary street signs. It was a decade later, after she had moved to Philadelphia to study and then teach city planning, that she first stopped at the Vegas Strip on a cross-country drive and felt, as she put it, "my hair stand on end, and creep along my neck and I just knew, just take it." Photograph, then think.

At the time, the Strip was a kind of supercharged Main Street, pocked with motels and casinos and billboards. She saw Los Angeles as a like-minded cousin, but Vegas was the most extreme version of a new kind of city, one that stretched along desert roadways and sported lots of plain little buildings topped with big, bold signs. This sort of town, modest and messy, was very different from the era's mid-century modern metropolis, which was sprouting state-of-the-art expressways and sleek glass-and-steel skyscrapers. To Scott Brown, the modernist preoccupation with singular and massive design interventions was fundamentally flawed. In her 1965 article "The Meaningful City," she imagined a visitor entering the high walls of a medieval town: they wandered the tiny streets, passed dense rows of homes, crossed the central market square, gazed up at the big, ornate church, and deciphered the city not by focusing on any one building, but by reading and interpreting the meaningful relationships between the small and the towering, the alleyways and the streets, the courtyards and the plazas.

Her interest in context and meaning was timely: theorists like Roland Barthes and Claude Lévi-Strauss were writing about symbols and sign systems. Skepticism of the outsize modern project was fashionable too. By the early '60s, Andy Warhol was ironizing the ordinary in his pop paintings of soup cans and Brillo pads. Joseph Heller was satirizing the American war machine in *Catch-22*. Antiheroism was in the air. But looking deeply at the sprawling Vegas Strip was not—for architects, at least—an obvious move. It wasn't seen to jibe with the nascent environmental movement. Nor did it look suitably urban. When Jane Jacobs mythologized the regular city street in her 1961 book *The Death and Life of Great American Cities*, she wrote about New York.

The same year that Scott Brown began formally studying the Strip, 1968, she was invited to design a commercial strip in South Philadelphia, under contract with the Citizens' Committee to Preserve and Develop the Crosstown Community. In those years, city officials and planners and architects targeted poor and working-class, usually Black, neighborhoods and their Main Streets for demolition, to make space for tall towers and six-lane highways. Led by the housing activist Alice Lipscomb, the committee was fighting a proposed highway project set to bulldoze fourteen blocks of South Philly and displace more than six thousand mostly middle- and working-class Black residents. Lipscomb asked Scott Brown to design a future South Street, the neighborhood's commercial corridor, without a highway running through it, to help officials see the value and meaning of the colorful storefronts and the modest homes, the flowerpots on the stoops, and the hand-drawn hopscotch courts on the streets they were prepared to erase. Scott Brown worked with residents and developed a plan that rehabilitated housing for low-income owners and renters; supported local business ownership and employment; and prioritized libraries, health centers, and schools.

Scott Brown describes her South Street design in the final section of *Learning from Las Vegas*. In it, she recalls a week in which she was rejected for two grants: one for the South Street project, because it was deemed "too political," and one for the Vegas project, because it was viewed as "not socially concerned." Modernists saw them as opposed—one worked with a community to fight a highway; the other analyzed the architecture that forms around sprawling expressways—and liked neither. But to Scott Brown, they were similarly good. They both illustrated how "beauty could emerge from the existing fabric," she writes, and how a "not-too-apparent order should be sought from within rather than an easy one imposed from above."

This is one of the reasons *Learning from Las Vegas* was so controversial when it was published. It ran up against a way of looking at cities that prized stripped-down, ordered spaces and that saw colorful or chaotic areas as lacking beauty and functionality, as ripe for either disregard or a top-down intervention involving a bulldozer. Modernists couldn't see that chaotic streetscapes could be functional. They didn't get that ornament is where the feeling lives.

Scott Brown and Venturi explained how architecture conveys meaning and emotion through a neat typology of ducks and decorated sheds. A building expresses its purpose, its modus operandi, in one of two ways, they observed: It embodies the form of the thing it does; the building, say, sells ducks and duck eggs and is the shape of an enormous duck. Or it is plain and sports a big sign declaring what it does; the above enterprise is a little shed with a sign depicting a duck atop it. Modernist buildings, they explained, are ducks; they are like big ornaments on the cityscape. The Vegas Strip is the land of decorated sheds, which in their assessment is a more flexible, sophisticated mode of communication. Scott Brown and Venturi claimed as a precedent for their vision the eminent Roman Forum: "Like the complex architectural accumulations of the Roman Forum, the Strip by day reads as chaos if you perceive only its form and exclude its symbolic content. The Forum, like the Strip, was a landscape of symbols with layers of meaning evident in the location of roads and buildings, buildings representing earlier buildings, and the sculpture piled all over. Formally, the Forum was an awful mess; symbolically, it was a rich mix."

In her 1973 review of *Learning from Las Vegas* in *The New York Review of Books*, Ada Louise Huxtable wrote that the book "passes the one conclusive test of art and history: we are never going to look at the world the same way again." *The Ohio Review* was equally effusive but in a panic-stricken sort of way. *Learning from Las Vegas*, the critic wrote, "threatens those things that we use to distinguish between us, the cultured, and them, the vulgar"—a quote Scott Brown and Venturi subsequently put on the back cover of the book's paperback edition. In *Learning from Las Vegas*, Scott Brown defended the implicit politics of her work. She explained that studying Vegas and South Street had taught her that, in cities, social and aesthetic realms go together, a lesson that "most planners and many architects find hard to accept."

I met Scott Brown for the first time in the early aughts, when I was a graduate student interested in the history of urban renewal and her South Street design. I was curious why the Citizens' Committee had solicited her expertise, her eye. It seemed her affection for Vegas had been part of its consideration. As she recounted in the project write-up, the committee told her: "If you can like the Las Vegas Strip, we trust you not to try to neaten up South Street at the expense of its occupants."

She told me to come see her at her design studio at 9 a.m. on a Saturday morning, the only time she had free. Venturi answered the door, smiling and bespectacled. As he walked me down the corridor to her office, he leaned in, as if to whisper a secret. "It's great you're interviewing her," he said. "People don't pay her the attention she deserves." I laughed awkwardly, not expecting to be praised for interviewing a famous designer. I didn't know at that point about the erasure of her work over the years, or that she had been treated cruelly by her peers. Once I was in her office, Scott Brown recounted her collaboration with Lipscomb and the Citizens' Committee with focus and precision; she did not stray from the assigned topic.

I would later learn that Scott Brown and Venturi first met at a faculty meeting at the University of Pennsylvania. It was 1960. Venturi was teaching part-time in architecture and thinking about opening his own firm. Scott Brown was a brand-new professor and a young widow: her first husband, Robert Scott Brown, had recently been killed in a car accident. At the faculty meeting, the dean introduced a proposal to tear down the School of Fine Arts Library for a bigger, more modern space. Scott Brown raised her hand and told the dean that he was making a mistake, arguing that the original structure should be preserved and renovated. (Ultimately, the library stayed.) Venturi approached Scott Brown after the meeting, introduced himself, and told her he agreed with her. Pleased and piqued, she responded with what would prove to be an evergreen question for them: "Well, why didn't you say something?"

After the faculty meeting, she and Venturi became friends. When they met, he was designing a modest house for his mom, which critics would later call the world's first postmodern building. At one and a half stories, it has a pitched roof and a double-wide chimney. Over the front door sits a slim arch, cut in half, which means it holds no weight: history's first, and maybe only, ironic archway. A large picture window to the door's left is countered to its right by four small windows in a horizontal row, upending the expected symmetry. As a whole, it's a constellation of exaggerated and manipulated elements that draw attention to the legible features modernists were back then throwing by the wayside. Scott Brown loved it. As she and Venturi wrote in *Learning from Las Vegas*:

At the time, the iconic male visionary loomed large in the art world, and designers epitomized him.

"The familiar that is a little off has a strange and revealing power."

They taught courses on architectural theory together and dined platonically. He was shy; she was social. They shared a dry sense of humor and an intense work ethic and liked to talk shop. Scott Brown was photographing and studying commercial strips and Main Streets, while Venturi was writing a monograph called *Complexity and Contradiction in Architecture*. Today, the book is canonical for its pithy critique of modernist style. "I like elements that are hybrid rather than 'pure,' compromising rather than 'clean,'" Venturi wrote. "I prefer 'both-and' to 'either-or.'"

At the time, the iconic male visionary loomed large in the art world, and designers epitomized him—when Ayn Rand needed a profession for her hero Howard Roark in *The Fountainhead*, she came up with "modernist architect." But such prejudice certainly wasn't unique to design. Just before *Learning from Las Vegas* came out, Linda Nochlin published her famous article "Why Have There Been No Great Women Artists?," investigating the structural circumstances of art production. As she wrote: "It seems probable that the answer to why there have been no great women artists lies not in the nature of individual genius or the lack of it, but in the nature of given social institutions and what they forbid or encourage in various classes or groups of individuals." In 1968, a year after they married, Scott Brown and Venturi published their first jointly written article, in *Architectural Forum*, on A&P parking lots; the contributor bio noted that Denise Scott Brown "is also Mrs. Venturi." When an acquaintance asked, "Are you an architect too?" Denise said, "No, Bob's the 'architect too.' I'm the architect."

One of the most inhospitable places for them would end up being where they landed professionally as newly married partners: the acclaimed Yale School of Architecture, where Venturi had started teaching, and where they brought Scott Brown's idea to do a studio on the Vegas Strip. The famous and wealthy modernist architect Philip Johnson—whose legacy is currently under scrutiny, given his enthusiastic support for the German Nazi party—was their colleague. When he judged a design competition for an apartment complex in Brighton Beach, Brooklyn, Johnson dismissed their firm's entry as "a pair of very ugly buildings." It was a set of multi-tiered, midsize towers, crafted to ensure that the maximum number of apartments had a view of the sea (only one in each building did not) and not to stand out from their surroundings. A few months later, an official in another competition called a different entry of theirs "ugly and ordinary." Since the criticism was part of the point, they thought, they made it their own. "Ugly and Ordinary" became their tagline, their vision, contra what they labeled the "Heroic and Original" ethos of the moderns.

The renowned art historian Vincent Scully, who was a Yale colleague and an early champion of Venturi's (he loved *Complexity and Contradiction*), greatly disliked this tagline. But when he expressed his displeasure to *The New York Times*, he did so in a way that diminished Scott Brown. "The Venturis impishly carry on about being boring and ugly. I understand why they do it, but it isn't true," Scully told the paper in 1971. "Bob Venturi is very much a traditional designer; he's extremely aesthetic." Scully didn't even mention Scott Brown's name.

Scott Brown and Venturi addressed the way their colleagues marginalized her, but they didn't quite seem to understand how the marginalizing functioned. It wasn't just about making her invisible, after all, but about associating with her the parts of their joint work that the establishment didn't like. At the beginning of *Learning from Las Vegas*, in a special, single-authored note, Venturi attested to Scott Brown's contributions: "Denise Scott Brown, my collaborator for twelve years, has been so intertwined in our joint development that it is impossible to define where her thought leaves off and mine begins," he wrote. "We both find it painful when her work as a designer or theorist (or our shared work) is ascribed to me, as it so often is. When I try to set the record straight, I seem to play Hearst to her Marion Davies." Venturi folded his declaration within a discussion of the virtues of collaboration more generally, diluting his specific message about her: "We look best when we stand as we are, a group of strong individuals who share enthusiasms and work well together, not as a pyramid with the figurehead of an Architect at the top." They even made one of their students, Steve Izenour, a third coauthor on the book, a generous decision that reflected Izenour's contributions but likely undermined Scott Brown, now poised to be aligned with the student rather than with the rising star.

In 1975, a few years after *Learning from Las Vegas* came out, Scott Brown wrote her own essay titled "Sexism and the Star System in Architecture," reflecting on her negation. It contains one of the few vulnerable moments she has put to paper. The marginalizing made her feel "self-doubt and confusion," she wrote. She would tell herself, "My husband is a better designer than I am. And I'm a pretty dull thinker," before trying to talk herself out of such negative thinking. "The first is true, the second probably not," she continued. "I try to counter with further questions: 'How come, then, we work so well together capping each other's ideas in both design and theory? If my ideas are no good, why are they praised by the critics (even though attributed to Bob)?'"

The pinnacle of this splitting came in 1991, when colleagues awarded Venturi the Pritzker Architecture Prize, the preeminent award in the field. The Pritzker jury wrote that "he has expanded and redefined the limits of the art of architecture in this century, as perhaps no other has, through his theories and built works." The citation highlighted the house he designed for his mother, as well as *Complexity and Contradiction*. It noted, at the end, his partnership with Scott Brown, their practice and scores of projects, and *Learning from Las Vegas*. Scott Brown boycotted the ceremony in protest.

Scott Brown has frequently said that she and Venturi considered refusing the award because of her exclusion but decided not to because their firm needed the accompanying hundred-thousand-dollar prize. Their practice designed award-winning museums, university halls, and civic buildings but not lucrative commercial skyscrapers. In his acceptance speech, Venturi struck a less emphatic, more wry tone than he had in his earlier front-of-the-book note—there was no big statement of protest. After listing numerous people and places to which he was indebted, Venturi said, "You will notice during this loosely chronological description I have used more and more the first-person plural, that is, 'we'—meaning Denise and I." He did, however, recognize her as an artist. "All my experience," he said at the end, "would have been less than half as rich without my partnership with my fellow artist, Denise Scott Brown."

In recent years the architectural establishment has made an effort to address and undo Scott Brown's erasure. In 2013, Women in Design, a student-led group at the Harvard Graduate School of Design, launched a petition to add her retroactively to the Pritzker; it garnered over twenty thousand signatures from architects around the world. In 2016, the American Institute of Architects awarded both Venturi and Scott Brown its Gold Medal: they were the first couple ever to receive it. But ripples of backlash have followed. In the fall of 2016, just months after Scott Brown accepted the Gold Medal, the Museum of Modern Art in New York City held a weekend-long fiftieth-anniversary celebration for *Complexity and Contradiction*. The festivities included panels and tours in New York and Philadelphia, with standing-room-only crowds and wait lists. Venturi did not appear—he had been suffering from dementia for many years at that point—but Scott Brown participated in the closing session, and the weekend's panelists mentioned her. During Friday's Q&A, architect and author Robert A. M. Stern, then seventy-seven and a contemporary of Venturi and Scott Brown, raised his hand from the audience and said that the panel was giving her credit she didn't deserve. He didn't remember her having anything to do with *Complexity and Contradiction*, he said. The panelists, he suggested, were rewriting history.

Word of the outburst made its way back to Scott Brown, with whom I was emailing at the time, hoping to pick up where we had left off in the aughts. She was responsive to my queries, but also consistently distant. In the early spring of 2018, I wrote to her with another update, noting an upcoming appointment I had to interview Robert Stern. An hour after I clicked SEND, my phone rang.

"Hello," a smooth, steady voice said on the other end. "This is Denise Scott Brown." A few weeks later, she invited me to lunch.

For nearly fifty years, Scott Brown has lived in a two-story art nouveau beauty at the end of a narrow residential street in Chestnut Hill, a neighborhood on the northwestern edge of Philadelphia. It's stately but not fussy. On the day of my visit, some peeling paint decorated the second-story balcony; the old stone fountain out front, surrounded by a gravel driveway, was not working. At the front door, a household organizer led me into the roomy, natural-light-filled foyer, where, against one wall, a dark wood bench provided a seat for a life-size doll wearing a crisp checkered dress, clutching a bouquet of fake flowers. If the doll had spoken, she might have said: *Welcome to my cluttered, curated home; please look first and think later.*

In the living room, connected to the foyer, the walls were covered in earth-toned, big-flowered wallpaper, a replica of the print Scott Brown and Venturi created for Best department stores in the early '80s. Miniature models of the chair they designed for Knoll, pink-and-yellow-flecked, stood or lay askew on a few side tables, like forgotten dollhouse furniture. Atop stacks of books on the room's large, round coffee table were three old soda cans, their rims threaded with rust: they were "decorative Cokes." On the rack of a piano in the corner, two copies of *Learning from Las Vegas* took the place of sheet music, each opened to one of the skyline shots they took of themselves.

As we settled on the sofa, Aalto, an eight-year-old English springer spaniel named for the Finnish architect Alvar Aalto, sat at our feet. "On occasion I call him Aalto-y or Otto-y," Scott Brown said, "but mostly I call him Poochela, which is 'Pooch' with a Yiddish ending."

She was chattier and more digressive than she had been in the aughts, but still directed. She recalled her childhood in South Africa during World War II, and then, a few years later, during apartheid, when she was hyperaware of being both white and Jewish. "I'm being a white oppressor, as well as being bullied in my school for being Jewish," she said.

Photography offered Scott Brown the possibility to reach into and stretch beyond the thorny barriers of the time, and she was eager to show me the images she was preparing for *Wayward Eye*, nearly all of which had sat boxed up and out of sight in her closet for five decades. She largely stopped photographing after her son, Jimmy, was born, in 1971, which was also when *Learning from Las Vegas* was being published and she began to receive more negative attention from her peers—and, in turn, when she and Venturi decided to devote less time to writing and more time to their firm. *Learning from Las Vegas* brought them "disciples," Scott Brown said, but not work.

On a dark wood table in the dining room, which was connected to the living room, a computer and two large monitors were set up to display her photographic layouts, and after lunch, we turned to the screens. Image by image, Scott Brown's meaningful city, the urban patterns and forms and adornments that inspired her work, came into view. An aerial shot of the outskirts of Johannesburg showed rows of small, identically designed square houses, not unlike a tract of US suburbia, with decorated porticos that Scott Brown had admired. In Philadelphia, the sign for O. R. Lumpkin, a family-owned mechanic, contained what she called a "sonnet": BODY AND FENDER STRAIGHTENING, AUTO REFINISHING, WRECKS OUR SPECIALTY, TAKE THE DENT OUT OF ACCIDENT. An orange-and-yellow food stand advertised chili dogs in Santa Monica, California; a motel's neon vacancy sign lit up Vegas's nighttime sky.

Looking at the photos was engrossing but also jarring, and at moments even gasp-inducing. The screens displayed Scott Brown's vision before it was clipped and, at the same time, the spaces of a social class that America doesn't really have anymore—what was, what could still have been. It was Main Street on the eve of its decline. Scott Brown photographed most methodically in the 1960s, on the cusp of cultural, economic, and political change. Through the '70s, thanks partly to *Learning from Las Vegas*, art and architecture became more open, colorful, and lavish, with over-the-top glitter and pop; meanwhile, governments privatized, corporations globalized, and media companies scaled up. Looking at Denise's images felt almost like glimpsing moments of an alternative future, one that sees a city's ordinary places as they actually are: as pieces of a larger, related whole.

In one photograph of South Street, a father in a hat and overcoat gently guides his toddler through the entrance of a plain storefront. As we looked at it, Scott Brown told me how she used to engage officials who were keen to bulldoze South Street for the highway: "I used the cult of the expert the other way around. I'd say, 'You say these buildings are very ugly. I'm an architect and an expert and I say they're beautiful.'"

It was the fullness and sincerity of Scott Brown's photographs that most surprised Christopher Hawthorne, the former architecture critic for the *Los Angeles Times*, who is today chief design officer for the city of Los Angeles. He had visited Scott Brown at her house a few years before my visit, and she'd shown him her images of LA. Hawthorne, a California native, almost always scoffs at outsiders' visions of LA, he told me, because they can't see past the stereotypes of glamour and Hollywood. But her photographs cut through the starstruck haze to reveal the places real people live and play. "I was stunned by them," he said.

In the '80s, scholars and theorists connected *Learning from Las Vegas* to the moment when Wall Street eclipsed Main Street in the public imagination. But back then, the capital-*A* Artist spotlight was pointed only at Venturi. By 1984, when the literary critic Fredric Jameson published his seminal essay "Postmodernism, or the Cultural Logic of Late Capitalism" and singled out *Learning from Las Vegas* as critical to his thinking, both Scott Brown's name and her vision—her way of looking at both the social and the aesthetic realms—had been written out of the canon. Jameson glossed the book as "Venturi's influential manifesto" and emphasized the "aesthetic populism" referenced in its title, the way the art world had become enamored with lowbrow styles.

The sharpest critique of Scott Brown and Venturi is that they failed to anticipate this twist, the way their critiques of modernism could be taken up by the capitalists but stripped of their social core—in a sense, that they failed to anticipate their colleague Philip Johnson. In the mid-'70s, Johnson, till then a famous modernist, tried his hand at the new decorative fashion and designed a pink granite-clad skyscraper for AT&T's new Manhattan headquarters. Scott Brown wrote that the tower was "self-indulgent" and part of a movement that was failing to grapple with the era's social upheaval; Ada Louise Huxtable dismissed it as "a standup joke." But in

> **Looking at Denise's images felt almost like glimpsing moments of an alternative future, one that sees a city's ordinary places as they actually are: as pieces of a larger, related whole.**

1979, *Time* magazine put Johnson on its cover holding a model of the building, and it quickly became the avatar of the new postmodernism. It also caught the attention of a young developer and future US president, who in the early '80s hired Johnson to make a "Trump Castle." (The castle was never built, but the two men embarked on a long business relationship.)

At her house, sitting in front of the screens, Scott Brown was brusque on the topic of losing control of her work and its reception. When I asked her what she thought about Johnson's AT&T creation becoming synonymous with the postmodernism she and her husband had helped create, and about Johnson then working with Trump, she parried. She reminded me that Johnson had an affiliation with Nazism. Was she surprised or upset that Johnson coopted their ideas? Her answer was short and sharp: "What we were surprised to see is how little our work was understood." This recalled a pointed comment of hers from the '80s: "Postmodernism did change the views of architects but not in the way I had hoped," she wrote. "The architect as macho revolutionary was succeeded by the architect as *dernier cri* of the art world. This made things worse for women because, in architecture, the *dernier cri* is as male as the prima donna."

In our chats, the architects, theorists, and critics who had most capitalized upon her and her husband's ideas maintained a persistent presence. They were like a gray mist hovering about, obscuring the view. She recounted with disdain a critic's characterization of her and Venturi "that Bob wrote poetry and Denise has her feet on the ground." She scoffed: "And he thinks it was a compliment." In past interviews, Scott Brown had said that she just wants to talk about her work, not her erasure, which makes sense; the latter has undermined the former. But they also go together, which perhaps is why in our conversations she wanted to discuss everything, the ideas and designs and misreadings and snubs and mistreatments.

One event that contained it all came up nearly every time we talked: the after-party that followed the opening night of Scott Brown and Venturi's fall 1971 exhibition on *Learning from Las Vegas* at the Whitney Museum, in New York. Parties are where the power plays unfold, where the more solitary work of making art meets the social scene, the status quo, the kingmakers. And this one, which was hosted by Robert Stern, lives on.

In 2016, Stern, who was concluding his appointment as dean of the Yale School of Architecture, gave an exit interview with the student magazine. When he was asked to share his "most traumatic experience with another architect," he recounted a moment at that party, when, as he described it, "I had to peel Denise Scott Brown away from fighting with Paul Rudolph in my apartment." Rudolph, a famous modernist, was also a former dean of the Yale School of Architecture. "That was pretty scary," Stern said. The gossip around this alleged incident circulates five decades later; I recently read a tweet with a more ebullient take: "denise scott-brown punched paul rudolph at a party and that is cool (even tho I like paul's work more.)"

Stern confirmed his characterization when we met. It was a "fistfight," he said. I had gone to see him because I was thinking about writing a book about Scott Brown and Venturi, and Stern had known them both early in their careers. As we talked, he echoed the old establishment line about the two. "I loved the Venturi approach," he said. "It was all this high-art, very sophisticated take on contemporary architecture." He added, "Of course, I hated the direction that the Venturis took." I asked him what he hated, and Stern said, "Well, I thought that they—and it was Denise, of course..." Stern saw *Learning from Las Vegas* as typical of what he considered a regrettable trend from that era: that of bringing politics into graduate design studios. "Every advanced studio had to be based on an issue," he said. Most recently, Stern penned the preface for a new edited volume assessing the legacy of *Learning from Las Vegas*, published in anticipation of its fiftieth anniversary; his essay downplayed the book's influence, praising it, oddly enough, for its pedagogical contributions to the field.

Scott Brown was primed to tell me her version of the story. She said there had been no punch, but there was a heated argument. The evening's exhibition had displayed the book's core art and ideas and critiques. When she and Venturi arrived at the after-party at Stern's spacious apartment, Scott Brown went into the library and saw Paul Rudolph sitting alone. She and Venturi had used one of Rudolph's buildings as their example of "establishment" architecture, and she approached Rudolph to explain that this choice wasn't personal. But Rudolph was upset. He accused her and Venturi of saying that everyone wants the same architecture and no one could possibly like his building; she replied, with characteristic honesty and bite, that, no, what they were saying was that his work was no longer relevant.

Then Scott Brown went into the dining room and ran into another aging modernist, Colin Rowe, who taught at Cornell. Rowe had recently written a critical review of their new Vegas work, naming only Venturi, so Scott Brown penned an essay in response, taking Rowe to task for leaving her out. At the party, Rowe, an avid drinker, approached her, whiskey in hand, and leaned in, as if to greet her with a kiss on her cheek. "Denise, cara mia," he said. "Fuck you, bitch." Then he poured his whiskey down her back.

Every time we discussed this party, Scott Brown was composed, even-tempered. She wanted me to know about Rowe's attack, which isn't part of the lore. "Colin was absolutely outraged that I should think that this battle of titans could include me," she said. Scott Brown also wanted me to know that she and Rudolph repaired their rift. After the whiskey transaction, she found her husband, who had been talking to a colleague in another room, and as they readied to leave she locked eyes with Rudolph and saw a look of sympathy on his face, one that conveyed to her, *I see what you have to go through*. The next morning, Venturi wrote a note to Rudolph, which I came across in his archives, reiterating that there was nothing personal in their discussion of his building; "We are sorry that what resulted was a misunderstanding," he wrote. There was no mention of a fistfight.

Regardless of what did or did not go down, I couldn't help but think about the evening's strong crosscurrents. It was, after all, a triumphant night for Scott Brown, or should have been—the first public display of the groundbreaking ideas she had developed with her husband, and at a major New York museum, no less. LEARN FROM WHAT YOU DON'T LIKE read a sign at the exhibition's entrance. But the night was rife with conflict, with peers who didn't like her or her antiestablishment ideas. And it was those conflicts, not the ideas, that have lived on in the gossip mill and social media timelines. Listening to stories from that night, I found myself engaging in wishful speculation: What if misogyny hadn't been such a readily available tool for her detractors? What if she had been less easy to dismiss? What if she had been legible as an Artist?

Over the past five years, Scott Brown's photographs have attracted increasing interest from galleries. An exhibition of images, primarily of 1960s Las Vegas, showed at the Venice Biennale's International Architecture Exhibition in 2016. A show of ten photographs followed two years later in London, at the Betts Project, a version of which then moved to the Carriage Trade gallery, in New York City, for her first US show. Peter Scott, owner and curator of Carriage Trade, recalled that few people knew of her when he was talking up the exhibition. "But then you say 'Venturi' and you get a bit more, and then you say, '*Learning from Las Vegas*' and it's like, *Right, for some reason I know that*," he said.

The show was one of Carriage Trade's most successful, he told me, selling multiple ten-print sets. He noted that Scott Brown signs each of her photographs in the lower right corner, like a painter. "It's very quirky," Scott said, adding that he found her name's prominence to be part of the photographs' appeal, what he described as their non-professional authenticity. The show received more than a dozen write-ups, including in *The New Yorker*, where, rather uncannily, the critic simultaneously paid it a compliment and continued to withhold from Scott Brown the status she seeks. "The works aren't art," he wrote. "They're more interesting."

The show ran through the fall of 2018, which was a momentous season for Scott Brown. That September, Venturi died after suffering for years from dementia. In October, Scott Brown received the Soane Medal, from London's Sir John Soane's Museum, awarded annually to a preeminent architect or critic who has transformed the field. Also in October, demolition began on an addition to a museum that she and Venturi had designed in San Diego.

It's not unusual for a famous architect's building to be destroyed, but what was strange was the timing: her work was being undone just as she was being internationally recognized for the first time in her career—and for photographs and theories that heralded the meaning and significance of the existing built environment. She was fielding press requests to talk about her award while trying to scrounge up coverage of the architectural destruction, all of which was taking time away from working on her book.

"I have so many deadlines," she told me on the phone that November. When I asked what her deadlines were, she corrected herself: "Well, the deadline is my death."

When we last sat together, in January 2020, just before the stay-at-home orders scuttled us all apart, Scott Brown spoke to me a little more freely about her partnership and marriage. Historically, she has allowed for little daylight between her and Venturi, directing her frustrations toward institutions and colleagues. And for the most part, Scott Brown held tightly to "we" when talking about her design work. "The truth is that Bob and I—it's not that he does this and I do that. We do this. His experience and my experience make a very rich combination," she said. "It's like lacing up a very great shoe." It's both-and. But she took issue with the way Venturi endorsed the 2013 petition to add her to the Pritzker. When he signed his name, Venturi also wrote, "Denise Scott Brown is my inspiring and equal partner." But Scott Brown detected an absence. "He said, 'My partner, my inspiration,'" she told me, "but what he didn't say is *my codesigner*." I asked Scott Brown if they had talked privately about how he saw her. After a pause, she answered in a way that suggested that she, too, tended to his capital-*A* Artist status. "Yes," she said. "But you know, in the end he's an old man, and people in the office were saying, 'We can see where the bright design ideas are coming from now.' I didn't want to rub all that in."

We were back in the dining room. Up near the ceiling, wrapping the entire room, was their elegantly stenciled frieze of the last names of famous architects: Soane and Borromini; Lutyens and Le Corbusier; Michelangelo and Wright. Scott Brown was showing me some changes she had made to her book layouts. She told me Venturi would frequently remark to her that because they were never not working, they would inevitably "die with work unfinished." But *Wayward Eye* was too important. "I cannot let this be unfinished," she said.

We clicked through a few images of Los Angeles and the Nevada desert, modest and beautiful. The next was a selfie: a photograph she took of herself in 1968 as reflected in the glass pane of a Vegas storefront. Her large camera obscured her face. It was a play on transparency, she said, à la the early modernists. "They loved reflections," she said. "There was, to them, such a precision with glass. That's just an old shack, really, but it looks like a wonderful early 1930s vision." Scott Brown could riff for hours on practically any image. But our time was limited. "Let's go on," she said, and clicked forward. ✯

PORCH LIGHT

LITERARY ARTS CENTER
+
WRITER'S RETREAT

We build community through the nexus of Image, Word, Performance and Outreach.

Book a writing retreat at our 1900s farmhouse within walking distance of downtown Iowa City.

Visit us at: porchlightliterary.org

ROY WOOD JR., "RECEIPT" JOKE

The Process

In which an artist discusses making a particular work

In his Twitter bio, Roy Wood Jr. says he tells the truth like "white draws," which seems to be his mystical calling, pointing out the excrement in our lives. As a correspondent since 2015 for Comedy Central's The Daily Show with Trevor Noah, *a veritable white pop-cultural institution, Wood Jr. is particularly subversive and incisive because he universalizes the specifics of everyday Black life in the form of dramatic and explorative narratives. And his wry, observational humor, skits, and absurdist commentary elucidate American life, particularly as it relates to race and bigotry. Take a segment he did after white supremacists held a deadly rally in Charlottesville, Virginia, in 2017. The joke shifts from the comedian ignoring the shock and horror of the rally to the farcicality of what it means to be a master race. Wood Jr. mocks the racists' bravado, and suggests that if white supremacists were truly indomitable, then the rally should have been held in a Black city instead of a white college town. He then critiques the redundancy of a master race that can't craft torches and instead has to buy them from a gardening store.*

In addition to working on The Daily Show, *Wood Jr. is crafting his as-yet-unnamed, third one-hour stand-up special for Comedy Central, which is set to air this year. It follows his previous two specials: 2019's* No One Loves You *and his first, 2017's* Father Figure. *(Both premiered as the network's highest-rated original stand-up special.) Wood Jr. had just celebrated his forty-second birthday when we spoke by phone in December 2020.*

Illustration by Samar Haddad

It was close to dinnertime, and Wood Jr. was setting up cameras in a bedroom in the Harlem apartment he shares with his girlfriend, shoe designer Salone Monet, and their young son. We talked about his writing process, comedy as a form of journalism, and one joke he tells in Father Figure, *which details why he always asks store clerks for a receipt and a plastic bag. This joke is framed as a tug-of-war with a concerned Best Buy clerk, who insists Wood Jr. doesn't need a bag for a purchase. When confronted by the cashier about not caring for the earth, Wood Jr. has to decide between saving the environment and risking a dalliance with security. He retorts, "It's about safety. I'm Black. I don't get the luxury of just walking out with shit in my hand." The concept resonated so much with the audience that they joined in to say the punch line at the end of the setup: "I need the receipt!" Leaving without conspicuously holding a bag—and a receipt—could result in a deadly misunderstanding with store security. The joke illustrates the small ways racism affects how people move through the world, especially in stores with high-value items. It's an observation that's at once hilarious and heartbreaking because it is so clear that many of us live in two separate Americas.*

—*Soni Brown*

THE BELIEVER: Your father was a radio broadcaster and he covered the Civil War—

ROY WOOD JR.: Civil War? Yeah. He is really old.

BLVR: Sorry, the Civil Rights movement. He covered stories on racism against Black soldiers in the Vietnam War. Your brother's also a broadcaster. You studied broadcast journalism at Florida A&M University. How did this training in the family business prepare you for stand-up comedy? What was that leap like?

RWJ: Comedy is a form of journalism. You are either reporting on the world or you're reporting on your own feelings and thoughts. You're a documentarian talking about your own inward journey. In journalism you're in the business of asking questions, really trying to get to the root of things. That's where journalism helped my stand-up comedy.

BLVR: Writing a political joke is different from mining your own life for observations and material. How do you sketch out jokes differently for your stand-up, Twitter, and *The Daily Show*?

RWJ: Twitter is more "brown and serve." Twitter is more about the conversation that is happening now. *The Daily Show* is more about the conversation happening this week or this month. And stand-up is about what has happened or what is happening. I think the best analogy I could give is that it's like talking about the weather versus the climate. The day-to-day is Twitter. It's very much, *Hey! This happened today. Here's a joke that fits what the conversation is today.* Twitter is kind of a barbershop. You walk in, grab a couple of jokes, and get the hell on. With *The Daily Show*, we definitely want to get to the root of real issues that people are dealing with as tactfully as possible, but we use humor as a way to move the conversation. My stand-up, that's definitely a place where I try to present different perspectives on something that people may not have considered. The standard difference between stand-up and *The Daily Show* is that at least with stand-up I have the freedom to analyze a problem without presenting a solution. Whereas at *The Daily Show*, you cannot do that.

BLVR: How do you workshop your jokes? What's your process?

RWJ: I'll tell you the one way Twitter is like stand-up. Twitter is a great place to eliminate thoughts. I can't confirm that something is funny on Twitter, but I can confirm that somebody else is thinking the same thing and I can use that platform as a place to rule out a particular angle of attack on the topic. As far as workshopping material, pre-COVID, at least, the process was getting up onstage and going back and listening to the material. A normal kind of wash, rinse, repeat. It's a process of eliminating words that are unnecessary, identifying the parts where people laughed, the parts where people felt something. It is just a constant refinement process of shortening your statements and figuring out places where you can touch it up, make it funnier. Once I have the joke deets worked out the way I want, then I watch myself perform the material. Once I know the verbiage of the joke, it's just: Is it funnier if I say this word faster or slower? Is it funnier if I'm standing near the front of the stage or the back of the stage? Then I start playing around with the sequencing of the jokes: Is it too soon for this joke? Is this too edgy to start out with? Those are the questions I can start exploring, but I can't do any of that until the jump is solid.

BLVR: What does comedy absolutely need in order to work for you?

RWJ: Mike Birbiglia said something I agree with. He said that in order for a joke to work, everyone has to agree. In order for the punch line to work, we all have to agree on the premise. That's where comedy is starting to have a lot of differentials now, because we all come from different truths, which is what makes political comedy so difficult. You could start a joke: "The election was crazy." Well, is that from the perspective of a Democrat or a Republican? There's a lot of people who feel like Biden stole the election. There are other people who feel like Biden won. Which angle of attack are we looking at? The thing I find interesting about comedy now is that we lack that agreement. I think that makes things very, very difficult. Jokes definitely have to inform people. I think the best jokes are informative about either who you are or how you feel. That's just for me. I'm not going to say that's the be-all and end-all of a good joke. The jokes I appreciate most inform me about either the performer's life or the performer's perspective.

BLVR: You've done *Def Comedy Jam*, BET's *ComicView*, and *Showtime at the Apollo*. This is the trifecta of Black comedy spaces. Black comedians say it's harder to make Black audiences laugh, like we make you work for a laugh, right? You're able to do it and you get mainstream audiences to laugh too. Your stand-up happens in front of a racially mixed audience and everyone's laughing. Is there an element of code-switching involved in what you do?

RWJ: I don't think there's an element of code-switching in what I do. I did *Def Jam* and [*Late Show with*] *David Letterman* in a short period of time. I did the same joke on both shows and didn't change a syllable. That was about presenting an observation I have about the world. I am a Black man. My comedy is definitely informed through the view of Blackness. I think I just remained myself. Black people will find me. Like any comedian, there's going to be people that don't find it funny, especially on the Black side of things. I think the thing that we as Black people reject is fakeness, because we've been lied to so much as a culture. Come to me with your honesty, the most honest version of yourself. If it makes me laugh, cool. If not, that's cool too. That's something I was very proud of. I went to shows with two different demographics and didn't change anything. There are topic selections I did differently for *Letterman* versus *Def Jam*. A lot of that just boils down to relatability. No, I don't think there's any level of code-switching. Look at what I did with *Father Figure* and that material. That was 100 percent about the experience of being Black in America. I feel like that material could have worked on any show.

Early on, I couldn't afford to code-switch. As a road comic in the South, I performed for so many people. If you want to perform every week, you can't perform just for Black people. Can't do it. I came up with an ideology: What are the things I can talk about that a Black audience would want to hear and that these fucking rednecks that I've got to perform for next week would also want to hear? Then a day later, I'm at a casino performing for people over the age of seventy. I'm not code-switching just from Black to white. I'd have to code-switch from rural to urban to rural. Then I had to code-switch from young to old, and that was just too much to be concerned about.

I had more fun trying to find the connector. What is the connective tissue between all of these different races and demos and economic classes? It made how I perceived the world a little broader. I don't have to come out and go: *Black, Black, Blackety, Black, Black, Black*. That just ain't me. It's obvious I'm Black. I don't have to go, *Black people everywhere*, or *I, as a Black person*. I just think eliminating that qualifier gave me the freedom to talk about stuff like that. That's the thing I enjoy, actually: it's talking about race. That's on a good day. My comedy is for Black people to know they're not alone in feeling the way they feel and also informing the people who are ignorant of the journey of a Black person in this country.

BLVR: My sense of your work, be it your prank phone calls from your radio days, as a contestant on *Last Comic Standing*,

> **Comedy is a form of journalism. You are either reporting on the world or you're reporting on your own feelings and thoughts.**

or hosting *This Is Not Happening*, is that you tell very detailed, highly nuanced stories that pull back the curtain on the absurdity of racism and inequality, but we don't know that until after the joke. Can you articulate the common element in your work? What is the DNA of your jokes?

RWJ: Emotion. We can all relate to emotions. I'm not necessarily trying to be right or wrong. I told the story on *This Is Not Happening* about the time that a guy tried to pay us in cocaine. He pulled a gun on us. That is fear and regret. We all have moments of fear and maybe moments or situations when we wish we could have had something. I enjoyed being able to pull that out of people. If you're emotionally naked with the audience and you share your fears and the things you're happy about, the things that confuse you, that stuff becomes relatable. I'm not here to project to the audience. I'm not here to explain to you why I'm right and you're wrong. I'm just here to explain to you why I think like this. You don't have to agree [despite what you think you already agree with]. That's the thing that made George Carlin so beautiful: that you could find yourself laughing at shit that you didn't even agree with.

BLVR: In *Father Figure*, you did this bit about never leaving a store without a plastic bag and receipt. The audience said "receipt" just as you were uttering the word. It was unprompted. When I was viewing it, the people who were saying "receipt" were Black. I immediately got what you were saying, because I do the same thing. I never leave the store without a plastic bag and receipt, but I also didn't realize these are the universal things Black folks do in America. It's kind of like when you get pulled over by the cops, you switch your music from rap to classical or smooth jazz…

RWJ: Yeah! Yeah!

BLVR: Or when you're in the emergency room you start saying to the nurse: *Well, I have a degree and I volunteer for stray animals and I play violins for cats.* Black people try to humanize themselves so they'll be seen as individuals and hopefully get unbiased treatment. When you make these jokes, I feel like there's a "wink, wink, nod" to Black folks. Do you have an imagined audience in mind when you write them? Do you care if white folks understand?

RWJ: I don't care if people don't understand the inside jokes I have with Black people onstage. Because for them, the joke is the moments of discovery and seeing that there are droves of people that experience a different America from them. Like I said, a lot of my material, that's just to confirm to Black people that they are not alone in thinking like this. This allows me to go onstage and say, *I don't care about recycling. I don't care about reusing bags. I'm not leaving the store without a bag, because I will be suspected of shoplifting and I may be shot by the police.*

That's essentially a joke about race, but I use recycling as the way in because that's what will hook a white person. It's also the more curious entry point into that topic, because the joke, of course, is about a Black person getting into an argument about conservation. I find it fun to take these Black things and Trojan-horse them into stuff I think some white people are more concerned about. Also, it's a more fun journey to the punch line because it's more atypical. I came up with a bizarro premise and then took it to a place where you completely understood my stance.

BLVR: When you are in stores and cashiers resist giving you or other Black folks a receipt or a bag, do you riff on this joke? How does this joke echo in the real world for you?

RWJ: I don't generally joke with strangers, 'cause I just don't know them and it's going to be weird. I don't know what kind of mood a stranger is in, and if they're going to take the joke as a joke or take it seriously, and I don't want to argue. I leave people alone. There are times when I see other people being told they don't need a receipt, but I just mind my business. I think that's just coming from New York. But I am stern about getting one. If I want a bag, there is a brief hesitation when I'm considering, What did I buy? What is the likelihood of me looking like I stole this when I walk out of the store? So I always get one.

BLVR: Given your work on *Stand-Up Playback* [a weekly video series for Comedy Central where comedians watch and critique sets from earlier in their career with Wood Jr.], do you watch the response videos that are made for your routines? Do you feel a sense of satisfaction in seeing people immediately identify with and dissect your jokes? What is your feeling when you hear people laugh and in some cases cry at the astuteness of a bit?

RWJ: I've seen some of the response videos. People tag me in them sometimes. I'm happy people find joy in my comedy and I'm more thankful that people give me credit for the material and that these people aren't just joke vultures stealing stuff for their own gain. At the end of the day, you want your comedy to resonate with people and to have something that leaves them viewing society differently or confirming for them the way they view society. When I see people putting those bits out there and then having people come behind them and go, "Oh yeah, that's Roy Wood Jr.," that's dope. That's dope all around.

BLVR: You eulogized Dick Gregory in a touching, emotional piece for *The New York Times*. How did opening twice for Dick Gregory change your comedy?

RWJ: I worked with him once in Nashville, and before that in Selma, Alabama. I was hosting a brunch function and shit was beautiful, man. They presented him as a speaker but it was something deeper than that. I mean, talk about an emotional connection to an art form. Then, when he performed at the comedy club, it also felt like I was watching this speech, this dissertation. It's just magic. It made me completely let go of any fear I have of trying to make a point and not comedy. Or, how can I put it, the fear of silence… being afraid of that silence. Because Dick Gregory embraced silence and made it part of the performance.

When you talk about leaving the show more informed, you are talking about a Dick Gregory performance. He definitely put me in a different head space to write material. And also the age range at a Dick Gregory show was something I clocked. You have the sense that he was appealing to so many different generations with something very specific to the Black experience. There were white people there. The things that Black people go through aren't complicated things to understand; you just have to be quiet and listen. I feel like the white people who can show up to these types of shows—if they're quiet and pay attention—they will catch on and figure it out. I don't feel the need to really sit down and do anything for them personally. So I don't.

BLVR: What is your writing ritual? Do you go somewhere quiet? Do you need noise? Are you in the back of a comedy club?

RWJ: [Dave] Chappelle talks about how comedians need to identify their joke machine. I only write material maybe three, four months a year. That becomes the material I workshop the rest of the year. I just have a collection of thoughts on my phone. I transfer all of that over to a Mead Five Star notebook. Kind of write the bullet points. I still like to handwrite because it commits it to memory better, even better than typing. I go onstage in fifteen-minute intervals and just work through everything in my notebook that I collected during what I like to call "high tide." So high tide is the period of time during the year when my creative juices are flowing and when joke premises are popping into my head. What follows is low tide, when I really can't think of anything.

I can't, after twenty-two years, tell you when high tide comes and when it goes away. It just comes and goes. Always has. When it's low tide, I can't think of new jokes. That's when I start looking through what I harvested during high tide. I sift through those premises, work those out onstage, watch the tapes, then hear the audio. Refine! Refine! Refine! But, you know, generally when I'm still onstage, I am working out ideas from the last creative high tide.

Journalistically now—this is where *The Daily Show* has changed some of my writing style—I like to research topics before I start talking about them. I often try a premise just to think, but if I really want to start getting deeper into it, then I want to do some research.

There's a bit I'm working on about how when people do horrible things in America, we often blame the parents. That's the default behavior in this country: to assume that this horrible person, like a mass shooter, didn't have decent parents. But you would be surprised that there's some mass shooters that actually had a really good childhood. There isn't anything that the parents could have done differently. That's the premise I presented to the audience. I have to have solid, solid information after that. That requires research. After I collect the information I also now have to make it funny. If I can't do all that, then I can't put that onstage. That's just some shit for a TED Talk.

When you start getting into edgier topics, you can't misstep, because comedy is the one art form created in front of the consumer. And when people are ready to cancel you for doing or saying something they didn't agree with, they're not considering the degree of difficulty and the trial-and-error required to say something edgy or to get right up to the line. You have to be a little bit more skilled when developing edgier material.

BLVR: How do you become skilled in developing edgier material?

RWJ: By being wrong. Crossing the line. That's how you learn where to scale it back and where to become a little bit more appropriate. But that's also where Twitter helps. Twitter shows you the holes in your premise and the blind spots you may have on social issues. Being able to address those social issues within your joke makes you more of a well-rounded comedian. Twitter lets you know what you'll be pushing back with in the new material: If I say this, I know this group of people is going to feel this way. I need to be able to address that in the next part of the joke, if I still see fit.

Look at the mass shooter premise, right? That joke is essentially about parenting and the expectations of parents and the presumption that parents are in full control. They are not. I have to make sure that remains the target and not me at any point, making fun or making light of being a victim of a mass shooting in this country. Someone is sensitive to that and sensitive to gun violence. That's a slippery slope. I cannot at any point be dismissive of the tragedies that the mass shooters dealt to so many people, right? But at its core, it is a joke about how everything isn't a parent's fault. There was a mass shooter in his forties and people attacked his mom. She was in her seventies. This man was forty-six years old. This isn't the same as a teenager. This is a different situation. I mentioned that, and that was the original punch line of the joke. Part of the joke was just about: When are you done being a parent? If your child is forty-six and acting out, is that a seventy-year-old woman's fault?

Someone made a very fair point. There could be things that happened in his childhood that he never unpacked that led him to unfurl at forty-six. In a lot of ways, the forty-six-year-old is just as unstable as the eighteen-year-old shooter. It just took him time to come out of his shell, you know; it's terrible. That's the punch line I have to rework. That's the angle I have to rework. That's something where if I'm wanting to mention a forty-six-year-old man, I cannot mention him without talking about his childhood. The joke as it was originally constructed disregards everything else that happened in his life up until that point. Or I have to do the research on his name and see the type of childhood he had to see if it upholds my original thesis. This is not a joke that could just be thrown up really on a five-minute open mic. I have to sit and do research and set a block on it. And once I do all of that, eh, maybe I still have a joke. Maybe I don't.

That's a joke I've had in my head since before COVID hit. I've kind of turned my attention to writing scripts and doing a lot of other things. I missed the stage, but not enough to go onstage.

BLVR: You are producing a sitcom with *Boondocks* creator Aaron McGruder called *Jefferson County: Probation*. [*In the sitcom, which is based loosely on events in his life, Wood Jr. plays a probation officer willing to bend the rules to prevent his clients' recidivism.*] Can you talk about the creative process between the two of you? How do you work it out?

RWJ: We shot that pilot last year [in 2019]. Unfortunately, we shot the pilot and then Viacom merged. There's a shit ton of back-and-forth work figuring out what they want to do, what projects they want to achieve. We're in a holding pattern right now with the network, but in the meantime, I'm doing my best to write a whole bunch of other shit.

Aaron is a gentleman that keeps to himself. It's a cool thing to be a part of, just to be able to collaborate with someone who I think understands the issues underneath all of this. At the end of the day, *Jefferson County: Probation* is the television show that, while making you laugh, can show you how recidivism happens in this country. There are more people on probation than in prison. A lot of this prison pipeline stuff is rooted in terrible probation officers and terrible judges. To be able to shine a light on that, that's something I don't take lightly. I needed to collaborate with someone who had a degree of understanding about the Black experience in this country. ★

A POP-CULTURAL AUTOPSY OF THE BLACK WOMAN MEDICAL EXAMINER

Crime dramas, one of the most enduring television genres, have revolutionized US popular culture with each hit series. But increasingly, programs that once enjoyed cultural immunity have had their popularity dissected. Charged with propagating "copaganda," crime television has been scrutinized for its continual use of charismatic yet flawed characters to avoid systemic criticisms of policing. Drawing on the nation's oldest narrative tropes regarding harm and heroism, they rehearse an American theater of morality and criminality.

In these dramas, the figure of the medical examiner is often peripheral yet indispensable to the sagas that unfold. Medical examiners do the tedious and thankless work of detailing the dead. MEs on TV are often clad in a crisp white medical coat or scrubs, and are equal parts sarcastic and sardonic, serious and spirited. These characters rely on one-liners and brief dialogue to assert their liveliness, their personalities serving as a contrast to the grotesque and morbid nature of their professions.

The Black female investigator enters this discourse as one of the more common representations of Black women in crime television. This casting pattern suggests a compelling connection between Black women's unique and unsavory history of caretaking in the Americas and Western ideas about our relationships and responsibilities to the deceased. Through their vibrancy in the face of often premature death, these fictional Black women model professionalism as a metaphor for the poetics of mortality.

—*Jordan Taliha McDonald*

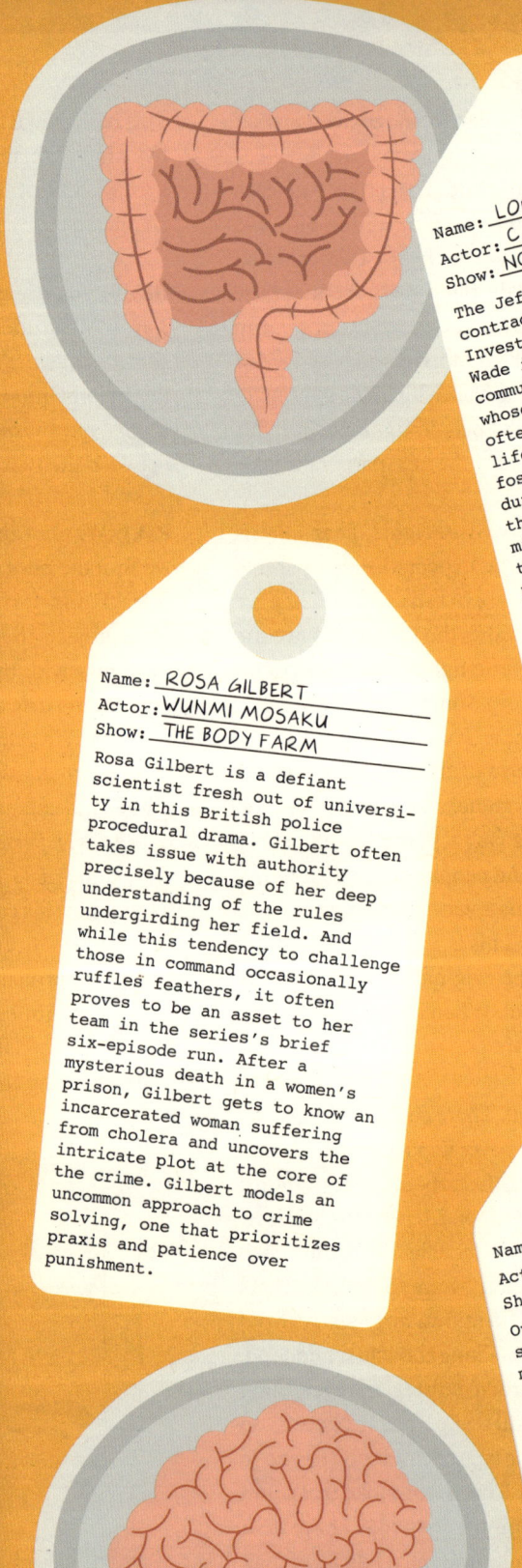

Name: LORETTA WADE
Actor: C. C. H. POUNDER
Show: NCIS: NEW ORLEANS

The Jefferson Parish coroner contracted by the Naval Criminal Investigative Service, Loretta Wade is a highly intelligent and community-oriented autopsist whose dedication to the job often bleeds into her personal life. Wade goes as far as to foster children she encounters during an NCIS case, and over the course of the series, one might argue that she has adopted the whole of the New Orleans parish as well. She is attentive and accessible to an impossible and perhaps illegal degree, and though she is offered the opportunity to join the New Orleans parish on numerous occasions, Wade routinely declines. It is as if she derives a distinct joy in servicing a parish that is not her own.

Name: ROSA GILBERT
Actor: WUNMI MOSAKU
Show: THE BODY FARM

Rosa Gilbert is a defiant scientist fresh out of university in this British police procedural drama. Gilbert often takes issue with authority precisely because of her deep understanding of the rules undergirding her field. And while this tendency to challenge those in command occasionally ruffles feathers, it often proves to be an asset to her team in the series's brief six-episode run. After a mysterious death in a women's prison, Gilbert gets to know an incarcerated woman suffering from cholera and uncovers the intricate plot at the core of the crime. Gilbert models an uncommon approach to crime solving, one that prioritizes praxis and patience over punishment.

Name: MELINDA WARNER
Actor: TAMARA TUNIE
Show: LAW AND ORDER: SVU

Over the course of the show's staggering twenty-two seasons, medical examiner Melinda Warner appears in nearly half of the show's 486 episodes. She is a measured and committed autopsist, and her observations of victims' remains often serve as the first clues about the life that led to their demise. There are few details provided about the woman behind the job. In one episode, she cites the hardships of her profession as the reason she got a pet: "It's nice to come home to something alive." Through autopsy, she is tasked with publishing the autobiographies of the deceased. And thus, her story remains untold.

Name: LANIE PARISH
Actor: TAMALA JONES
Show: CASTLE

NYPD medical examiner Lanie Parish excels with the dead due to her zest for life. After a full shift spent with corpses in her morgue, she spends her hours off the clock surrounded by the warmth of the living, whether at a nightclub or on a hot date. Parish encourages her coworkers to develop rich social lives, occasionally meddling and playing matchmaker. She is unafraid to mix business with pleasure, and finds love at work in homicide detective Javier Esposito. A romantic in life and love, Parish takes special care with the deferred dreams of the deceased, as they inspire her to tend to her own.

Name: CAMILLE SAROYAN
Actor: TAMARA TAYLOR
Show: BONES

Despite plans to kill her character off in Season 2, Saroyan's no-nonsense attitude proved quite popular among viewers. The straightlaced medical examiner has another shot at narrative life, by Season 12, and she has evolved into an empathetic leader and mother to several foster children. Ten seasons after her character's near-death, the work-obsessed, law-abiding high achiever we met at the start of Season 2 takes a leave of absence from the grueling work that once defined her. Saroyan is reborn once more. This time she is not "killed off" but set free.

Name: ALEXX WOODS
Actor: KHANDI ALEXANDER
Show: CSI: MIAMI

A New York girl who settled into the Miami-Dade County Police Department, Alexx Woods is best known for bringing a bubbly disposition and vibrant fashion sense into an otherwise stiff line of work. A married mother of two, Woods notoriously refers to the dead using terms of endearment: "baby," "honey," and "sweetie." She allows the corpse to serve as an authority on the life of the victim. Though her methods and mannerisms may be regarded as unorthodox and are at times blamed for her lack of professional promotions, Woods remains a pillar of the show's world-building. After she resigns from her post in Season 6, she continues to return, her dynamism making her an exceptionally hard act to follow.

Name: FLO DUNIGAN
Actor: MICHAEL HYATT
Film: THE LITTLE THINGS

This California-based crime thriller stars Denzel Washington as Deputy Sheriff Joe "Deke" Deacon, who investigates a string of murders. When it's revealed that a surviving victim was killed by Deke during a rescue gone wrong, it's Flo Dunigan's revisionist record of events that ultimately shapes the film's narrative arc. In covering up Deke's culpability, the medical examiner rewrites history. Though she is a secondary character, Dunigan's final act ensures that the film's lead, a culpable cop, remains free from accountability and incarceration. She reminds us that the role of the medical examiner is not a neutral one. She who writes the state's death records holds great power.

Name: ELAINE DUCHAMPS
Actor: LORRAINNE TOUSSAINT
Show: CROSSING JORDAN

Elaine Duchamps is initially introduced as a new coroner who struggles to build relationships with her coworkers. Though she's written as an antagonist, her early engagements with the office staff are marked by conflict with those who refuse to see her as anything more than management's replacement for her troubled predecessor. When the morgue staff is exposed to a seizure-inducing toxin in the midst of an unprecedented autopsy, Duchamps works to discover an antidote. As a result of her effortful attempt to save the life of a new recruit, Duchamps succumbs to a fatal E. coli infection. In the end, her death simultaneously redeems and removes her character from the show's narrative arc.

THE INNOCENT

A poem by Jennifer Chang

For weeks we watched for hatchlings to come
of three smug eggs tucked into a nest,
the nest tucked into the crook
of a neighbor's honeysuckle. Time nodded,
was nodding—the shred of living, how offhand
the wind teeters toward erosion. Hard at work,
on guard in two backyards, the robins mothered
and fathered their territory daily. And beyond,
our block's alley stretched aimless as fields,
where watching happens by accident,
by nature. They'd squawk on a streetlamp,
a cedar fence, our back stoop, warning off
the tabby, my two young sons, everyone
stuck at home. I lost my mind with watching
and thought it grief or egotism, the bruise
of yesterday, not least the sky
unraveling another season. It was easy
to mistake the bared skeletal pinions
as lawn clippings, old leaves. That circle
in the grass, a massacre of feathers. That
terrible cat. It was easy to lose my mind.
One neighbor said, let's not tell the children,
why know the world as always fated
toward remnant. Another said, go,
take the nest, set it under glass, and make it a lesson.
Instead, I watched our habits pass, the honeysuckle
fade from sickly sweet to nothing but heat.
Call it science. It's summer again, and then
everything's remnant. What did we do those days,
stuck at home, my sons might some day ask. We lived
or tolerated living. We looked away from death.

The Places We Lost

by KATHY MACLEOD

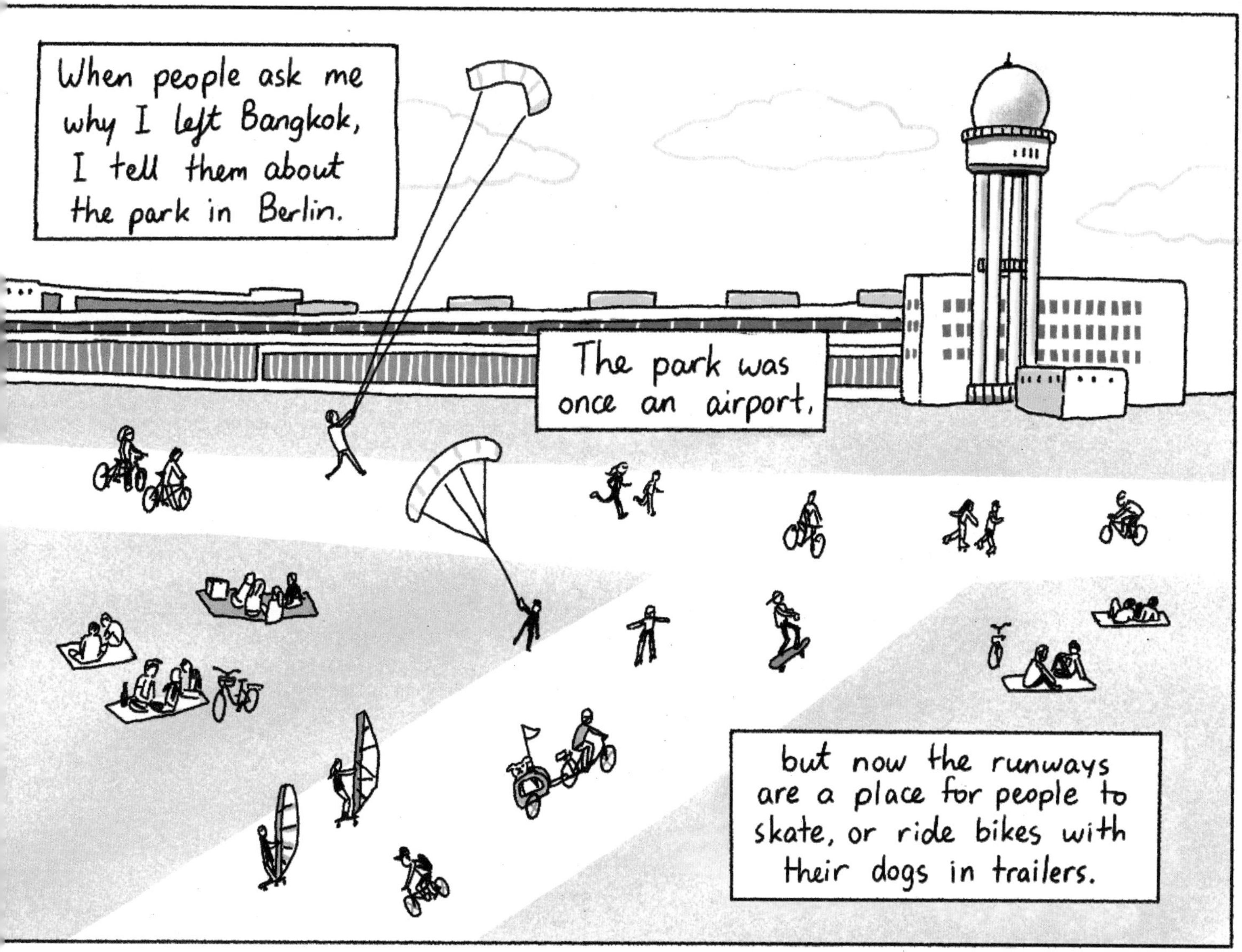
When people ask me why I left Bangkok, I tell them about the park in Berlin.
The park was once an airport,
but now the runways are a place for people to skate, or ride bikes with their dogs in trailers.

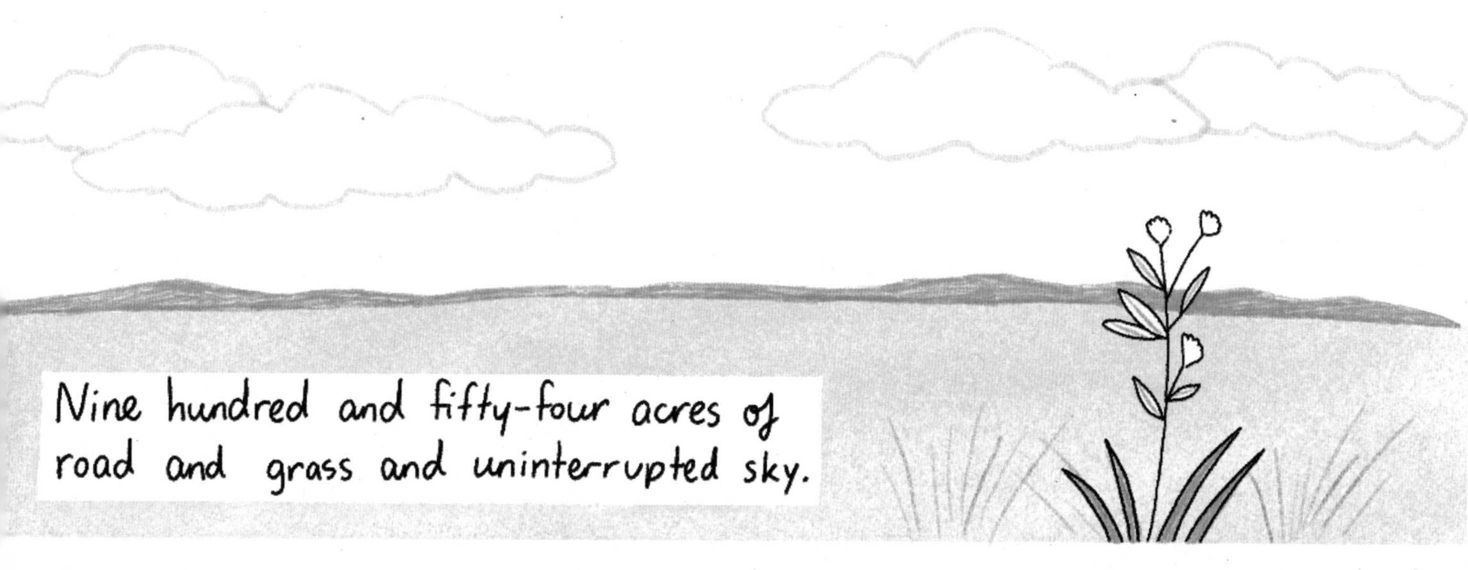
Nine hundred and fifty-four acres of road and grass and uninterrupted sky.

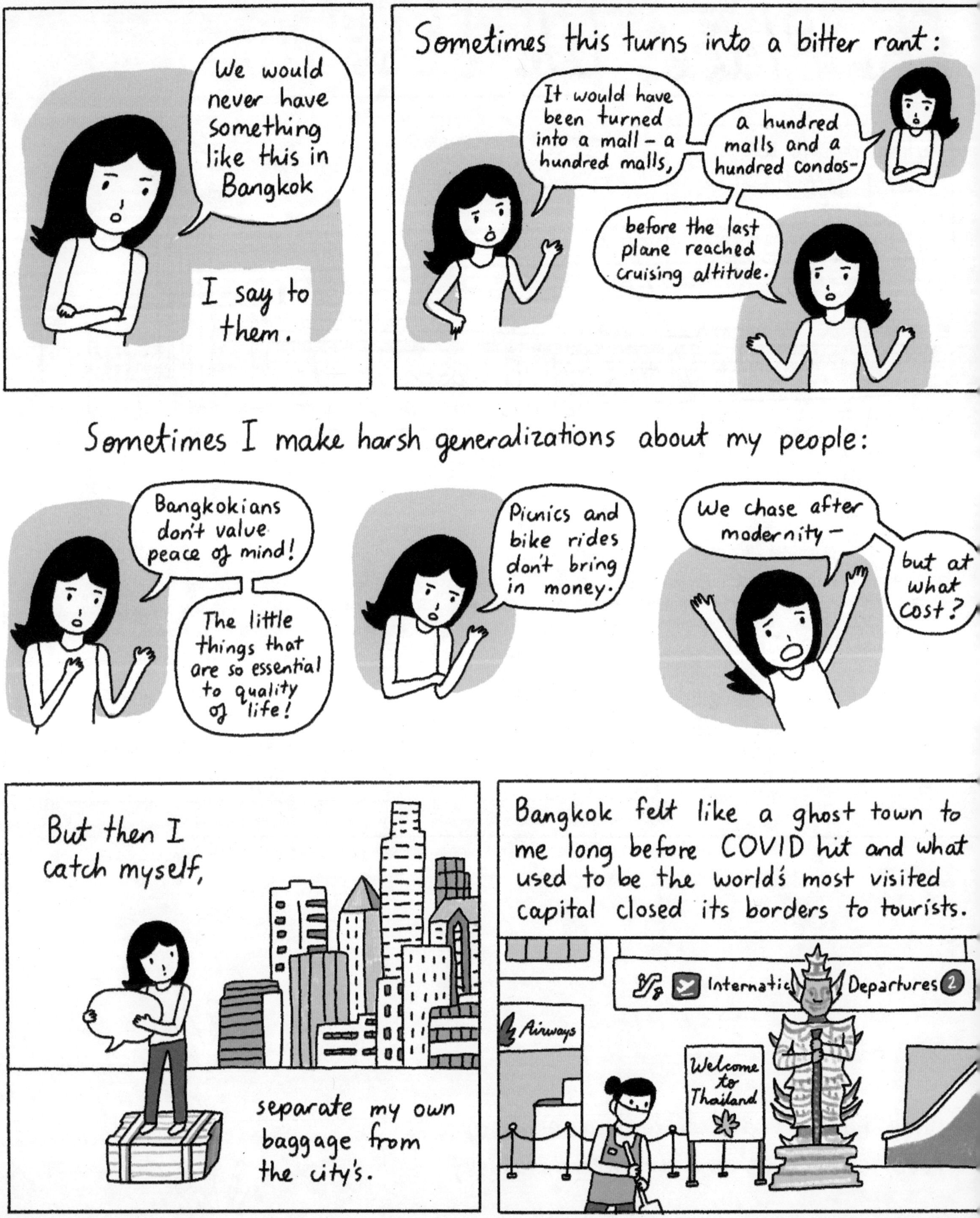

We would never have something like this in Bangkok
I say to them.
Sometimes this turns into a bitter rant:
It would have been turned into a mall – a hundred malls,
a hundred malls and a hundred condos-
before the last plane reached cruising altitude.
Sometimes I make harsh generalizations about my people:
Bangkokians don't value peace of mind!
The little things that are so essential to quality of life!
Picnics and bike rides don't bring in money.
We chase after modernity –
but at what cost?
But then I catch myself,
separate my own baggage from the city's.
Bangkok felt like a ghost town to me long before COVID hit and what used to be the world's most visited capital closed its borders to tourists.
Departures 2
Airways
Welcome to Thailand

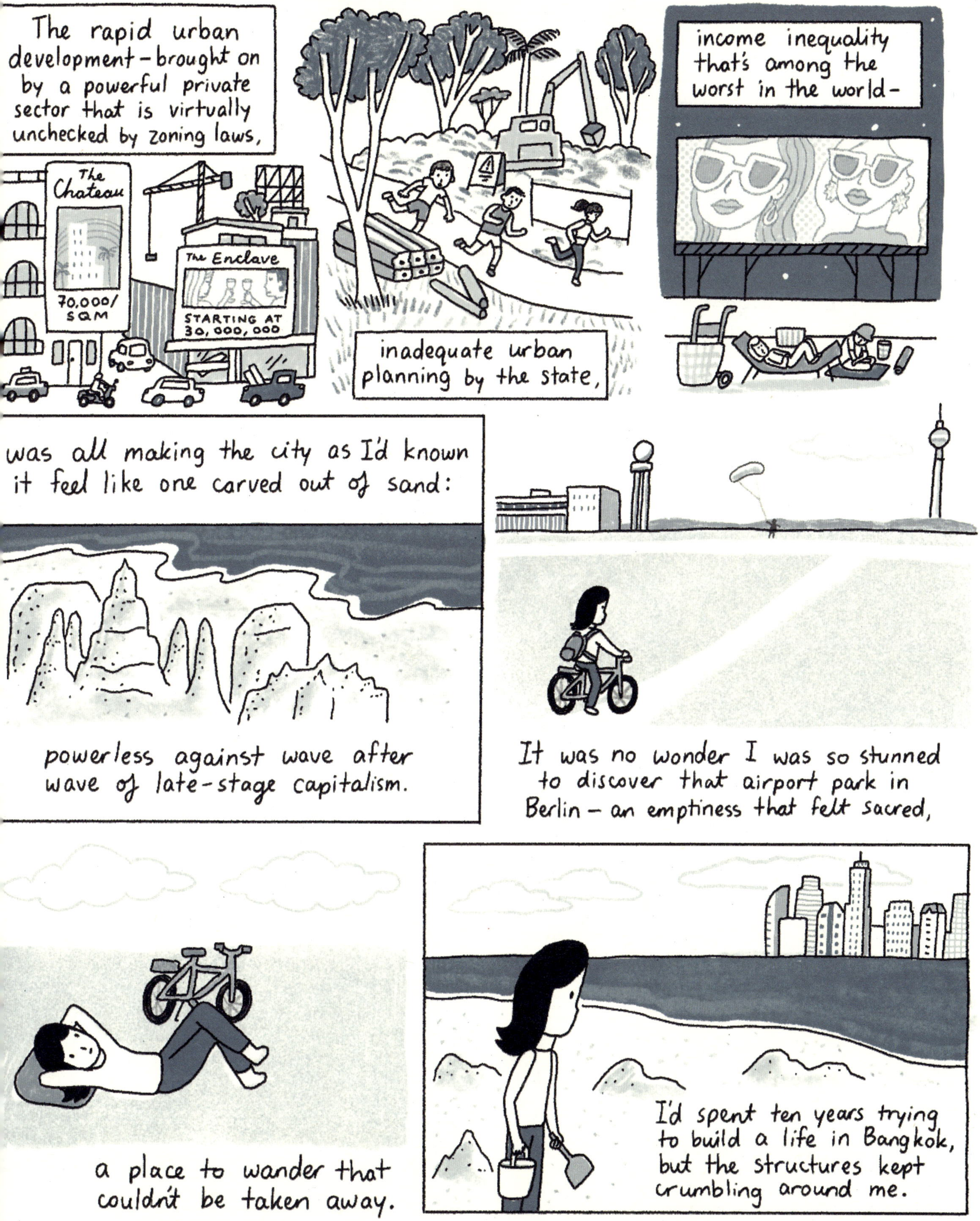
The rapid urban development – brought on by a powerful private sector that is virtually unchecked by zoning laws,
The Chateau
70,000/ SQM
The Enclave
STARTING AT 30,000,000
inadequate urban planning by the state,
income inequality that's among the worst in the world –
was all making the city as I'd known it feel like one carved out of sand:
powerless against wave after wave of late-stage capitalism.
It was no wonder I was so stunned to discover that airport park in Berlin – an emptiness that felt sacred,
a place to wander that couldn't be taken away.
I'd spent ten years trying to build a life in Bangkok, but the structures kept crumbling around me.

The Rex Hotel

Built in the '60s to accommodate American GIs (so the story went), the hotel had a twenty-four-hour diner inside that I imagine had not altered a detail since the war.

Spacious, curved vinyl booths, servers in bow ties, two menus: Thai and Western.

There weren't many places in Bangkok that were open all night, and where you could get a shitty club sandwich with a side of spicy century eggs.

The hotel was across the road from our favorite bar, a cozy little dive called WTF.

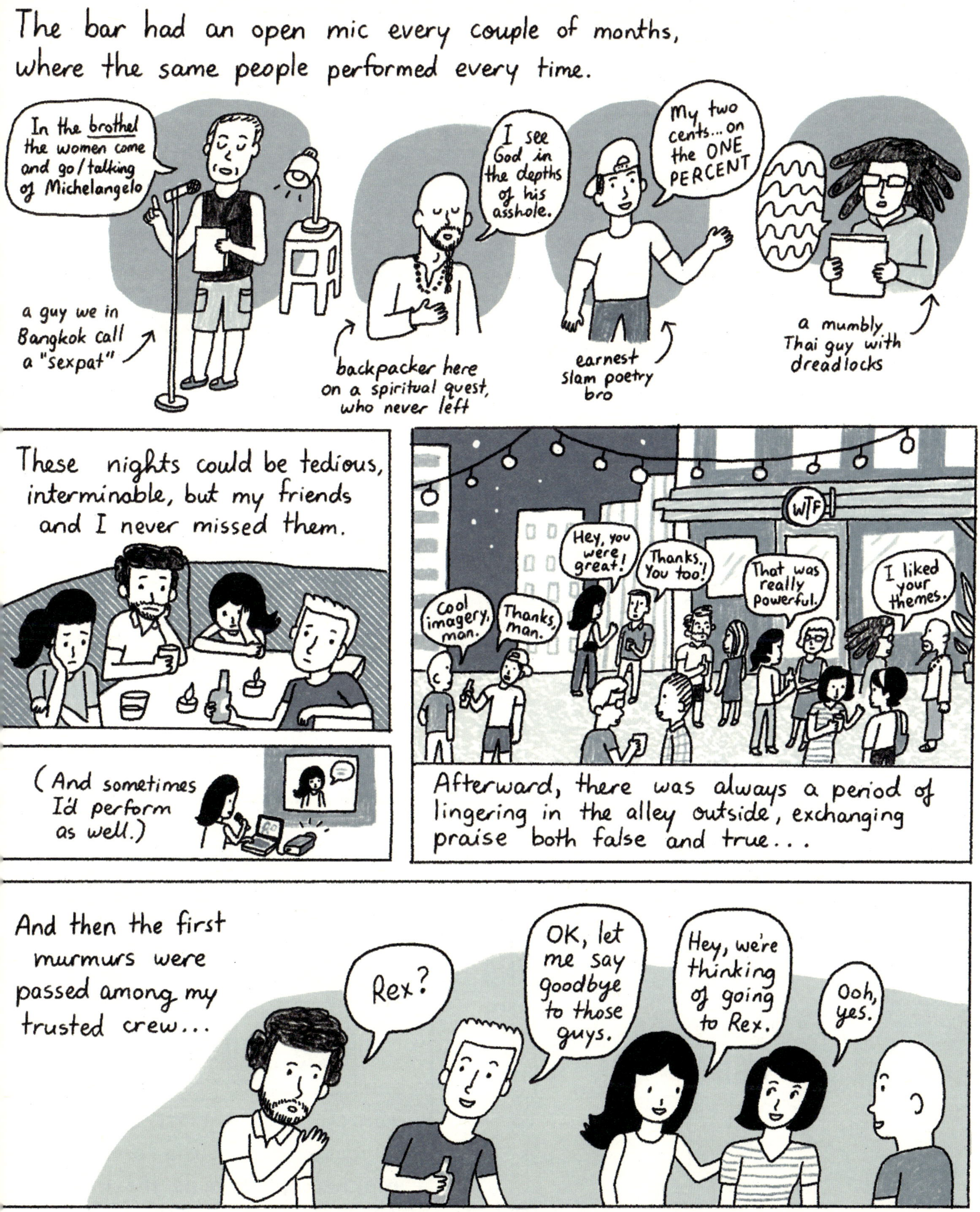
The bar had an open mic every couple of months, where the same people performed every time.
In the brothel the women come and go / talking of Michelangelo
a guy we in Bangkok call a "sexpat"
I see God in the depths of his asshole.
backpacker here on a spiritual quest, who never left
My two cents... on the ONE PERCENT
earnest slam poetry bro
a mumbly Thai guy with dreadlocks
These nights could be tedious, interminable, but my friends and I never missed them.
(And sometimes I'd perform as well.)
WTF
Cool imagery, man.
Thanks, man.
Hey, you were great!
Thanks. You too!
That was really powerful.
I liked your themes.
Afterward, there was always a period of lingering in the alley outside, exchanging praise both false and true...
And then the first murmurs were passed among my trusted crew...
Rex?
OK, let me say goodbye to those guys.
Hey, we're thinking of going to Rex.
Ooh, yes.

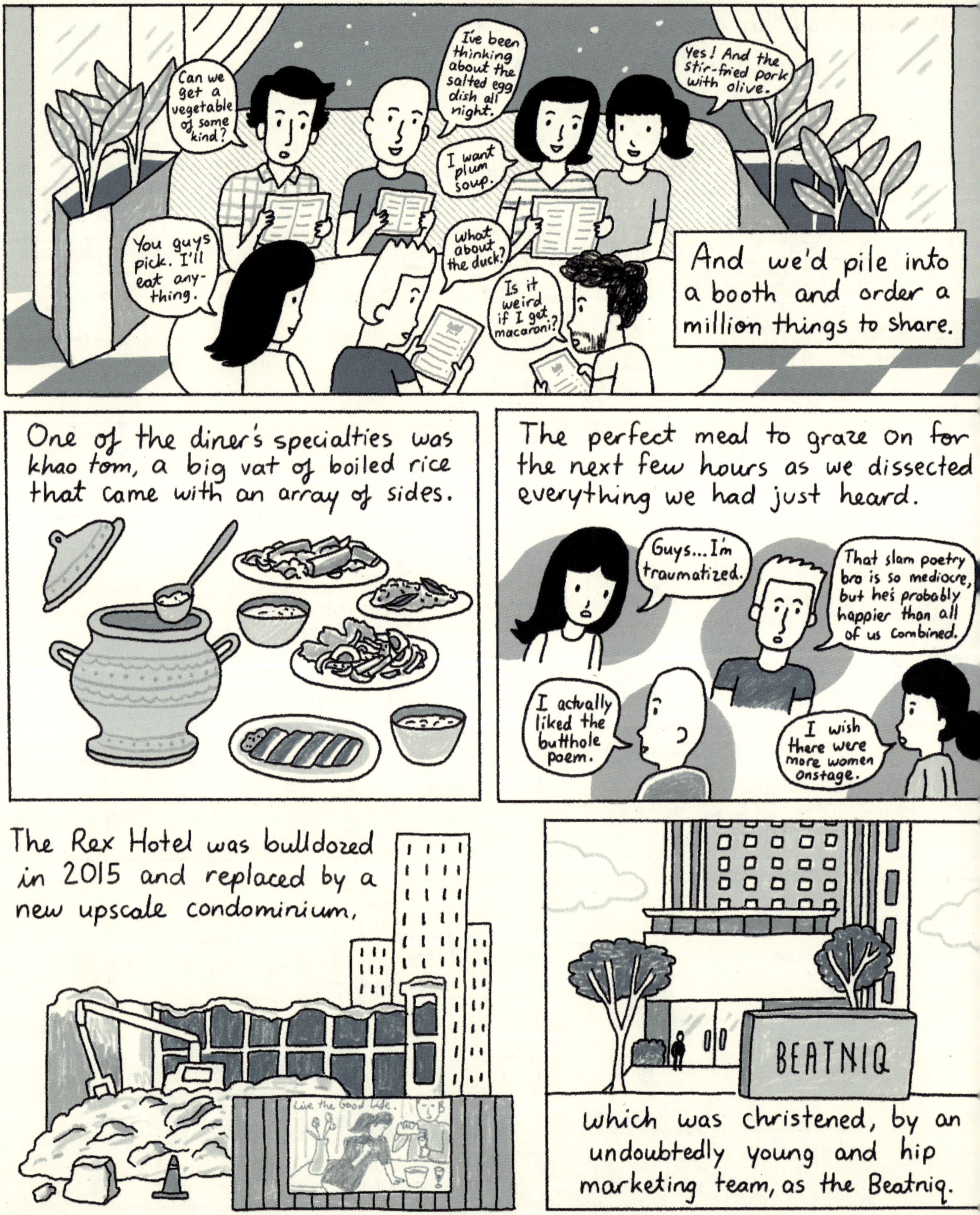
Can we get a vegetable of some kind?
I've been thinking about the salted egg dish all night.
I want plum soup.
Yes! And the stir-fried pork with olive.
You guys pick. I'll eat any-thing.
What about the duck?
Is it weird if I get macaroni?
And we'd pile into a booth and order a million things to share.
One of the diner's specialties was khao tom, a big vat of boiled rice that came with an array of sides.
The perfect meal to graze on for the next few hours as we dissected everything we had just heard.
Guys... I'm traumatized.
That slam poetry bro is so mediocre, but he's probably happier than all of us combined.
I actually liked the butthole poem.
I wish there were more women onstage.
The Rex Hotel was bulldozed in 2015 and replaced by a new upscale condominium,
Live the Good Life.
BEATNIQ
which was christened, by an undoubtedly young and hip marketing team, as the Beatniq.

Chalermsuk Court

Any apartment complex in Bangkok whose name ends in "Court" will inevitably be a mid-century low-rise structure with hardwood floors and terrazzo stairways.

An apartment in a Court is hard to find, and I was overjoyed to land one, back in 2012.

It was the first apartment of my very own — a shockingly cheap, light-filled one-bedroom in a central part of town.

I'd decided it was time to stop living at home, like so many unmarried Thai twentysomethings do.

"Take care of yourself"

My cat, Penny, had traveled with me from Connecticut to Florida to Philly to Georgia and finally to Bangkok, so I thought she was used to new places, and good at adapting.

"Come on, buddy."

"How did you even get up there?"

But she never warmed up to Chalermsuk Court (roughly translated as, like, "glorious happiness"), never loved it like I did.

Still, I never thought I could be so happy in a place, with my own couch to laze upon.

Penny, on the other hand, was always on edge. Whenever my mother came to visit, Penny would get into her carrier and wait to be taken back to the big house. It broke my heart.

On my thirtieth birthday, my then boyfriend filled it up with houseplants — one of the few times I truly felt that he loved me.

Then Penny got sick. She was twelve years old.

Within a month she was gone — the only witness to all my twenties.

The thing about Court life is that a Court's days are always numbered. The eviction notice couldn't have come at a better time.

I was feeling Penny's ghost in every corner.

I left well before I had to, and moved into a smaller, darker place down the block.

Every day I walked past my first apartment as it gradually turned to rubble, to make way for some kind of condo showroom.

One day I stopped longer than usual, thinking about what used to be, when I noticed a little visitor in the ruins.

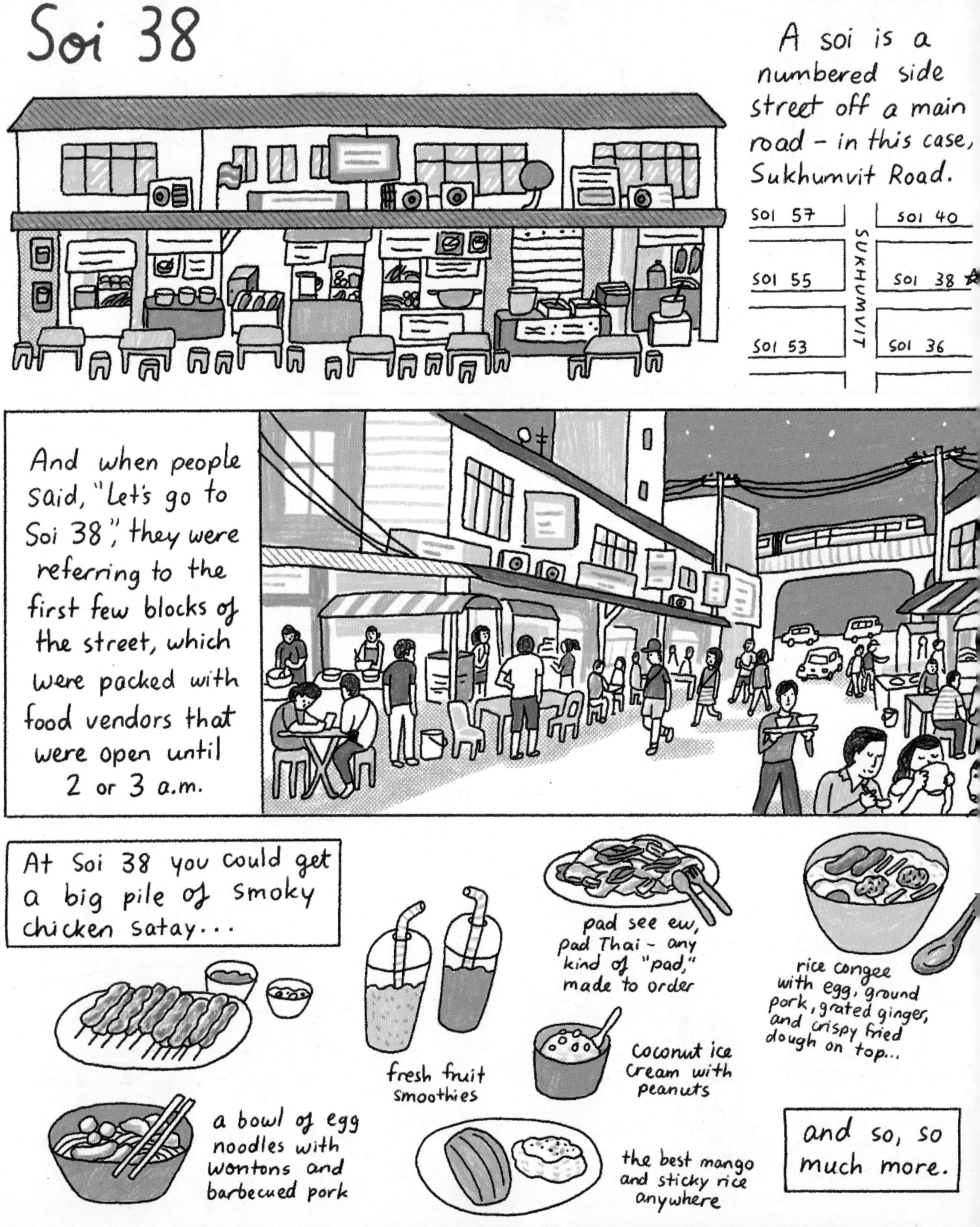
Soi 38
A soi is a numbered side street off a main road - in this case, Sukhumvit Road.
SOI 57
SOI 40
SOI 55
SOI 38
SOI 53
SOI 36
SUKHUMVIT
And when people said, "Let's go to Soi 38", they were referring to the first few blocks of the street, which were packed with food vendors that were open until 2 or 3 a.m.
At Soi 38 you could get a big pile of smoky chicken satay...
fresh fruit smoothies
pad see ew, pad Thai - any kind of "pad," made to order
coconut ice cream with peanuts
rice congee with egg, ground pork, grated ginger, and crispy fried dough on top...
a bowl of egg noodles with wontons and barbecued pork
the best mango and sticky rice anywhere
and so, so much more.

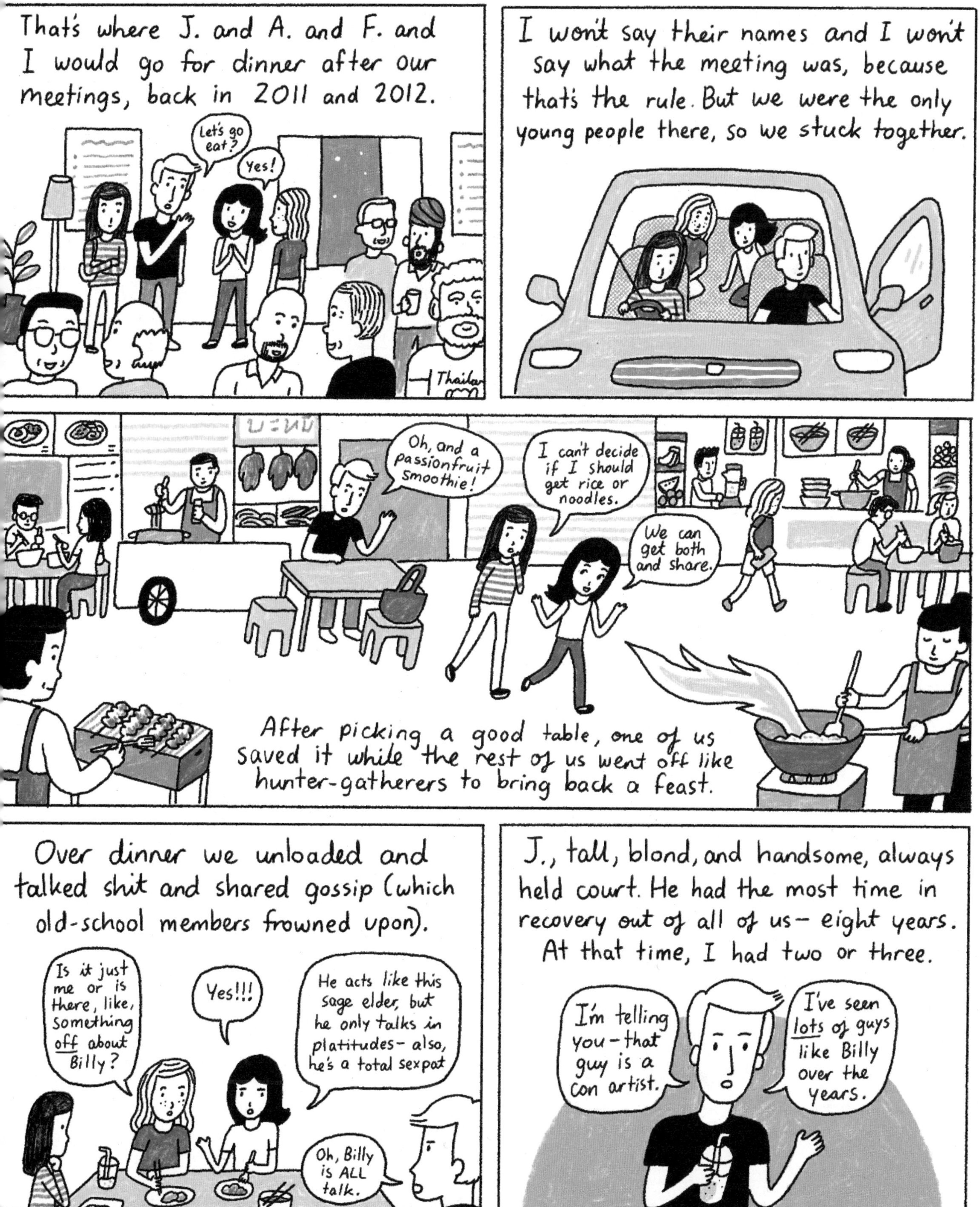

That's where J. and A. and F. and I would go for dinner after our meetings, back in 2011 and 2012.
Let's go eat?
Yes!
I won't say their names and I won't say what the meeting was, because that's the rule. But we were the only young people there, so we stuck together.
Oh, and a passionfruit smoothie!
I can't decide if I should get rice or noodles.
We can get both and share.
After picking a good table, one of us saved it while the rest of us went off like hunter-gatherers to bring back a feast.
Over dinner we unloaded and talked shit and shared gossip (which old-school members frowned upon).
Is it just me or is there, like, something off about Billy?
Yes!!!
He acts like this sage elder, but he only talks in platitudes- also, he's a total sexpat
Oh, Billy is ALL talk.
J., tall, blond, and handsome, always held court. He had the most time in recovery out of all of us- eight years. At that time, I had two or three.
I'm telling you- that guy is a con artist.
I've seen lots of guys like Billy over the years.

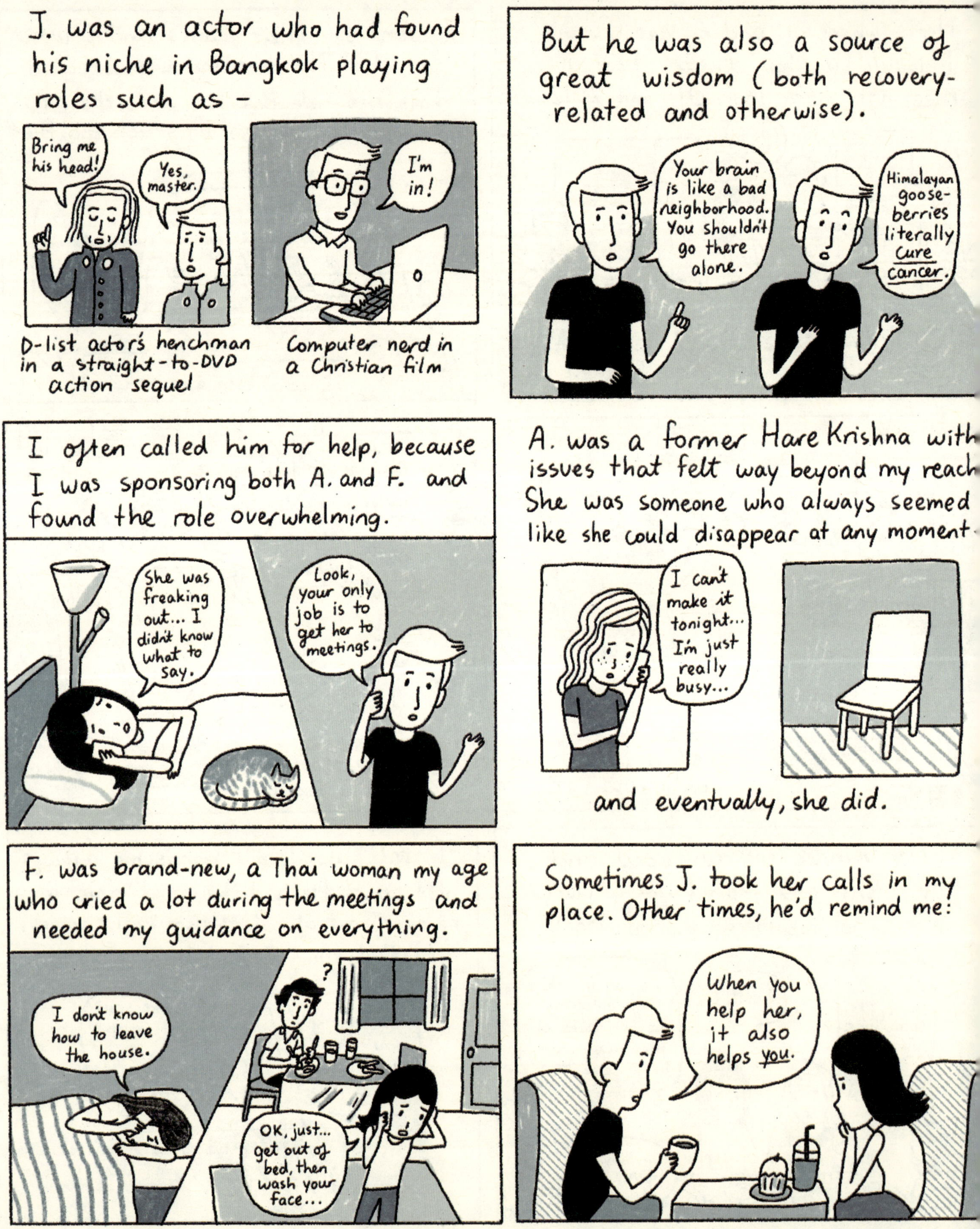
J. was an actor who had found his niche in Bangkok playing roles such as -
Bring me his head!
Yes, master.
D-list actor's henchman in a straight-to-DVD action sequel
I'm in!
Computer nerd in a Christian film
But he was also a source of great wisdom (both recovery-related and otherwise).
Your brain is like a bad neighborhood. You shouldn't go there alone.
Himalayan goose-berries literally cure cancer.
I often called him for help, because I was sponsoring both A. and F. and found the role overwhelming.
She was freaking out... I didn't know what to say.
Look, your only job is to get her to meetings.
A. was a former Hare Krishna with issues that felt way beyond my reach. She was someone who always seemed like she could disappear at any moment.
I can't make it tonight... I'm just really busy...
and eventually, she did.
F. was brand-new, a Thai woman my age who cried a lot during the meetings and needed my guidance on everything.
I don't know how to leave the house.
?
OK, just... get out of bed, then wash your face...
Sometimes J. took her calls in my place. Other times, he'd remind me:
When you help her, it also helps you.

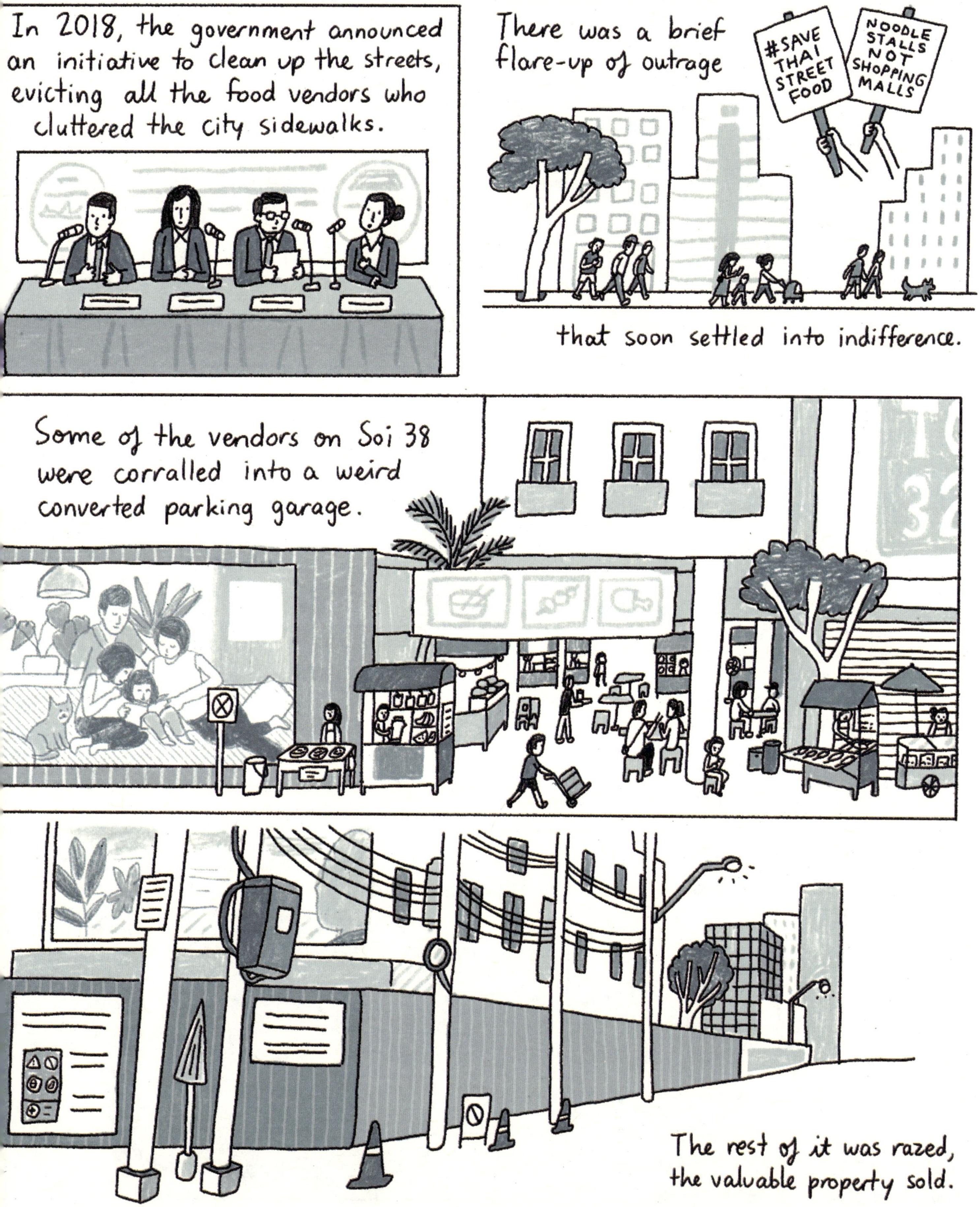
In 2018, the government announced an initiative to clean up the streets, evicting all the food vendors who cluttered the city sidewalks.
There was a brief flare-up of outrage
#SAVE THAI STREET FOOD
NOODLE STALLS NOT SHOPPING MALLS
that soon settled into indifference.
Some of the vendors on Soi 38 were corralled into a weird converted parking garage.
The rest of it was razed, the valuable property sold.

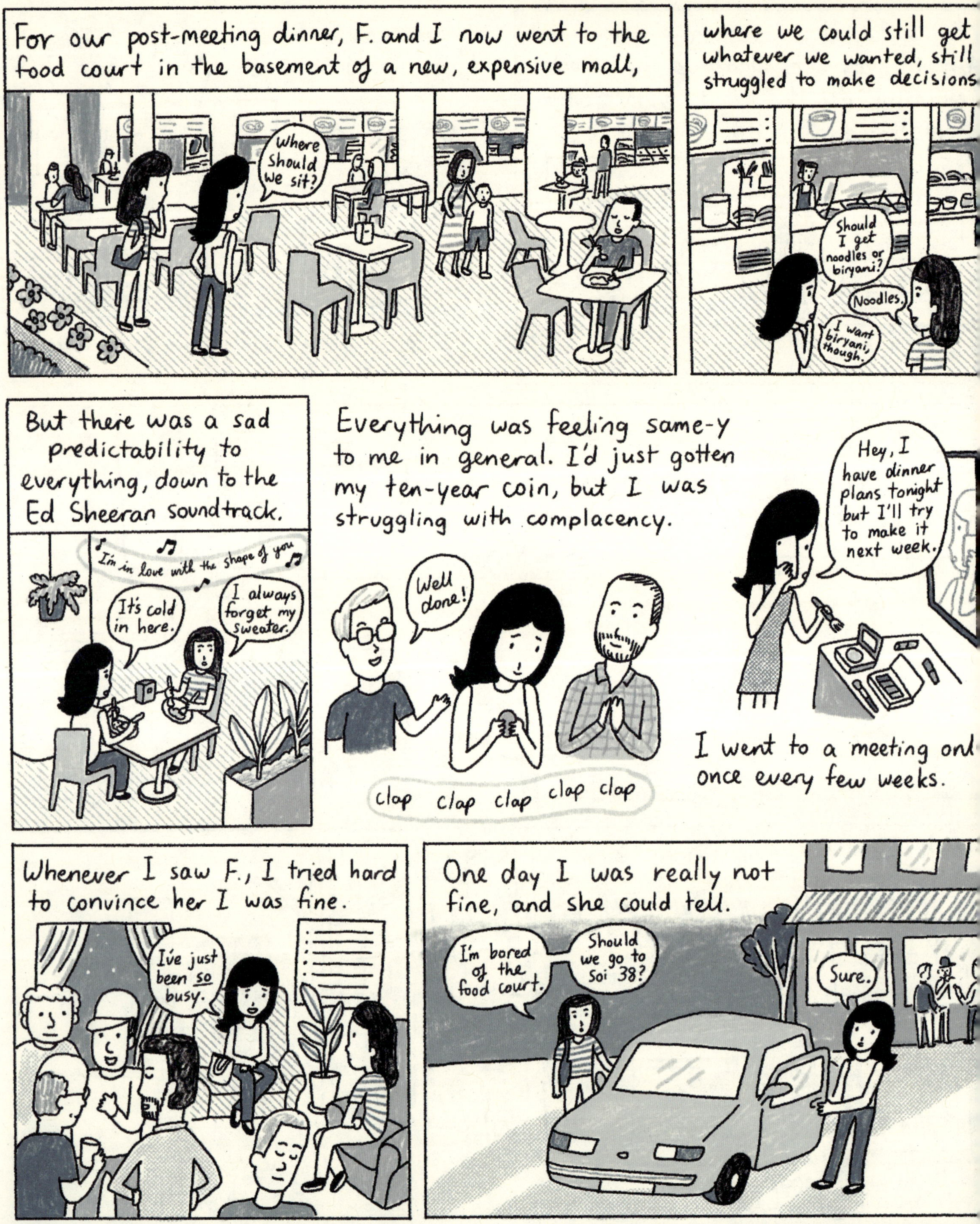
For our post-meeting dinner, F. and I now went to the food court in the basement of a new, expensive mall,
Where should we sit?
where we could still get whatever we wanted, still struggled to make decisions
Should I get noodles or biryani?
Noodles.
I want biryani, though.
But there was a sad predictability to everything, down to the Ed Sheeran soundtrack.
I'm in love with the shape of you
It's cold in here.
I always forget my sweater.
Everything was feeling same-y to me in general. I'd just gotten my ten-year coin, but I was struggling with complacency.
Well done!
clap clap clap clap clap
Hey, I have dinner plans tonight but I'll try to make it next week.
I went to a meeting onl
once every few weeks.
Whenever I saw F., I tried hard to convince her I was fine.
I've just been so busy.
One day I was really not fine, and she could tell.
I'm bored of the food court.
Should we go to Soi 38?
Sure.

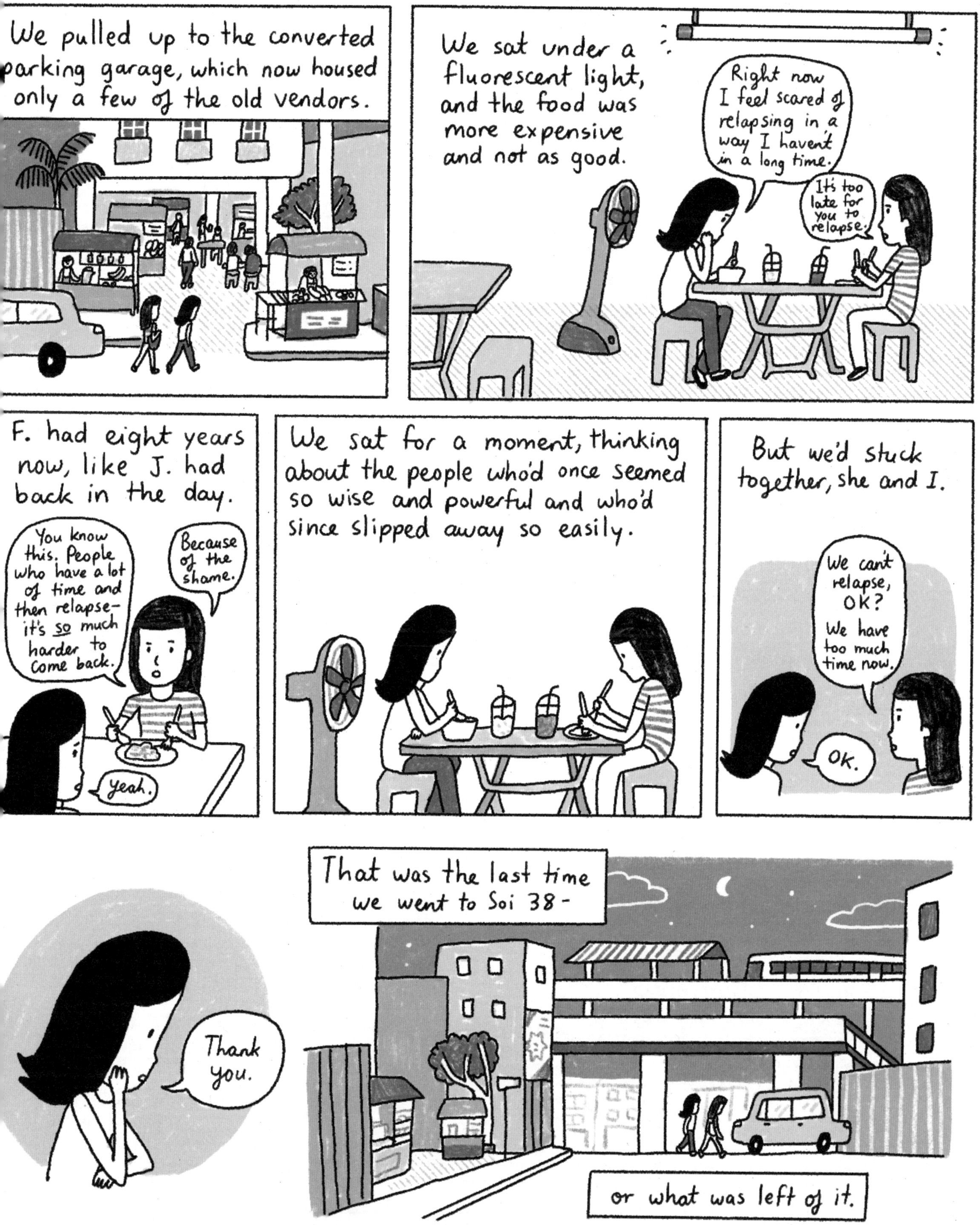

We pulled up to the converted parking garage, which now housed only a few of the old vendors.
We sat under a fluorescent light, and the food was more expensive and not as good.
Right now I feel scared of relapsing in a way I haven't in a long time.
It's too late for you to relapse.
F. had eight years now, like J. had back in the day.
You know this. People who have a lot of time and then relapse- it's so much harder to come back.
Because of the shame.
Yeah.
We sat for a moment, thinking about the people who'd once seemed so wise and powerful and who'd since slipped away so easily.
But we'd stuck together, she and I.
We can't relapse, OK? We have too much time now.
OK.
Thank you.
That was the last time we went to Soi 38-
or what was left of it.

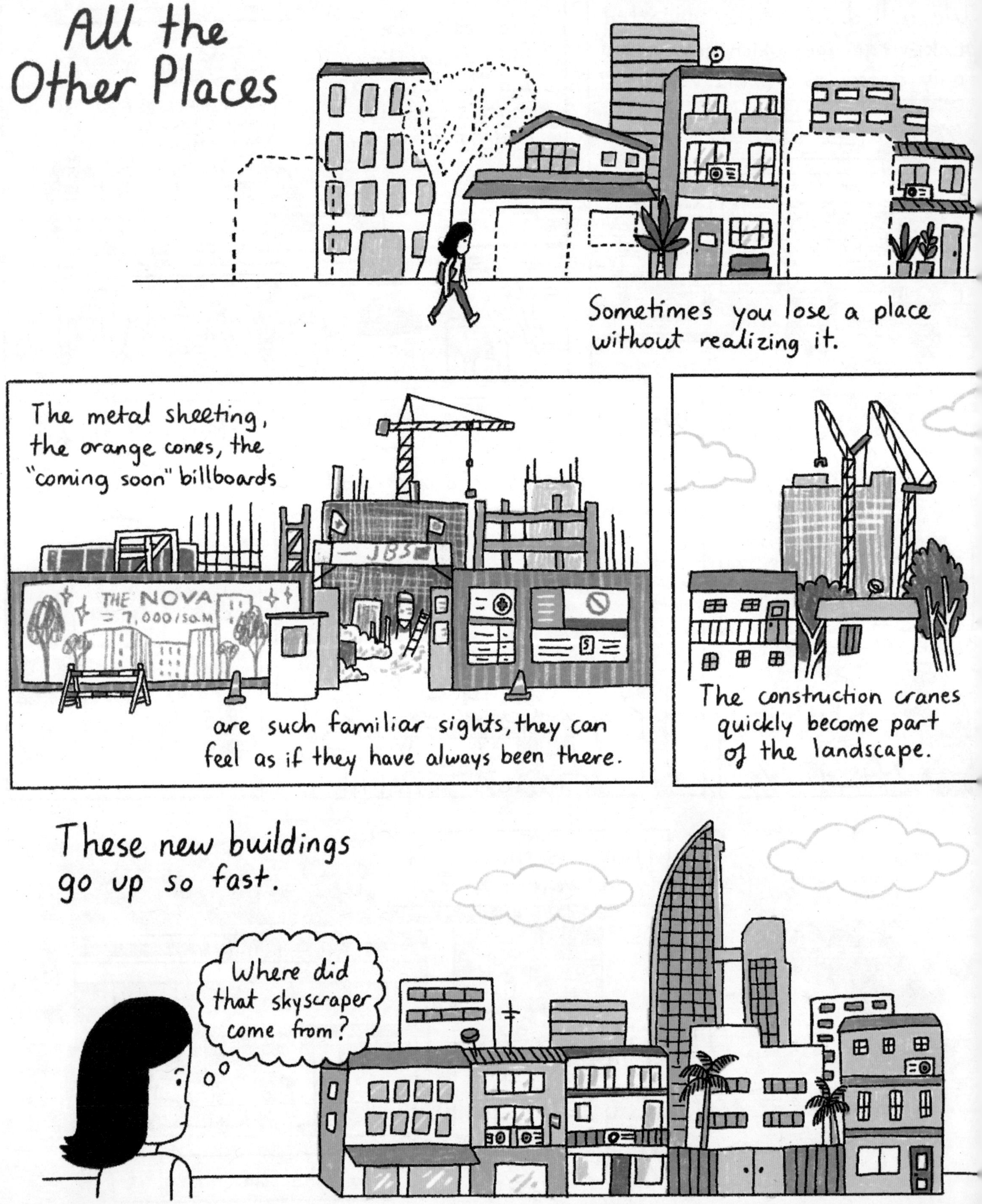
All the Other Places
Sometimes you lose a place without realizing it.
The metal sheeting, the orange cones, the "coming soon" billboards
THE NOVA
= 7,000/SQM
JBS
are such familiar sights, they can feel as if they have always been there.
The construction cranes quickly become part of the landscape.
These new buildings go up so fast.
Where did that skyscraper come from?

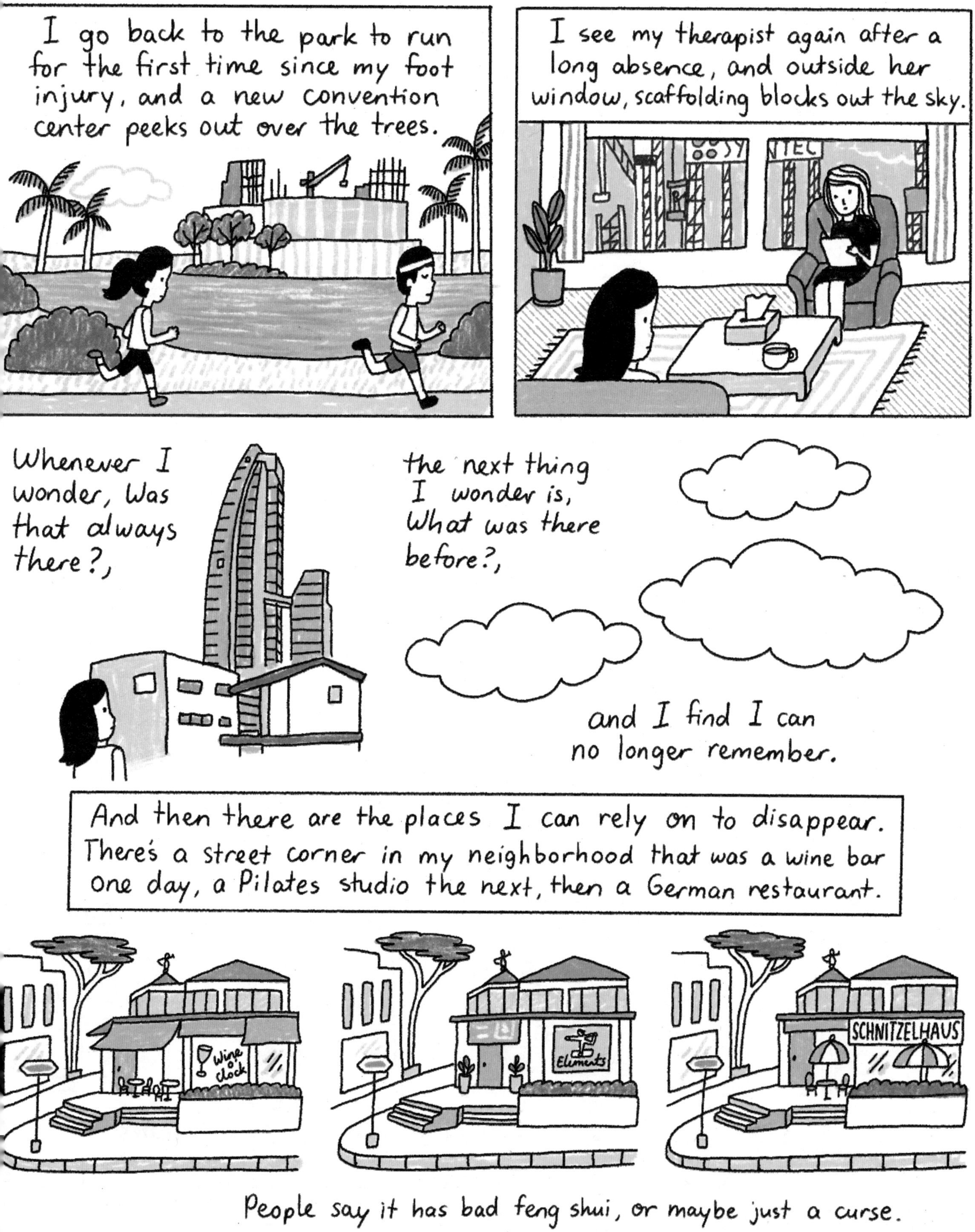
I go back to the park to run for the first time since my foot injury, and a new convention center peeks out over the trees.
I see my therapist again after a long absence, and outside her window, scaffolding blocks out the sky.
Whenever I wonder, Was that always there?,
the next thing I wonder is, What was there before?,
and I find I can no longer remember.
And then there are the places I can rely on to disappear. There's a street corner in my neighborhood that was a wine bar one day, a Pilates studio the next, then a German restaurant.
Wine o clock
Elements
SCHNITZELHAUS
People say it has bad feng shui, or maybe just a curse.

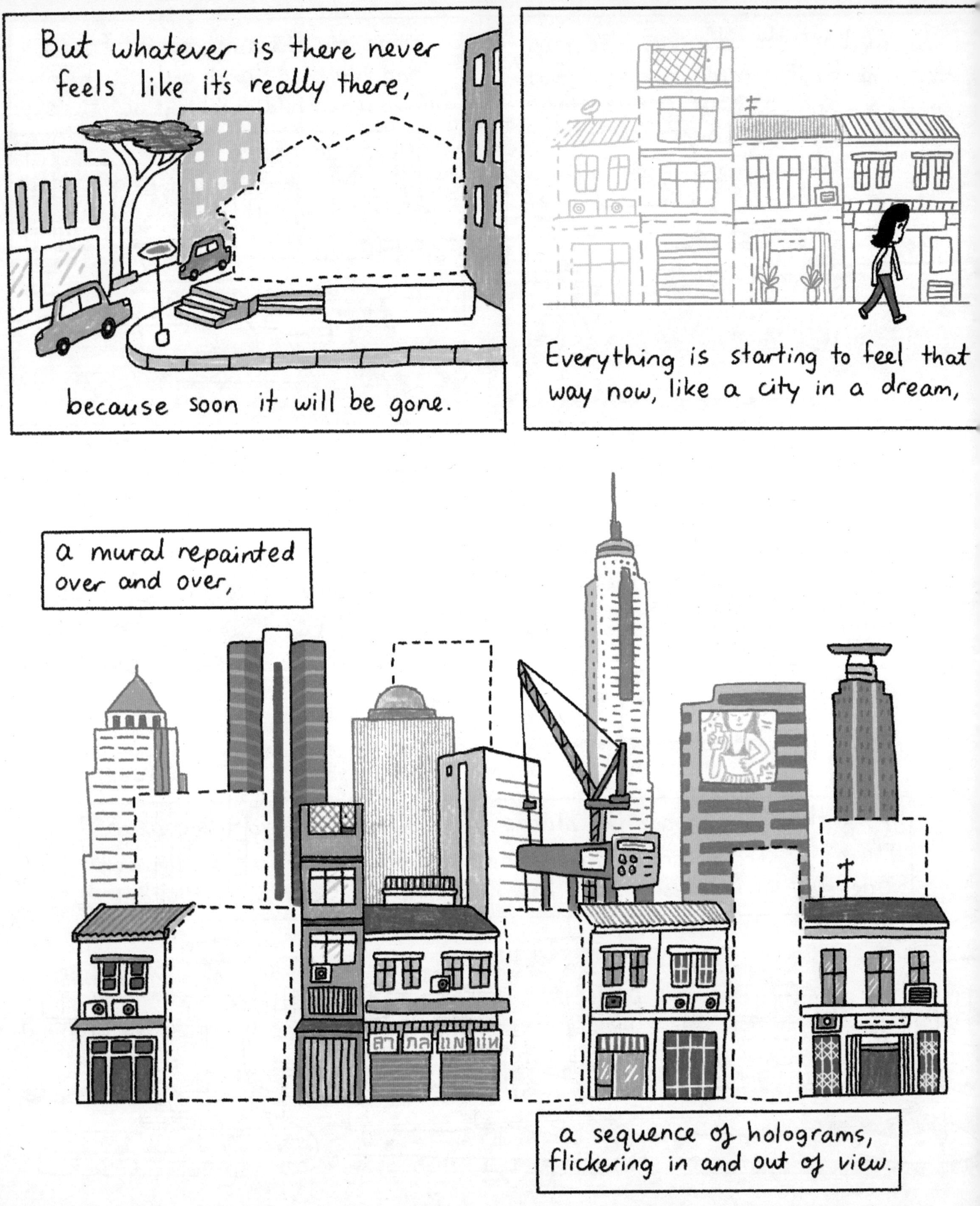
But whatever is there never feels like it's really there,
because soon it will be gone.
Everything is starting to feel that way now, like a city in a dream,
a mural repainted over and over,
a sequence of holograms, flickering in and out of view.

"THE JOB OF A SONGWRITER IS TO ILLUMINATE SOME DISCUSSION ON THINGS THAT PROBABLY WOULDN'T BE TALKED ABOUT."

CHUCK D
[MUSICIAN, ILLUSTRATOR]

Chuck D always has something to say. Yet I wasn't expecting the Public Enemy founder to have a lot to say about President Dwight D. Eisenhower's push for a national interstate highway system. When we sat down to chat, the rapper who told generations of young people, "Don't Believe the Hype," launched into a detailed history of the Eisenhower National System of Interstate and Defense Highways. Turns out that driving those roads mapped out by a bygone administration has played an integral part in Chuck D's songwriting process and thus is central to Public Enemy's and hip-hop's history.

Born Carlton Ridenhour, Chuck D, who is now sixty-one, spent a lot of time behind the wheel as he meandered along the highways and byways around his childhood home in Long Island, New York. He was studying graphic design at Long Island's Adelphi University when he cofounded Public Enemy in 1986. Chuck D teamed up with DJ Terminator X, Professor Griff, and clock-enthusiast rapper Flavor Flav, and the group released their politically conscious debut rap album, Yo! Bum Rush the Show, in 1987. Public Enemy quickly established themselves

Illustration by Samar Haddad

as a no-holds-barred, opinionated rap group who didn't mind pissing the right people off. Their song "Fight the Power" was memorably blasted out of Radio Raheem's boom box in Spike Lee's film Do the Right Thing, while songs like "Don't Believe the Hype," "Fear of a Black Planet," and "Bring the Noise" have been in heavy rotation for decades. All this has helped cement Chuck D's spot in the Long Island Music Hall of Fame, alongside Billy Joel and Mariah Carey.

Over the last three decades, the band has not skirted controversy, preferring to wade right into the thick of it. Their lyrics are provocative and contemplative, and Chuck D's unmistakable baritone delivers a dose of medicine tucked inside the sweet beats. Even after three decades and fifteen studio albums, not to mention a host of live and compilation records, the band hasn't slowed down, releasing a stream of new music, including 2020's What You Gonna Do When the Grid Goes Down? They generate headlines and make their opinions heard—and Chuck D certainly has a lot of opinions. Opinions he expresses in his books, his music, and his artwork, which is part of the permanent collections at the Smithsonian Museum of African American History and Culture and the Oakland Museum of California. We spoke on the phone about the Monkees, The Great Gatsby, facial recognition software, and, of course, the Interstate Highway System.
—Melissa Locker

I. ANGRILY CURIOUS

CHUCK D: Let's start with the name of your magazine, *The Believer*. Let's talk about the Monkees. I'm a believer. Let's talk about the songwriters that wrote for the Monkees and for other people and TV shows. Let's talk about Gerry Goffin and Carole King.

THE BELIEVER: Are you a Monkees fan?

CD: I grew up with the Monkees. I was one of the ones that believed. I believed they wrote their own songs and sang their own songs.

BLVR: Did you know that the Monkees were on an FBI watch list because they were worried the band was anti-government or something?

CD: I didn't know that. One thing my daughter just told me, like ten minutes ago, while I was taking my 2021 passport pictures, is that there's a policy that will no longer allow pictures with smiles. Did you hear about that? That's a new problem. I think maybe it has something to do with facial recognition software. Your face contorts when you smile.

BLVR: Do you get nervous about the government using facial recognition software?

CD: *Nervous* is not a good word for that. I don't get nervous about it. I might get unhinged. Unhinged and nervous are two different things. I'm like: I'm a citizen here. I demand some kind of explanation.

BLVR: Are you worried about your phone using facial recognition? Are you worried about the government using facial recognition to monitor you out in the streets? Or are you just conscious of it?

CD: Worried? *Worried* is not a word I would use. I don't get "nervous" or "worried" about any of this. I don't want to just throw my machismo up in this thing, but I'm just saying that when you're worried and you're nervous, that means you're dealing with the unknown. We demand the right to know who's pushing the buttons on some of these things that are peculiar. And, actually, it makes me, you know, angrily curious. Like, Who the hell? What the hell? WTH is this? Like, Yo, man, give me an explanation for this bullshit.

BLVR: In China they're using facial recognition technology to monitor whether kids are skipping class.

CD: Wow. They've got to find new ways of monitoring youth, especially in this century.

BLVR: Are you a big tech person?

CD: I'm a big tech person who says we should do our best to manage the technology we have. Upgrades and new gadgets piss me off because they should be managed and work well instead of just being consumed like a meal. They upgrade faster than our capabilities. You know, when things upgrade at such a high speed, they tend to make the *masses asses*. They just move the *m* over.

BLVR: Is your album *What You Gonna Do When the Grid Goes Down?* related to the same idea of technology moving so quickly?

CD: Yeah, you got to figure out how you're going to manage these gadgets and not be dependent upon them, because if you don't manage the gadgets, they'll master you. You'll become dependent on them and won't be able to do without them, and that means they will master you. Then when they do disappear, you can't adapt. The song "When the Grid Goes Down" is not so much of an anti-gadget, anti-technology thing. It's more: Beware of the way the government's playing games with the grid thing. They could *make* the grid go down. They *could* make anything happen, so just be privy to what's happening.

BLVR: One of the things you mention specifically in that song is "No GPS, what will you do?," so I was wondering what you would do in that situation? How are your map-reading skills?

CD: My map-reading skills are probably better than those of anybody you could ever find in your life. I already have an inside GPS. I was trained with maps, with latitude and longitude readings and the parallels and all that stuff. I have an understanding of the roads in the United States and the Eisenhower interstate system. I'll give you a little trivia that will make you understand what the Eisenhower interstate system is, if you don't know already. Where do you live?

BLVR: I live in New York.

CD: You always lived in New York?

BLVR: Originally, I'm from Oregon.

CD: OK, and what road runs north to south in Oregon?

BLVR: I-5.

CD: Right. Now what road runs north to south in New York?

BLVR: I-95.

CD: Exactly. So you understand that the fives run straight up and down. And they run perpendicular to the roads that go east to west. So if you go from Oregon all the way over to New York, you're going 5, 15, 25, 35, 45, 55, 65, 75, and 85 to the east. I don't know if you've driven anywhere else in the country, but when you're down south, and you go from Florida to Los Angeles, you're going on the 10, right? When you're up north going from New England to Seattle, you're on the 90. Those

> When I'm on a dark road in the car with the pad and my pen, that's where the ideas come from, along with the music.

numbers go 10, 20, 30, 40, up to 70, 80, 90, from the south to the north. And anything with three numbers in it is a beltway that runs around a city, but most people don't know that.

BLVR: So why do you know all this?

CD: Because I had to go to all those places on tour and I was curious. I played in all these cities.

BLVR: Were you the guy sitting right next to the bus driver, following along with a map?

CD: Yeah, and having a conversation with the driver. But, you know, I would know just as much as the driver.

BLVR: Do you have a favorite road to drive, since you've driven so many of them?

CD: Well, I've written my best records while driving, ever since my first record, in 1986. So it's been the energy I use to write a song with my hand on the passenger seat with the pad. The number one thing is to keep your eye on the road. The number one thing is to be safe. But when I'm on a dark road in the car with the pad and my pen, that's where the ideas come from, along with the music. So my favorite road? I love driving the 101 up the West Coast. It's beautiful.

BLVR: I always threw up on that road as a kid. It's too curvy!

CD: You did? It's not as curvy as the Southern State [Parkway] in Long Island. Here's another road thing: in Long Island, the

Southern State and the Northern State [Parkways] curve and swirl, but you know why?

BLVR: No.

CD: Because in the '20s, driving was a rich person's luxury. So when they took their drives on Long Island, they sashayed and swayed and did loops and curves with their new-order automobiles. So that was a rich-person thing until Henry Ford really popularized the Model T.

BLVR: You would think *The Great Gatsby* would have convinced the rich folks not to drive crazy on the roads in Long Island.

CD: No, he was on the North Shore. He didn't go to the south. *The Great Gatsby* dealt with the North Shore—that's where all the big mansions were—but the rest of Long Island dealt with, you know, agriculture and farms and stuff like that, and a lot of those roads are still there. But the Southern State and the Northern State are beautiful to drive on, and they were built for the leisure and the luxury of driving. But if you've been on the LIE [the Long Island Expressway], it makes no bones about it. It's like, *What's the shortest distance between two points? A line*. And that's what the LIE is. A line that goes straight out, no curves, no turns. Cut right to the chase on the Long Island Expressway. Also, another thing is they are called "parkways" in New York. Have you noticed they don't call them parkways in Oregon? That's because the rich [in New York] set up parkways to look like they were driving to a park like Central Park. That's why the overheads are so low too. You can't drive commercial vehicles on the Southern State. If you drive a commercial vehicle on the Northern or Southern State, it is going to crash into the overhead passes, which are less than ten feet in height. And that's why when Eisenhower set up the Interstate Highway System in 1956, the overpasses were made higher so they could move military trucks and gear, which they took from the Autobahn, which was set up by Hitler and his boys. OK, enough of that.

II. OSTRICH FARMING

BLVR: So back to your songwriting. You said you would drive and write your songs simultaneously. How?

CD: Yeah, I would never look into my seat; I would look at the scribble after. But I could read my writing.

BLVR: Is there one song you remember writing while driving?

CD: Yeah, "Bring the Noise."

BLVR: What road were you driving down?

CD: The Meadowbrook State Parkway, driving from Roosevelt to Long Beach. And then I wrote "Prophets of Rage" [also the name of the supergroup who performed the song, made up of members for Rage Against the Machine, Cypress Hill, and Public Enemy] while being stuck on the Kosciuszko Bridge driving up into Manhattan.

BLVR: I hate that bridge. I can definitely understand writing about rage on it. Do you have any rituals in the car to get yourself in the mood to write, or is it just the act of driving that inspires your creativity?

CD: The act of driving and having time and being left alone. That's the ritual. Start the car up and I'm good.

BLVR: Do you listen to music when you drive?

CD: Well, I have to if I'm writing a song.

BLVR: When I was watching the video for "When the Grid Goes Down," I kept thinking about apocalypse preppers who have outfitted bomb shelters so they can live for years after the apocalypse. Are you a prepper? Do you have, like, ten thousand dollars in cash and four hundred cans of soup to ride out the apocalypse?

CD: Maybe I do. [*Laughs*] But how you gonna ride out the apocalypse?

BLVR: With a can of soup and a can opener?

CD: And then what you got to do about your blood pressure? A can of soup, man: the sodium will kill you.

BLVR: I was doing some research before we started chatting, and I read on Wikipedia that Terminator X left Public Enemy to raise African black ostriches. What are those?

CD: I don't know. Although what he really said was they weren't ostriches; they were emus.[1]

BLVR: Is that the weirdest reason to leave a band?

CD: It ranks up there. But I don't think that's the real reason he left the band. I think he left the band because he was tired of the road, tired of certain things that happen in a group and also in hip-hop.

BLVR: So it wasn't really the ostriches.

CD: No, I think the emus were a great venture. He was told it was a good venture to go into, but the emus all got wiped away by, I think, Hurricane Andrew, which went through North Carolina.

BLVR: Oh no! That is sad.

CD: Yeah, that was the end of that story line.

BLVR: I went to the post office the other day and they had hip-hop stamps *and* Harlem Renaissance stamps. Do you think this is in response to the Public Enemy album *Most of My Heroes Still Don't Appear on No Stamp*?

CD: It's actually a statement that first came out in "Fight the Power." I mean, the job of a songwriter is to illuminate some discussion on things that probably wouldn't be talked about. So, yeah, possibly. But it takes a lot more to pass a bill into a law. I do understand that my realm is in popular culture, not in law-making and -breaking. We make suggestions and hopefully the social sphere will be able to turn them into real things.

BLVR: I just thought it was so strange to be able to go in and buy a stamp that has "B-boy" written on it. That it went through whatever the stamp approval process is and suddenly I can put a B-boy or graffiti art stamp on my electric bill.

---

[1] Terminator X raised ostriches. He left the group in 1998. Terminator X's ostrich farm was a family business, but he stepped away because he didn't agree with the way it was being run.

CD: Well, B-boys have been around for, like, forty or fifty years. Things evolve and, you know, the fact that you could see rock and roll on a stamp was definitely mind-boggling to somebody who was born in the '20s or '30s. So they kind of looked at it the same way people look at hip-hop and rap music now. But it's not a young person's music, so to speak. While it initially came out of the young people's idioms, that's no longer true. In fact, it might be the old people's music, because young people are into a whole different other thing.

BLVR: Are you on TikTok?

CD: No, I'm only into Twitter. I don't even do Facebook. You're not going to see me on TikTok; you're not going to see me on Instagram.

III. [INSERT LOGO HERE]

BLVR: I read on the internet—so it must be true—that you drew the logo for Public Enemy in the '80s?

CD: Yes. I've drawn a lot of logos, and I consider myself an illustrator.

BLVR: So what inspired you to make a band logo?

CD: I believe that hip-hop should have logos, just like the Rockettes. And my influence was what Iron Maiden was doing, what the Rolling Stones were doing with their tongue [logo]. I believe that rap artists should have logos that are identifiable.

BLVR: Did you want to be an illustrator, in case your music career didn't work out?

CD: I am an illustrator. And I wanted to be an illustrator to do album covers. So I was going to get into the record business one way or another. But I wasn't necessarily trying to record. I just tried to get in and use my skills in the art department. That was my first goal, anyway, but Rick Rubin requested I do records. He thought I had something, and after two years of him running and chasing me down, I conceded to *Bum Rush the Show* and brought my homeboys to the party.

BLVR: Do you still draw regularly?

CD: Yeah, all the time. I plan to have gallery shows right through my sixties, and I have a couple of art aliases out there. Really one art alias out there.

BLVR: What's your preferred medium?

CD: Watercolor, Sharpies, and those BIC Wite-Out Shake 'n Squeeze correction pens. Acrylics are too messy and can't travel too much on the plane. I have also spent all my hotel time on tour setting up my room as an art lab.

BLVR: So you don't really live up to that musician-destroying-the-hotel-room stereotype, huh?

CD: Yeah, I'm not going to go to the lobby or the bar. I mean, I do that for the camaraderie, but my hotel room is set up like an art lab. A lot of that influence came from being inspired by people like [Rolling Stones guitarist] Ron Wood. Have you ever seen Ron Wood's art? It's phenomenal.

BLVR: Who else inspires your art?

CD: Pete Beard, who does all the documentaries on YouTube of all the great illustrators. He has almost sixty documentaries on the great illustrators of all time. I have a team called mADurgency, which is like a collective of graphic artists and illustrators. We're a worldwide team and we're growing. And the beautiful thing, Melissa, is that because of the internet, you can actually see artists show their art in a very transmitted way. And it's a great way of using the internet instead of getting on there for drama.

BLVR: You've been on *Space Ghost Coast to Coast*. You've been on *Johnny Bravo* and *Aqua Teen Hunger Force*. Cartoons are clearly a fan of you, but are you a cartoon fan?

CD: No. I'm grown. I ain't gonna look at a cartoon the same way as I did when I was six. I'm sixty. I mean, I'm an illustration fan.

IV. THE QUOTA

BLVR: The original public enemy number one was Al Capone, and I was just curious if you knew he wanted to be a songwriter.

CD: Well, that's kind of what did him in, huh? The celebrity of it all.

BLVR: Yeah, that was apparently his true passion. You hadn't heard that one before?

CD: No, no. I mean, I knew Charles Manson wanted to be a rock star and a songwriter too. Songwriters are a little different.

BLVR: Do you remember what the first rap video you ever saw was?

CD: Yeah, the first video was, I think, "The Message." Grandmaster Flash and the Furious Five did "The Message" in, I think, '82, and it was something I kept staring at. Because it wasn't so much about seeing the video but who was broadcasting it. So in 1981, '82, a few more affiliates were touching rap. I'm trying to remember if I saw something before that. Was "Planet Rock" a video? Was "Rapper's Delight" a video? I remember seeing their performances, but I don't recall the videos.

BLVR: I read that the first "rap" video ever played on MTV was Blondie's "Rapture." What are your thoughts on that?

CD: Blondie was no joke, ever. Debbie Harry was no joke. They were really New York City cats. Tina Weymouth and the Talking Heads too. They were really hip people, you know. They were hip and they got turned on to rap. If it wasn't hip, they wouldn't have fucked with it anyway. "Flash is fast, Flash is cool." I was blown away when she said that, because Flash *was* fast, and Flash *was* cool. We knew that. It was fascinating coming from this white woman, coming from a record, and then coming from Blondie, no less, who were already getting some heat in New York and around the country. So we thought that was good, that was props.

BLVR: And the video had Fab 5 Freddy and Jean-Michel Basquiat, which is pretty amazing.

CD: Right? And the guy in the beginning that people always mix up and say is Flavor Flav. It wasn't.

BLVR: Do you remember the first time you saw one of your videos on TV?

CD: Yeah, it was on *Video Music Box* with DJ Ralph McDaniels and the Vid Kid [Lionel "Vid Kid" Martin].

BLVR: How has video-making changed from your very first video to your most recent?

CD: I always hated doing videos. But the music business has gone from a sound business to a sight, sound, story, and style business. People usually see their music first, before they hear it. The latest generation, they kind of see music. If they can't visualize music, it's almost like the song doesn't exist. So the big difference, I think, is that it's necessary to actually let people know that the song exists. Even if the song has been out for a couple months, people think it is brand-new because they haven't seen the video. I think we are at a time when people kind of listen a little bit too much with their eyes.

BLVR: Public Enemy was the first group ever to release an all-MP3 album [*Bring the Noise 2000*]. Did you have any idea that digital releases were going to be the future?

CD: Yeah, that's why I did it. We released it because we got involved in the internet revolution in '98, '99. We felt that the marketplace was too saturated. We wanted to be able to go peer-to-peer instead of going through [a process] that would reject our music. And so we wanted to be peer-to-peer on our own terms.

BLVR: You've been telling people to "fight the power" for over thirty years. Do you ever wish that particular song was no longer necessary?

CD: Thirty years is a long time ago as far as the music industry goes, but that's a short period of time when it comes down to real life. New generations have to have things taught their way. You can't say, *Man, did we do things this way before?* They say, *I wasn't there.* I wasn't in the '50s. But I could learn from the '50s, right?

BLVR: I remember you talking at one point about wanting to inspire one hundred minds that would go on to change the world. Do you think you've accomplished that?

CD: Yeah, that was the goal. I think we got those numbers. But, you know, life goes on. You can't bask in the numbers at all, like we reached our quota. Nah, life doesn't work that way. ✱

Subscribe to **McSWEENEY'S QUARTERLY CONCERN**

Sunday-sized newspaper issues, sweaty human head issues, Z-shaped double books, magnetically bound triple books, books disguised as party balloons.

Every issue features work by some of today's finest writers and artists, such as Lauren Groff, Chimamanda Ngozi Adichie, Lesley Nneka Arimah, Carmen Maria Machado, T. C. Boyle, and Valeria Luiselli.

McSWEENEY'S QUARTERLY CONCERN HAS TAKEN A HEAD-SPINNING VARIETY OF FORMS OVER THE PAST TWENTY ODD (SIC) YEARS, AND WE'RE JUST GETTING STARTED.

To subscribe to McSWEENEY'S QUARTERLY CONCERN, *visit:*

STORE.McSWEENEYS.NET

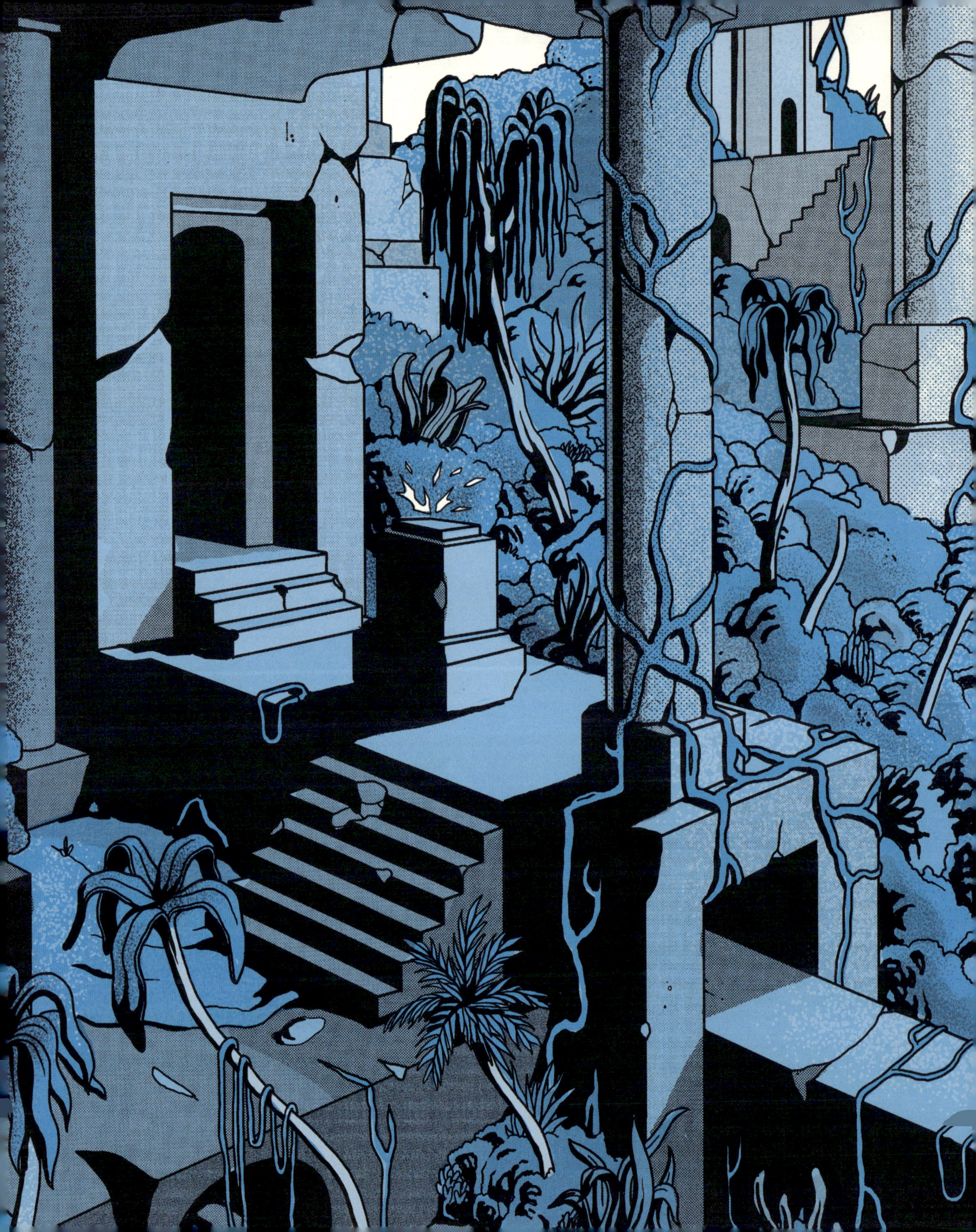

a citizen sleuth is tracking down India's stolen artifacts—but what happens to the idols once they're home?

idol threats

by shruti ravindran

illustrations by micha huigen

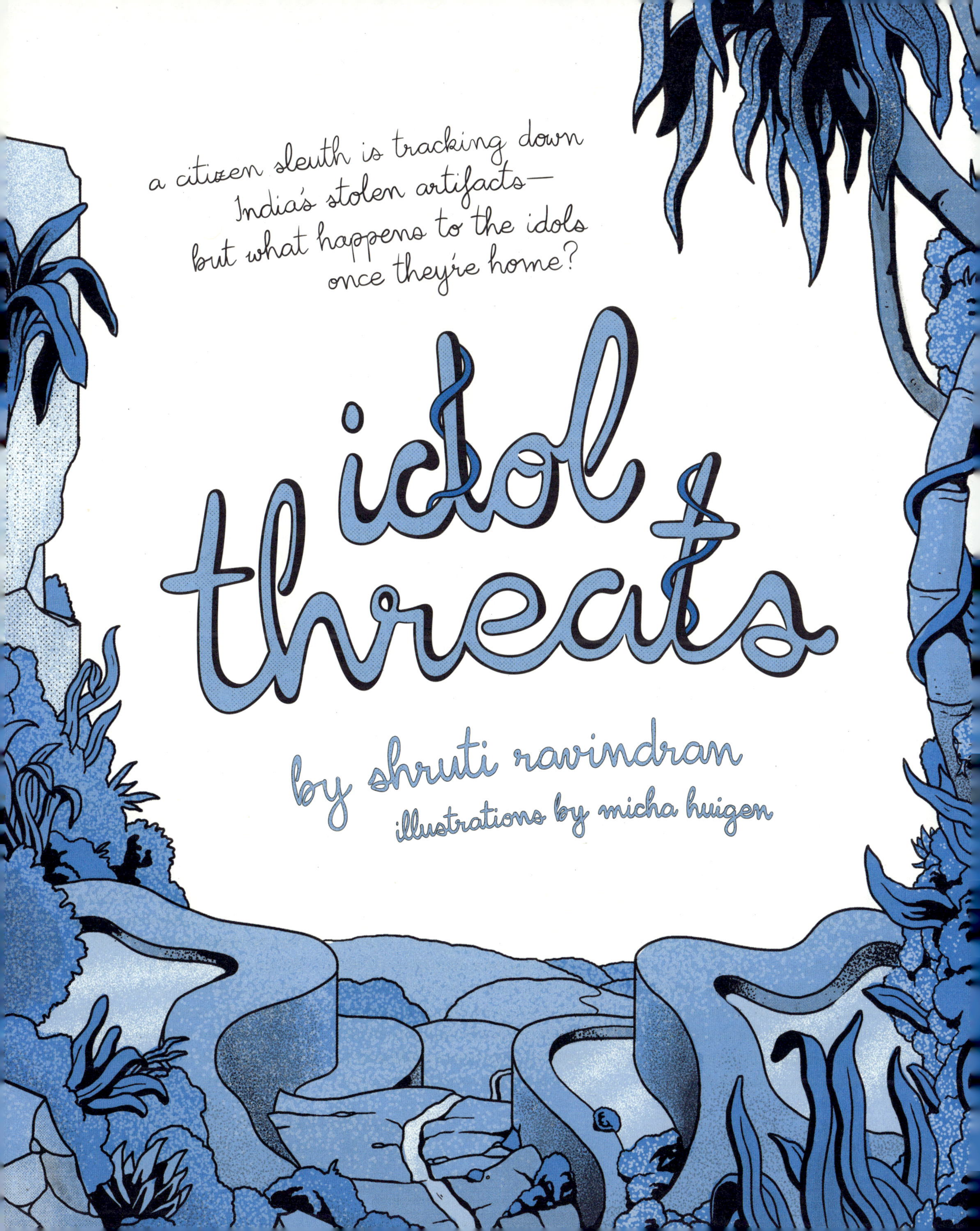

DISCUSSED: *A No-Handed Androgynous God; Photos Splayed Out TV-Detective-Style; Help!!! The Brits Have Kidnapped Me!; Displayed in the Nude; A Gentleman's Agreement Atmosphere; Nick Fury and His Avengers Club; Sites of Conscience; Borders to Nation-States, Museums to Empire; Hell, Yes, It Was Smuggled; A Disservice to All Visitors; Pucca Gentlemen; You'd Have to Take a Sweeper Along with You; A Visit to the South Indian Village of Virudhachalam; Not to See, Not to Touch*

Early one Saturday morning in the summer of 2013, Vijay Kumar, a shipping executive in Singapore, woke up to a news alert on his phone. A museum in Australia had, after protracted prodding and delays, finally disclosed how it came to possess an ancient Indian relic with a suspicious history. Kumar was eager to see what it had been so reluctant to reveal.

Kumar is a self-taught expert on Indian antiquities, traveling frequently to temples in his home state, Tamil Nadu, to document the sacred treasures they contain. He traces his interest to a trip he took to a South Indian temple, where he overheard a father misidentifying a god to his son. This both outraged and inspired him to write a blog on ritual art called *Poetry in Stone* as a kind of "dummy's guide" to ancient Hindu and Buddhist art and iconography.

On expeditions over the previous decade, Kumar had noticed many empty niches where statues once stood, and had peered at divinities through padlocked iron grilles. Theft of Indian idols for sale to overseas museums was rampant. The Australian news report seemed to describe one such case.

As Kumar read the details of the report, a particular image surfaced in his mind. The statue under investigation was described as an androgynous divinity. As it happened, Kumar had recently written a blog post about the androgynous avatar of the god Shiva—the Ardhanarishvara, or "the Lord who is half woman." As an illustration, he had used an image of an early medieval sculpture in a temple in Tamil Nadu. Carved from granite darkened by a thousand years of ceremonial smoke and incense, the statue depicted the beatifically smiling god with his matted hair piled in the shape of a crown. Kumar was transfixed by the way the languid curves of the deity's female side were counterbalanced by his taut male side, which reposed on a stately bull. The statue's astonishing beauty, though, was marred by damage: both its hands had been lopped off.

Sensing a connection, Kumar dug further and unearthed a photo of the statue in Australia—it also had missing hands. But as far as Kumar knew, the original sculpture was being worshipped in a temple in South India. He wrote to the journalist whose name was mentioned in the article, asking for more-detailed photographs. A closer look confirmed it was the same sculpture. "That's when I realized I was onto something," he says.

He needed more than his own eyes to convince authorities that the statue was stolen, however, so he logged on and asked his two thousand Facebook followers if any of them could go to a temple in Virudhachalam village and pay the statue a visit. Within minutes, he heard back from an engineer in Dubai whose friend ran a cell phone repair shop in the village. The friend went to the temple and sent back photos of the niche, where a suspiciously glossy statue with two intact hands now resided. "It was a modern fake," Kumar says.

Kumar's discovery added to mounting evidence against Subhash Kapoor, a New York City art dealer who owned an Upper East Side gallery called Art of the Past. Over three decades, Kapoor had sold thousands of antiquities to museums in Europe, Australia, and North America. Of these, his neighbor the Metropolitan Museum of Art had bought at least fifteen. But Art of the Past was a front. Its real business was conducted far from Museum Mile, in West Nyack, New York, through a company called Nimbus Import Export. A federal investigation found that the business amounted to "a black-market Sotheby's," its wares supplied by temple raids that Kapoor commissioned. The spoils found their way to buyers, curators, dealers, and private collectors via a browsable photo gallery. "Like prospective grooms looking for matches, these guys were picking and choosing the best of ancient Indian art," Kumar says.

Kumar's confirmation that the androgynous idol had been stolen cranked bureaucratic wheels into motion, the return of the sculpture was requested by the Tamil Nadu Police, and the androgynous god was at last sent home on a private jet. "A journalist contacted me to let me know when he was in the air," Kumar says. "I was ecstatic to hear he was coming home."

Over the past few decades, countries with ubiquitous but poorly secured temples and museums, like India, have proven easy targets for smugglers. The extent of the theft is enormous, but exact figures are hard to come by; about 5.7 million of India's 7 million antiquities are undocumented. A scathing 2013 report by the country's government watchdog blamed the custodian of national antiquities for not bothering to maintain a record of what it possesses. An estimated—likely underestimated—4,408 relics were stolen from sites under this organization's less than watchful eye over a recent four-year span. Such losses are nothing new; UNESCO estimates that prior to 1989, about 50,000 antiquities were removed from the subcontinent.

India is not especially spirited in the pursuit of its lost treasures, compared with countries like Italy, Greece, and China. Italy has a police wing dedicated to combating theft and the trafficking of cultural artifacts and maintains a database of stolen relics. Greece wages tireless and aggressive campaigns to recover its relics from numerous countries, including the United Kingdom, which refuses to relinquish its hold on the Parthenon marbles it took when Greece was under Ottoman occupation. And China has a state-run program that dispatches delegations to scour the archives of international museums for mislaid relics. The Indian government, meanwhile, has rarely pursued lost antiquities.

In some places, ordinary citizens have filled in for their governments in demanding the repatriation of their countries' art. Mwazulu Diyabanza, a Congolese activist, was arrested and charged with theft last year for seizing a Chadian funerary post from an anthropological museum in Paris. Likewise, in China, a group of unidentified bandits have organized over the past two decades to extract Chinese antiquities from a smattering of European museums and royal residences.

And since 2014, India has had Kumar. The retrieval of the androgynous god marked the beginning of his career as a stolen-artifacts hunter. After the case, he became increasingly convinced that his profession, in transnational shipping, was implicated in the frittering away of these treasures. One-ton bronze statues couldn't be tucked in a purse or stowed in airplane baggage. These statues were being transported by sea. Kumar decided to use his knowledge of global logistics to sniff out fraud in the paperwork.

He believes his efforts to catch smugglers have been more successful than those of any government agency in India: Kumar estimates his work has led to the majority of the fifty-one restitutions that have occurred in the country over the past eight years. His only compatriot in the field—a retired archeology professor named Kirit Mankodi, whom he sometimes collaborates with—has helped recover far fewer, just two antiquities around the same time frame.

The commitment of Kumar and other amateur sleuths is laudable, but their activities have also brought some uneasy legal and ethical questions to light. In the case of relatively recent thefts, like the handless relic, repatriation is the obvious course of action. But what about art that was spirited out of a country not a year ago but a century ago? Do people who have

Over the past few decades, countries with ubiquitous but poorly secured temples and museums, like India, have proven easy targets for smugglers.

never officially possessed it have the right to demand it back? And if, once returned, the art is forsaken, who is responsible then?

To Kumar, the experience of repatriating the androgynous god was exhilarating but sobering. It demonstrated to him that without his intervention, India's divinities would continue to be stranded abroad. He thought of Vaman Ghiya, an art dealer who funneled some twenty thousand antiquities out of the country before being arrested, in 2003. It enraged him to think of the bureaucratic lethargy that has caused countless sacred relics to remain dispersed throughout the world, despite easily locatable proof that they were acquired by questionable means. So, to complement his work as a repatriation hobbyist, he decided to conscript a lobbyist. Along with his colleague Anuraag Saxena, a former investment banker based in

Singapore, and dozens of like-minded nationalists, Kumar formed the India Pride Project, in 2014, with the stated mission of "bringing our gods home."

The group has two aims. One half of the crew, led by Saxena, leads awareness-raising campaigns intended to prick the conscience of—in his words—"societies that have normalized kleptomania." They organize protests outside museums that have collections of ancient Indian art in London and North America and make impassioned speeches to promote their cause. In a protest in 2018, Saxena and a handful of demonstrators went to the British Museum and photographed around twenty relics of Indian origin, with speech bubbles held up next to them: HELP!!! THE BRITS HAVE KIDNAPPED ME!; I'VE BEEN SNATCHED, SOLD, PARADED, AND SHAMED; and ASK YOURSELF: HOW DID I GET HERE?

Kumar's group is the black-ops branch of the movement. He leads a posse of volunteers who pose as prospective buyers of antiquities at auctions in Amsterdam, London, and New York, then send him pictures of potentially repatriable antiquities. ("I'm like Nick Fury, and they're my Avengers," Kumar says.) He prints out the photos and splays them across his bedroom wall in the style of a TV detective, until his wife tears them down. He stares at them for hours to see if any of the objects spark recognition. When one does, he searches for a matching photograph or other record of the object in its country of origin. If what he finds amounts to robust evidence to demand the object's restitution, he sends that evidence to Indian diplomats posted in the country where the relic surfaced, in coordination with antiquities authorities in New Delhi.

The press often likens Kumar to Indiana Jones, but he sees himself more like Robert Langdon, the symbologist hero of *The Da Vinci Code*. "We're both unfit," he says with a laugh. "We've both got a great memory: he recollects passages, I recollect images." Kumar claims

> **The press often likens Kumar to Indiana Jones, but he sees himself more like Robert Langdon, the symbologist hero of *The Da Vinci Code*.**

to have crammed his mental database with the contents of out-of-print art history books, which he slots according to a mental algorithm that moves from style to region to period to dynasty. Mentally filing away references helps him spot telltale correspondences between those references and objects that surface in auctions or museums. A blemish on a nose, a crack in a carved leaf. "It's like a game to me," says Kumar. "Other people play UNO; I play with idols."

Eidetic tricks aside, Kumar thinks the most striking similarity between himself and Dan Brown's hero is that they're both solitary figures facing off against a powerful, shadowy conspiratorial cabal. "Both Langdon and I are not scared to take on the big mafia," he says. "The only difference is that I do it without government support. And I deal with lots of red tape."

Demands for repatriation are far from a recent phenomenon. They date back as early as 1936, when the oba of Benin requested the return of ritual objects seized by British troops in their violent invasion and sacking of Benin City, in present-day Nigeria, in 1897. Repatriation requests rose in the '60s and '70s, when African states won independence. But the sorts of anthropological and "encyclopedic" institutions that amassed colonial-era loot—and the former imperial powers to which they belonged—long found it expedient to evade such demands. When the landmark UNESCO convention prohibiting the illicit trade in cultural property was passed in 1970, many countries including Britain tarried for decades before ratifying it. For the most part, Western museums operated under a philosophy popularly encapsulated as "What's mine is mine; what's yours is mine." This approach was exemplified by the 2002 "Declaration on the Importance and Value of Universal Museums," a statement put forth by the directors of the British Museum, the Louvre, the Prado, and fifteen other institutions to preempt repatriation claims. In the declaration, the directors emphasized the role of Western museums in inspiring the "universal admiration" for the ancient civilizations whose treasures they displayed. They exhorted their audience to "acknowledge that museums serve not just the citizens of one nation but the people of every nation" and argued that whittling down their "diverse and multifaceted" collections through repatriation requests, however legitimate, "would therefore be a disservice to all visitors."

In recent years, however, the clamor for repatriation has grown into something of an international movement, borne by powerful political and intellectual currents that challenge the stories these museums tell the public about themselves. To repatriation advocates, museums are not neutral storage containers that just innocently happened upon the treasures they possess. Rather, they were purposefully built by imperial powers to advertise and justify white supremacy, by juxtaposing "superior" Western art and archeology with the plundered relics of cultures and societies they subjugated and destroyed, and whose peoples' skulls they pseudoscientifically displayed as "primitive." "As the border is to the nation state so the museum is to empire," writes the archeologist and curator Dan Hicks in his book *The Brutish Museums: The Benin Bronzes, Colonial Violence and Cultural Restitution*. The solution he and his fellow advocates propose emphasizes "acts of transparency," starting with the restitution of ancestral cultural objects that were expropriated during colonial times. They point out that many of these objects were obtained through theft, violence, or duplicity, and assert that holding on to them would deprive formerly colonized people, including indigenous populations, of their living heritage, which forms a part of their identity. In 2018, the movement gained its biggest victory thus far in the form of a landmark report commissioned by French president Emmanuel Macron.

The report pointed out that over 90 percent of Africa's cultural treasures were found outside that continent, and recommended, as a corrective measure, nothing short of the swift and permanent restitution of thousands of artifacts acquired during France's colonial era. Two other former imperial powers, the Netherlands and Germany, were also galvanized into similar action.

Faced with increasing demands for radical action, directors at the largest museums in the world envision a "horror scenario": their rooms and storerooms emptying out overnight. To them, repatriation represents a kind of lawful robbery. They view it as an existential threat, one that could threaten their livelihoods and the objects they've studied and safeguarded throughout their professional lives. Neither are they convinced that repatriation is entirely justifiable. As they see it, since there is no clear "cultural continuity" between the ancient Athenians and the present-day Greeks and no traceable direct descendants

of Sumerian or Assyrian kings, Western museums are equally entitled to the relics these long-dead people left behind. Further, they argue that repatriation advocates tar all objects acquired in the colonial era with the same brush, adding that many treasures were gifted or willingly shared with colonial officers or missionaries. Finally, they say that not repatriating might often be in the interest of the relics themselves; as the first indigenous director of Paris's Musée du Quai Branly put it in a 2020 interview with *The New York Times*: "I'm not in favor of objects being sent out into the world and left to rot."

Whichever side of the debate you are on, one thing is certain. The fate of all antiquities, whether in the custody of museums, dealers, or auction houses, boils down to one arcane detail: their "provenance," or the paper trail that documents their history of ownership. These details, or the absence of them, can establish whether a relic is repatriable—if it left the source country after 1970, when the UNESCO Convention prohibiting the export of cultural property was passed, or may have been unlawfully seized from its owners. A clear, uncomplicated provenance can also bolster the case for a museum that wishes to hold on to an object. The problem, however, is that only a tiny percentage of antiquities currently residing in museums or surfacing in the art market have a well-researched ownership history.

The reasons for this depend on whom you ask. For Kumar, it's a willful obfuscation, an exploitation of a shoddy system by smugglers and the curators whose collections ultimately reap the benefits. "In most cases," he says of the museums, "they knew it

wasn't an innocent good-faith purchase. They knew it was fresh plunder, fresh loot." Victoria Reed, curator of the Museum of Fine Arts, Boston, has a less nefarious explanation: provenance is expensive to research, and it's a relatively recent field that came into existence in the late '90s when a number of cases brought to light art objects that had been illegally expropriated, including those by the Nazi regime during World War II. Prior to that, the acquisition process relied on a "kind of gentleman's agreement atmosphere," Reed says, "that you know the dealer, trust the dealer, the dealer will give us a good object, and if it has an 'interesting' history, we will ask about provenance."

Still, it is undeniable, and widely acknowledged, that many of these documents are entirely fictive, serving only to legitimize artifacts in the service of museum curators and private collectors.

Erin Thompson, an archeologist who researches art crime, says the vast majority of antiquities present an intractable challenge for provenance researchers: they're often from underdeveloped source countries where the circumstances under which they were excavated and owned are unknown or unknowable. The lack of information increases the chances that museums might unwittingly acquire fakes and also lose information on the place and time an object was disinterred or created. "We're so concerned about holding on to these collections," Thompson says, "that we've crushed the usefulness out of them."

Sometimes, staring at the photos on his wall, Kumar imagines himself alone, facing off against an assemblage of adversaries, composed of robbers, shady dealers, and corrupt connoisseurs. If any one person comes close to incarnating that shadowy enemy, it would be Pratapaditya Pal, a scholar and curator who built the Los Angeles County Museum of Art's extensive collection of Southeast Asian art. Pal has worked for more than four decades as an adviser to numerous private collectors, including the canned-food mogul Norton Simon, who in 1976 reached an out-of-court settlement with the Indian government over a tenth-century Chola bronze of Nataraja—the deity Shiva's dancing form—that had gone missing from a South Indian temple two decades earlier. Simon notoriously told The New York Times, "Hell, yes, it was smuggled. I spent between $15 million and $16 million in the last two years on Asian art, and most of it was smuggled."

I talked to Pal over the phone, after a lengthy correspondence, during which he scrutinized my CV and a number of writing samples and attempted to dissuade me from speaking with him. When we did speak, however, he shared his views with few reservations: "I am strongly opposed to the idea of repatriating art in general," he said. "This issue is becoming as absurd as that of abortion in the United States. We want to save the unborn child only to shoot them down mercilessly at schools or send them off to useless wars in their youth to die." He was gratified to see sacred Indian art well preserved and well displayed in museums in the global North, where, he said, they serve as "the silent ambassadors of the country." Repatriation, he believed, would doom these works to an ignominious fate. "Have you been to the oldest museum in Asia?" he said. "It's in Calcutta. Forget about the display, which is disgraceful, but if you wanted to see the thousands of objects in their storage, you'd have to take a sweeper along with you to dust the sculptures, or you won't see anything!" Of the repatriated objects, he asked: "Where will they put them?"

Pal strikes an almost defiantly anachronistic position in the antiquities world. He has spent his retirement writing a number of nostalgic essays chronicling a lifetime spent socializing over whiskeys with "pucca gentlemen" collectors with deep pockets and a self-cultivated taste for ancient Indian art. He celebrates the "extraordinary omnium gatherum" of ritual Indian art that crowded the darkened recesses of his aristocratic friends' Upper East Side townhouses.

Pal's insouciant persona seems designed to revolt Kumar. As he sees it, the work of curators like Pal, in helping museums in wealthier countries amass relics that go on to be preserved, studied, and admired, is not a worthy contribution. It does not, he thinks, signal their respect for sacred objects. In fact, as he sees it, it is a distinct lack of respect for "our gods" that permits curators to put them on display in galleries and museums, where supposedly admiring guests gather around them and pose with them, champagne coupes in hand. "To me, it is defilement," he says. A Nataraja ought not be reduced to "a showpiece curio," he says, adding: "A Nataraja does not want a focus light. Nor does he want a temperature-controlled environment." His exasperation then mellowed into reverie. "In my ancestral village," he says, "I've seen an old priest running from his home to the temple with a bowl of

The report pointed out that over 90 percent of Africa's cultural treasures were found outside that continent.

rice, fearing that God is going hungry." Every day, Kumar says, this priest rouses the Lord from sleep, bathes him "like his own child," dries him, and dresses him up in silk, flowers, and diamond necklaces. "Once you've seen that," he adds, "you would never want him to be displayed in the nude, with no rituals."

Kumar's distaste for men like Pal is palpable. But I'm struck by what the two have in common: both are drawn into a bit of a feeding frenzy at the prospect of acquiring these divinities, whether on behalf of a country or institution; both share tales of tireless, near-obsessive pursuit; and both are fond of rhapsodizing about the beauty of the relics they pursue. And both are proud of their hard work, accumulated expertise, and fierce commitment to their diametrically opposed missions.

Since Kumar's favorite androgynous relic with the lopped-off hands made it back to its place of "birth," many more smuggled sculptures have been repatriated to India. In Tamil Nadu, an obscure police department known as the Idol Wing has been confiscating hundreds of sculptures from private collectors and museums across the country. Kumar considers all returns positive, whether they're from abroad or from elsewhere in India. As he sees it, the icons are now back where they belong. But where is that, exactly? Pal, the curator, conjured for me a glum vision from the first Indiana Jones film, when the Ark of the Covenant gets shunted into a shabby crate that floats out into a sea of other shabby crates. "They're probably rotting in a storeroom somewhere," he says, "just like the bronze Nataraja that our poor country spent millions of dollars in legal fees to bring back in 1986. It was a cause célèbre, but today you can't see it anywhere."

I decided to pay a visit to the androgynous Shiva to see how it was faring. It had spent the past five years at an "icon center," a shelter for repatriated relics, housed at a temple in Kumbakonam, Tamil Nadu. One afternoon in August 2019, I entered the temple's towering pylon-like entryway, which featured brightly painted stucco gods seated on cows, rats, and peacocks, and surrounded by romping demiurges, sages, and princes. A soulful Tamil movie tune wafted out of a nearby tire shop, and a flower seller by the entrance dozed over a soft pile of jasmine and rose garlands.

I crossed a sunlit courtyard and asked a passing priest where the temple's administrative office was, and he waved me toward a tiny room, where a few functionaries were sipping filter coffee. When I asked to see the androgynous relic, one of them, an accountant, shook his head vehemently. He informed me that the idol was "undergoing a court case" and was therefore barred from view. "So no one can visit?" "It's a prohibited area, not a museum," he replied, adding that "general people" were not allowed in. "How about art scholars?" "No probability. No chance," he said.

In hopes of getting a glimpse nevertheless, I walked to the building where the relic was held. It was low-slung, painted petroleum green, and resembled a bank vault. The entrance consisted of a retractable security grille fortified with two padlocks, behind which was a heavy door with a heftier padlock. Twice a week, the building is opened by a security guard, and a priest and two accountants armed with mops and brooms are allowed entry. The three get unimpeded access to more than a hundred repatriated relics, unclothed due to risk of fire, inside the icon center's air-conditioned rooms. While the accountants mop the room and dust the shelves, the priest performs an abbreviated ceremony—without lamps, oils, or ash—in the general direction of the statues. "It's just for ritual purpose," one of the accountants told me. "Not to see, not to touch."

I left without seeing any of the idols, and not quite knowing how to feel. It seemed a sorry fate for sculptures that were once on public display, admired and revered by thousands. I saw the case for a middle ground, one wherein relics that are culturally and religiously meaningful are returned with the promise of custodians to adequately preserve them, and other relics are left in place, where they are appreciated, instead of vanishing into an oversize walk-in closet.

A few months after my visit, in November, I read about a thousand confiscated wooden and stone relics that had been tossed into the backyard of the Idol Wing's branch in Chennai. Temple chariots were piled next to stone sculptures of nymphs and gods, and all had been rinsed by several monsoons and exposed to bird droppings. These objects seemed caught between lives. Once ritual objects, they had transitioned, by theft or gray market transactions, to become valuable commodities. They were then displayed—for clinical study or aesthetic pleasure—in a collector's home or museum. The act of seizure, however legal, caused a perturbation in their status. They are ritual objects haunted by their time spent as commodities; they can no longer be on open display.

Kumar doesn't find the fate of these relics so dispiriting. He hopes they will soon find their way back to the temples they came from, but in the meantime, he considers them just fine in a dismal backyard. "What difference does it make? They're not better off in a rich man's bedroom in Europe," he says. "Besides, these sculptures survived four hundred years of Islamic invasions. Their thousand-year lineage was broken only by greed. Still, they survived. They will survive forever." ✶

"LISTENING CAN NEVER BE A WASTE OF MY TIME. IT CAN NEVER DISHONOR MY ATTENTION, BECAUSE THIS IS WHAT I'M HERE FOR."

ALEXIS PAULINE GUMBS

[WRITER]

Alexis Pauline Gumbs describes herself as a "Queer Black Troublemaker and Black Feminist Love Evangelist and an aspirational cousin to all sentient beings." And while this naming is expansive and almost comprehensive, as she reminds me in our conversation, "I'm not witness to all of me." She is the one who embraces that which is "kindred beyond taxonomy," as she writes in her book Dub: Finding Ceremony; she is also an oracle, a teacher, and a gardener. She is the author of a triptych of experimental poetic works published by Duke University Press: the aforementioned Dub (2020), a book of prose poems that "explores the potential for the poetic and narrative undoing of the knowledge that underpins the concept of Western humanity"; Spill: Scenes of Black Feminist Fugitivity (2016), which stages moments of Black women activating their own freedom; and M Archive: After the End of the World (2018), which "speculatively documents the

Illustration by Samar Haddad

persistence of Black life following a worldwide cataclysm we are living through now." Her new book, Undrowned: Black Feminist Lessons from Marine Mammals *(2020), is a meditation on what we might learn from the social life of whales, porpoises, dolphins, seals, and other mammals. A National Humanities Center Fellow, Gumbs is at work on her forthcoming book,* The Eternal Life of Audre Lorde: Biography as Ceremony.

Her literary work is only one element of her offering. For the past decade, Gumbs has worked alongside her partner, Sangodare, on Mobile Homecoming, an experimental and experiential archive "amplifying generations of queer Black brilliance." The project centers intergenerational community-building. Starting with a listening tour in a 1988 Winnebago over a decade ago, the couple has been traveling the country, facilitating retreats and compiling a multimedia archive; several participants have described these events as "healing," which speaks to their impact. (Every third Sunday, you can join live services with Mobile Homecoming.) Also with Sangodare, she cofounded the Black Feminist Film School, which is "an initiative to screen, study and produce films with a Black feminist ethic."

On a Tuesday in December 2020, I called Gumbs to talk about interspecies collaboration, listening practices, and Lucille Clifton in relation to Undrowned. *I feel lucky to have had a moment to speak with her. Our conversation felt like a reunion of sorts. I cannot tell you the exact moment I met Gumbs, almost a decade and a half ago, through her various online projects, but I can tell you it was an occasion of learning. And every encounter thereafter has been a generous opportunity to tenderly open a valve, return to a text with new antennae, or hold my body still in meditation. It was Gumbs who first introduced me to Kitchen Table: Women of Color Press. It was Gumbs who encouraged me to write. And it is Gumbs whose tentacular life work reminds me of several lines from one of my favorite Lucille Clifton poems, "i am not done yet" (1974): "i continue to continue / where i have been / most of my lives is / where i'm going."*

—Kameelah Janan Rasheed

I. DEEP LISTENING

THE BELIEVER: In the introduction to what are now several books, you talk about these voices that emerge during your writing process. I recently learned about Lucille Clifton's practice with spirit communication. How do voices emerge as you write? What do you think about Lucille Clifton's engagement with spirit communication?

ALEXIS PAULINE GUMBS: I love that question. Lucille Clifton is such a huge influence on me. This idea of hearing voices obviously has been stigmatized and pathologized. People have been institutionalized and incarcerated for admitting that they hear voices. This question brings me back to a really important time in my writing, in my creative and intellectual process, and also to an important moment in M. Jacqui Alexander's mentorship of me. I was in Atlanta because I had a dissertation research fellowship at Emory University at the time when Lucille Clifton's papers were just getting to their archive. They were in the boxes she'd mailed them in. She was alive. She had just cleaned out her office and sent them. I was looking through her papers, which were not at all organized. I was having this experience that I was trying to explain to Jacqui because it was similar to the experience I have when I'm in archives with Audre Lorde's papers and June Jordan's papers. Still, those were papers that were actually in some kind of order. Lucille Clifton's archive was the first archive—outside of cleaning out my own mentors' and family members' houses and garages—where what I touched and looked at and found was so random. But then it was exactly what I needed.

I had a question about June Jordan's economic philosophy, and I found this copy of a talk Jordan gave when she and Clifton were on a panel together. Clifton's talk wasn't anywhere to be found. This was the first time in my life that I was meeting Jacqui. It was a miracle that she was a visiting scholar at Spelman at the same time that I had this fellowship at Emory. Over dinner, I was talking to her about this experience of feeling so guided in the archive and about the listening practices I have, and about how I wear my grandmother's jewelry as part of my listening for her and our ongoing conversation. I was starting to understand that part of that receptivity to listening was going beyond my grandmother and carrying over to the people I was researching. I felt that June Jordan was speaking to me through Lucille Clifton's boxes of papers.

Jacqui was receptive to that. She really listened to that. Part of the reason I shared that with her was because she writes so powerfully about spiritual labor as labor in her work that I had already read and been influenced by. But she also gave a warning. She was like, "Alexis, those people who are walking down the street screaming and talking to themselves are not talking to themselves." And I had to really hear that. She was saying it's so important to actually respect the fact that we are connected to so much more than our own consciousness, and it's really important to honor that and to relate to that in ways that are balanced and healthy. And intentional.

So all that is to say I do feel I'm listening all day long; I would characterize everything I do as a form of listening. In terms of my writing rituals, I am very specifically up before the sun rises in a meditative practice of listening. The most intensive specific listening practice is that early morning practice. I didn't really know and have since learned that many different traditions have considered that time, from 2 a.m. to 6 a.m., a spiritually generative time to pray, meditate, or practice. I didn't necessarily know that. I just knew that asha bandele told me to make time for myself before anybody else needed my time.

But I understand it now. As someone who listens, I feel the messages are louder at that time of day for me. The rest of the time it's just general guidance like, *Turn left, don't turn right*; *OK, one more dash of turmeric*, or whatever. I know that was part of how Lucille Clifton worked. When her mother passed away, she still needed her mother's guidance, and she created ways to listen for her. Clifton and her children used a Ouija board, and she created her sense of rituals similarly to what I experienced. She started really listening to her mother, but then the transmissions became broader and she heard all these different historical figures and ancestors and the cosmic entities she writes about in "the message from the Ones / (received in the late 70s)."

The other thing is that another mentor of mine, Akasha Gloria Hull, spent years interviewing Lucille Clifton and documenting her process for Hull's book *Soul Talk[: The New Spirituality of African American Women]*. She also looked at the processes of other Black women artists, including Alexis De Veaux, Michele D. Gibbs, and Toni Cade Bambara. I found that work at the same time as I encountered Lucille Clifton's archive. I was [figuring out] my own intellectual offering and ways of being in relationship to the work after decades of being in school and looking at and critiquing and navigating the ways of being an intellectual that

I saw. I felt very supported by Lucille Clifton's example, as it was profoundly, miraculously available to me.

BLVR: This has me thinking about many things. Particularly about the ways we think about teachers as people who are physically on this planet with us at the exact moment we are, but we must also leave space to listen for mentorship and guidance that's not physically here with us in ways that are familiar.

There is this element of synchronicity and also this question around filtering in what you're saying. I'm interested in the

> **I'm not trying to judge whether what they're saying is worthwhile or if they're getting to the point. I may have no idea what you're talking about, but I know I am committed to listening.**

distinction between what's considered to be noise and what's considered to be productive sound. And I use the language of productivity very specifically to think about the context of capitalism, which distinguishes between sonic engagements that "produce value." When you're listening, is there any noise, or is it all generative listening?

APG: I do feel it is all part of my assignment, right. I'm a listener, so I'm listening. Discernment happens because not every message I receive, piece I write, or thing I notice has anything to do with publication or sharing with other people. There's only so much I understand. What I heard this morning has an impact on my day, and that's important. So I am recording. I'm writing. I'm honoring that and, actually, I think it's very important to my practice of listening that I don't need to know whether anything has to do with anything else. That discernment comes later. In my active listening to anyone who's in a workshop I'm facilitating, or when I'm listening to my elders, I'm not trying to control what they say. I'm not trying to judge whether what they're saying is worthwhile or if they're getting to the point. I may have no idea what you're talking about, but I know I am committed to listening.

I'm specific about who I'm sitting with and listening to. I'm really prioritizing queer Black elders. I'm prioritizing Black feminist elders. I'm prioritizing Black kids. That act of priority is also what allows me to completely surrender and say there's nothing that Black children can do in front of me or say around me that I don't feel is worth my presence. So in that context, listening can never be a waste of my time. It can never dishonor my attention, because this is what I'm here for. I'm here to be with you. I'm here to learn from you. I understand that to be already decided possibly before I even got here.

II. WHALE WHISPERING

BLVR: Can you say more about noise?

APG: I've been paying attention to theorists who have been talking about noise, and I find the disruption of noise and forms of sounds that are not as easily co-opted very interesting. I would say that in my listening process I experience a lot of clarity, but what I hear and what I write are not always clear to me in the moment. I don't find myself experiencing very much dissonance even though I'm often experiencing something I can't categorize. But I don't feel like what I hear is hurting my ears or giving me a headache. Even when I feel overwhelming sadness and I can't necessarily index it or note what exactly is causing it, I understand that it is for me. I don't feel like it reached the wrong address. And that to me is a form of harmony. Even if it's so complex that I can't detangle or understand it in a linear sense. And, honestly, I think it's helpful to view what I'm experiencing as an ancestral reclaiming of my presence, attention, and time. I just want to make more space for the experience

that has led to me making less and less time for some of the linear demands that capitalism and the narrative of capitalism had already taught me.

BLVR: I am thinking about the poet Bhanu Kapil. She wrote this book called *Schizophrene*, which I'm reading now. It was suggested to me because of her writing process. She wrote this manuscript, wasn't happy with it, threw it into her backyard, and then seasons went by. She grabbed it out of her backyard and sort of wrote from the fragments that were left behind.[1] There was this collaboration with the soil and the water and the bugs in her writing process. She listened and maybe didn't expect everything that came out of that holistic process.

What role does revision play in your practice? In *M Archive*, you write about this idea of an "ancestrally cowritten text" that sort of defies single authorship. You include so many footnotes and endnotes and in-text citations in all your works. What drives your citational practice?

APG: What drives my citational practice? Honestly, I'm so repetitive. I find repetition really helpful, and maybe that's part of how I'm organizing my listening. So with *Spill*, *M Archive*, and *Dub*, my prompt for listening every single day was work by one person. Now, of course, that's never true. That's why in *Spill* and *M Archive* there are lists of many, many other texts besides the one I was listening to daily, because sometimes the listening prompt from Hortense Spillers's work brought me into the middle of an Alice Walker story. I'm just super, super repetitive, and so if I realize there's something important to me, like, *I really need to listen*, one of the ways I give myself what I feel is ample and abundant space is to do it every single day for hundreds of days. And so I didn't realize necessarily until after the fact that, in the case of *Spill*, *Dub*, and *M Archive*, this results in a very performative citational practice that resonates with my values of citing Black theorists, and Black women theorists in particular.

So many Black women theorists are not being cited, when what folks are doing would never be possible without the work

---

[1] At the beginning of her book *Schizophrene*, in a section titled "Passive Notes," Kapil writes, "On the *night* I knew my book *had failed*, I threw it—in the form of a *notebook*, a hand-written final *draft*—into the garden of my *house* in Colorado. Christmas Eve, *2007*. It snowed that *winter* and into the *spring*; before the weather turned truly *warm*, I retrieved my *notes*, and began to write again, from the *fragments*, *the phrases and lines* still legible on the warped, *decayed* but curiously rigid *pages*."

they did. Because of this, there is a reparative accountability that drives my citational practice. *Drive* is a good word because there is something in the work of Black women theorists that I want. I want to be with this work so much that this is the first thing I'm going to do every day. I mean, that was the case with marine mammals.

BLVR: Yes, the marine mammals.

APG: I guess we should talk more about *Undrowned*?

BLVR: I've obviously been following your work, and for the past couple of years I have been really interested in interspecies communication. I've been reading all these interesting studies about attempts to talk to dolphins, and I'm compelled by animal countersurveillance. I came across this hawk moth that basically vibrates its genitalia in order to interrupt the echolocation of a bat. I was excited because I wanted to see how other folks are thinking about our relationship to other species. So there is one point where I stopped, on page 9 of *Undrowned*, when you're talking about your vulnerability and the possibility of projecting onto other species. I want to start here because I'm hype about nonhuman animals and I'm wondering if they are excited about us too.

When we don't share a language with other species, how do we engage in this work of collaboration and consent, or how do we translate what we're hearing or what we think we're hearing?

APG: Yeah, I love that, too, about the countersurveillance. And, as you know, I just really love the opacity and ferocity of animals in the ocean. I love that sea otters will never allow scientists to measure their babies. I love that. I think there is something very important about that, and of course it's something I recognize. I recognize it from living my own survival strategies, and I recognize it in my family and community.

I definitely don't feel like I'm translating across species. When I'm sitting here, so often listening to the whale sounds and the seals and the dolphins breathing, I understand that I'm listening to recordings of them communicating with one another or expressing their own embodied processes. I'm not trying to translate them into English.

However, when you said that we don't have a shared language, what I heard is that I have allowed the several languages I know that are all spoken predominantly by human animals to be dominant in my experience of my own existence.

I think it's true that marine mammals clearly communicate with human animals on purpose and say things like *Stay away*, or, in the experience of a walrus, *I'm about to pop this naval ship*. That's clear communication, in my opinion. It calls out many things I cannot express, and each thing I wrote in that process was an opportunity for me to be close to that articulation.

It's not like I'm translating something marine mammals are saying. I feel myself driven toward the limits of my being on the basic levels of breathing; of fluid, insulation, and fat in my body.

BLVR: As you are speaking, the thing I'm appreciating most about this interview is the upending of these questions, because I think questions start from their own sort of schema. Even in the formation of a question, I'm still prioritizing human speech as the register of communication. I found really helpful the use of gestures and sounds that evade a notion of conventional language, where learning, but not fluency, is prioritized. The goal is not conquest, or comprehension. The goal is not mastery. That's one of the interesting things about the way *Undrowned* unfolds. It's not a taxonomy; it's not a scientific study that gives you specific, final comprehension or understanding. I was starting to count the number of questions you offered. There's a beauty in thinking about what science could be, in creating a scientific text that offers more questions and prompts than it does answers.

I'm curious: Have you been able to read excerpts of *Undrowned* to any marine mammals? I don't know if that's a strange question, but—

APG: I love that question so much because it never would've occurred to me to read it out loud to marine mammals, because of course if I'm near marine mammals, I'm listening. I didn't even think about it as a possibility. Now, I will say there were times when I was close to marine mammals while I was actually writing. I was writing in my journal about harbor seals, and there were harbor seals right there. There were harbor porpoises just playing with us while we were kayaking. I don't know if they could hear our conversation. You know what I'm saying? There are definitely moments like that. What would communicate to me that a marine mammal would want to hear this?

I think that could be possible. It's just that it has not happened. I don't know if you've been following the whale-whispering work of Michaela Harrison.

BLVR: No, but when you mentioned it, I got so excited. I'll be doing some listening tonight.

APG: Yeah, she is phenomenal. She's in a relationship with these humpback whales in the Atlantic, and they are singing together. They're singing old spirituals and creating new songs together. She's in a collaborative process and she's out on the water with underwater microphones and speakers. It's so amazing and I feel so happy she's told me about it and shared aspects of it with me.

III. "NO FISH LOOKS LIKE ITSELF"

BLVR: In *Undrowned* you talk about the dangers of being discovered. You also ask these important questions: "What if my swimming unseen sacrifices the wisdom that would waken within you if you saw? What if I've trained you to ignore the truth about me at your peril and mine?" Later, you reference Eric Stanley, whom I interviewed several years ago, so this is a nice moment of connection.

APG: Oh, I love Eric.

BLVR: Eric Stanley asks us to consider how one can be "known without being hunted."² And, of course, I'm connecting this to Zora Neale Hurston, writing in *Mules and Men* about the "particularly evasive" quality of Black people, and of course [Édouard] Glissant's ideas in *Poetics of Relation*. And I am also thinking about María Iñigo Clavo, who considers "confessional ontology" in the context of colonialism and surveillance. And you also mention this notion of the depth of recognition.

You ask, "What if the thing that I hide could also be something that liberates someone else or helps someone else wake up?" But also, you need to keep yourself safe. So how do we navigate this tension between opacity and transparency? How do we deal with surveillance and safety while also being in community?

APG: Yeah. And even to layer it, I've been studying the sky and looking at the moon, and what I see is just what's visible from a certain angle. I've had scoliosis since I was a child, so my spine is curved, and I've been doing Pilates, which I mention in the book, and I've changed the shape of my spine. But I don't know what it used to look like, and I don't know what it looks like now. My partner tells me, "I can't even find the curve in your spine anymore." I guess they could take a picture, but I'm not witness to all of me. I'm just not, and I think that is part of what community is. We say it, we know it. It's absolutely threaded in the vernacular of who *has your back*.

Part of why Eric's question resonates with me so much is because it reminds me that it's not like it's just a choice of how I'm perceived, when I'm perceived, if I'm perceived, and what somebody else perceives about me. It's actually not. Eric is talking about it very specifically in the sense of the precarity of trans folks who are being harmed by people who think they perceive something. I think the question has a liberation energy behind it—all of Eric's questions do. I feel like part of what Eric is liberating all of us from, but obviously centering on the community of accountability, is that we cannot always be in the practice of trying to be recognizable or unrecognizable, because, as Toni Morrison says, "Invisible to whom?"³

Recognition doesn't happen once, and it doesn't happen for all types of situations. I don't even recognize half of my own body. It's not agential in a simple way. It's so complicated, and it's always, always, always changing. I was talking to the poet Kathryn Nuernberger, and she was telling me about her husband, who identifies fish in a lake to try to measure the impact of pollution. He said, "No fish looks like itself." Right. They're working with a taxonomy and guidebooks that say, *This is what this fish looks like, so if you see it, it's called this*. But when you actually look at the fish in the lake, they don't look like that. How they are is not lining up with the taxonomy that's been created to recognize, interpret, catalog, and count them. So we don't even know what we're recognizing or *not* recognizing.

There is a lot there, which is why I love that question. Even if we weren't talking about—which we are—a pervasive

---

² In a 2017 essay for the *South Atlantic Quarterly*, scholar, author, and UC Berkeley professor Eric Stanley engages notions of trans representation and recognition and Stanley's own development of the idea of "trans opacity" amid ongoing anti-trans and anti-Black violence. "At the center of the problem of recognition lies this," they write: "how can we be seen without being known and how can we be known without being hunted?"

³ In several interviews, Toni Morrison questioned the mode of address for some Black writers, whose work, in her view, seemed written for the white gaze. She told one interviewer, "In this country, [in] many books, particularly then—'40s, '50s—you could feel the address of the narrator over my shoulder, talking to somebody else. Talking to somebody white. I could tell because they were explaining things that they didn't have to explain if they were talking to me." In a 2003 *New Yorker* profile, she said, "The title of Ralph Ellison's book was 'Invisible Man.' And the question for me was 'Invisible to whom?' Not to me."

comprehensive surveillance structure, where it's very possible that what we're talking about in this conversation is being algorithmized into Google results and ads that I'm going to see in the future, it's already the case that recognition is a myth that's useful until it's not.

I don't have control of whether or not people are going to recognize that I'm in the lineage of Hortense Spillers, M. Jacqui Alexander, Sylvia Wynter, Akasha Gloria Hull, Barbara Smith. I don't have control over whether people recognize that, but I repeat it so much that hopefully it becomes impossible not to recognize it in the context of that opacity.

IV. "A SCALE OF CARE"

BLVR: Before we leave each other, I wanted to talk about your definition of "school" as a "scale of care."

APG: That is what I feel like dolphins are teaching me. There are so many different ways [that their social patterns] are described by the people who research them, but do we know? We don't know. Animals are traveling all over the whole ocean and very effectively evading researchers. So we don't really know, but what I realize is that the same arbitrariness has shaped how we organize, what our institutions are, how we think about what it is to learn, and how to be alive and learn together. So even though, obviously, it wasn't fish who said, *Let's call it school*, there was some kind of resonance in the adaptation and the invention of that terminology that used *school* to describe groups of animals that are swimming together. I'm still learning from that poetic space. What is the point of learning? The point of learning is that we can take care of one another better, right? What else is there to learn?

Intelligence is not contextual until it's intelligible. Why did I learn critical thinking? What has been the relevance in researching and reading things over and over again and thinking as creatively as I can? I realized at a certain point, Oh, this is me trying to learn how to be a daughter to my mother. That's been my central research project. It's not the only one, but it's all relational in that way. How do I daughter these Black women theorists whose work generates my living consciousness? How do I hold space for all my communities of accountability? I'm using your word *drive* again. That's the drive. Why be creative? Why think critically? Because it matters how I care for you. That matters to me, and that is the point of it. I realized very early on, as a tokenized Black girl in prestigious white schools on scholarship, that other people thinking you're smart can only do so much, and there's also a lot it can't do. It doesn't stop people from being racist. I learned that a long time ago.

BLVR: Yes.

APG: A lot of people have learned that and are learning it right now. Some people think about the benefits of learning in a capitalist way. Some people, if you really ask them why they're in school, they say it's because they want to take care of their parents one day. That matters to them. A lot of what they're doing, even what they're majoring in, doesn't matter to them. Now, the fact that they think it's going to give them access to resources that will allow them to provide care in these very capitalist ways and also within the structure of a heteronormative family—that's there. That's a narrative that's written over it, but what we understand is that at the root of it is actually a desire to care and be cared for in a context where it seems like that's the only way to have that happen.

I'm trying to say that the structure of how we care for one another is something we're still learning. It's arbitrary, the ways that we've understood it. It's infinitely possible. We're learning ways that are generative to us. There are fish whose bellies light up; what are the ways we light up? What are the structures that allow us to learn that? You've written about this: it's hard to separate learning and care, but we can do it.

It's so interesting that what we've named educational structures really marginalize.

BLVR: What you're saying is making me shiver a little bit because I am thinking about this particular moment when lots of young people across the country and the world are being asked to log in online to receive schooling. Kids who don't want to log in don't hate school; they just can't receive the type of care they receive in person. I'm praying that this is a moment when we actually understand that care is a part of schooling.

APG: Yes.

BLVR: I hope this is a moment when we actually think about what it means to remove all the uncaring structures of a school day. When you walk into a building and the first person that encounters you is a police officer or a safety security guard, that is not a caring entry into the building. And if the first question is "Did you do your homework?" and not "How are you? Did you have breakfast?," that is an uncaring moment.

APG: To have a conversation with you is such a gift. I want to be having conversations where I feel cared for, and I feel safe enough to learn something, and you [make me feel that way]. I love it, and please know I appreciate it. Just know I have time to talk to you, because this is what time is for. ✶

THE ACT OF SMELLING: CANNON FIRE
BY JUDE STEWART

GUNPOWDER RECIPES HAVE changed over time, but its bouquet has remained consistent: eggy, sulfuric black powder as the base note. A tang of urine from saltpeter. The particulate density of charcoal.

Another way to say it is that cannon fire smells kinetic. It fills the empty air with mass, boom, taste, and grit. It roils and churns the air, remixing its smells. If a street scene pixelated into rubble before your eyes, it would look as unreal as a movie. But the smells and dust clogging your nostrils would be undeniably real.

Illness isn't usually considered among the ills humans have fought with cannons. But cannon fire was once employed to ward off the plague. According to miasma theory, prevalent until 1880,[1] disease was caused by bad smells. Miasmas leaked from garbage heaps, privies, hospitals, and poorhouses, and also from cemeteries, swamps, caves, even cracks in dirt sidewalks. Some miasmas killed outright; others could be neutralized with aeration and by maintaining one's personal odor balance. Bathing was cautioned against: better to keep your skin's pores plugged against disease.

The prevalent strategies for fighting miasmas were wrong-headed in a way that only debunked science can be. Annick Le Guérer's book *Scent: The Mysterious and Essential Powers of Smell* traces their false logic. Some scientific factions favored counteracting miasmas with pleasant smells like scent boxes, cigars, lozenges, and syrups; a wealthy person could carry a tiny, fragrant citrus tree or wear a perfumed sachet near the heart. One sixteenth-century text advises physicians to approach patients armed with a juniper branch and a pomander ball. (One reason for the advent of the stethoscope was that it enabled the examination of a patient at a distance.)

Other factions fought miasmic smells with even worse smells. Jean de Lampérière, in a 1622 text, suggested a protective body rub of dried peacock dung and goat urine. There may have been some merit to this strategy, however—the smell of goats (and cattle, sheep, and camels) does in fact repel the fleas and ticks that transmit the bubonic plague.

Enter the cannon. In seventeenth-century France, professional perfumers carried out plague fumigations, decontaminating households after victims were carted off. Perfumers lit bonfires in front of the victim's house, shut all windows, and then set to work indoors. They burned perfumes in pans, gutted straw mattresses, put dirty linens in hot ovens to cook the bad odors out of them, and so on. The checklist was vigorous, extensive, and always smelly. Meticulous perfumers capped off their work by firing cannons in the streets to "dispel the infection that may linger in the woodwork or on the outer walls of buildings," according to one contemporary report. (Of course, the cannon firing caused its own problems, rupturing building foundations, breaking windows, and attracting looters.)

The fight against nasty odors often does more than eliminate them. The battle against miasmas—and noxious urban smells, in the era of germ theory—shaped the urban landscape. Invisible smells produced real and visible effects. Decisive moments of reek spurred swift reforms. In the summer of 1858, London suffered a heat wave that left the Thames running low and revealed that the river, from which the city drew its drinking water, was basically an open sewer. For six weeks, later termed the Great Stink of London, the city was suffused with the revealed stench of excrement. One self-styled "Sufferer in Thames Street" described the smells emanating from the waterfront as "a thick, warm steam, surcharged with odours from every imaginable abomination penetrating into the apartment, and into you." With blinding speed, Parliament greenlit a public works project that had previously been stuck in committee, creating a massive system of sewers, pumping stations, and water treatment plants. Similarly, Paris suffered its own Great Stink in 1880, resulting in similarly rapid and far-reaching urban planning reforms. To fight the smells, lawmakers on both sides of the English Channel paved sidewalks and whitewashed walls, engineered sewer systems, established health boards and zoning ordinances, introduced environmental reforms, widened streets, and planted public gardens to serve as "urban lungs."[2] Disgusting odors are nothing if not intensely motivating.

As a smell, cannon fire has a long and surprisingly varied backstory. It's the smell that used to waft over scenes of warfare and of plague. It has signified both destruction and protection. And now, in the modern era, you smell cannon fire almost nowhere at all, a poignant end for such a potent scent. ✶

---

[1] Miasma theory dates as far back as Seneca.

[2] Melanie A. Kiechle wrote an entire book about this topic called *Smell Detectives: An Olfactory History of Nineteenth-Century Urban America.*

THREE IMPORTANT LESSONS FROM *THE BELIEVER*

HOW TO GET RID OF YOUR USED CDS
(ISSUE ONE-HUNDRED FOURTEEN)

It's not all bad news.

HOW TO TALK TO BEARS
(ISSUE ONE-HUNDRED EIGHTEEN)

Bears eat flowers.

HOW TO SUPPORT THE BELIEVER
(RIGHT NOW)

STEP ONE
VISIT BELIEVERMAG.COM/SUPPORT.

STEP TWO
MAKE YOUR DONATION.

STEP THREE
WAIT FOR A WAVE OF PROFOUND THANKS TO REACH YOU, SENT FROM THE GRATEFUL PUBLISHERS, EDITORS, AND WRITERS WHOSE WORK YOU HELP MAKE POSSIBLE.

This magazine exists thanks to contributions from its readers.

SPECIAL THANKS
TO THESE SUPPORTERS OF *THE BELIEVER* AND THE BLACK MOUNTAIN INSTITUTE

BELIEVERMAG.COM/SUPPORT

Thank you

Scott Able, Michael Adams, Gail Anastasion, Peter Anderson, Phil & Leigh Aurbach, Maria Bakali, Frank Barbiere, Marguerite Barnett, Katherina Bateman, Stephen Bates, Jon Robin Baitz, John Bedecarre, Christine Meleo Bernstein, Nicholas Beyer, Dawn Biernacki, David Billotti, Elena Bird, Marika Birkby, Benjamin Bishop, Douglas Blandy, Rachel Blythe, Dylan Bontrager, Anita Bratton, Joe Brown, Michael Bryant, Brittany Burridge, Melissa Rachleff Burtt, Amanda Cadogan, Janet Calderwood, Joseph Cannon, Padmasini Chakravarthy, Hallie Chen, Roy Christopher, Lori Church, Daniel Coble, Hugh Collins, Hayley Cummings, Mk Czerwiec, Rahn Dagostino, Sarah Davis, Gemma De Choisy, Trey Delap, John Delap, Marlitt Dellabough, Saul Delmore, Keith Donohue, Christopher Drake, Toby Drake, Emily Dreyfuss, Hannah Duggan, Olivia Durif, Erin Dustin, Bryan Dziedziak, Thomas Easterson-Bond, Julie Ellison, Dina Emerson, Jay Endejan, Tara Engler, Scott Faingold, Daryl Fefee, Mac Freepo, Steven Friedman, Stephen Fuller, Joanna Fusco, Tom Gallagher, Mala Gaonkar, Gabriel Garcia, Juliet Gelfman-Randazzo, Carmen Gilbert, Justin Gilder, Kristina Gomez, Chris Gonya, Marina Gonzalez, Patrick Grantz, Robin Greenspun, Gretchen Grierson, Rachel Eliza Griffiths, Susan Haas, Brianna Haggard, Ann Hamilton, Jeanne Hamrick, Jonathan Hatch, Karen Harbour, David Hardin, Diana Hardy, Forsyth Harmon, Heather Harmon, David Hart, Philip Hart, Carol Harter, Lauren Haun, Emily Haynes, Dorothy Hearn, Christian Henning, Lisa Herrera, Rachelle Hill, Mike Hodgkinson, Mike Holm, Madeline Howard, Barbara Jeffress, Alec Kamra, Samantha Keller, China Kent, Jonathan Kiefer, Ioulia Kolovou, Milo Kostelecky, Jonathan Kriz, Leyla Kursat, Wendy Kveck, Mathilde Labat, Catherine Lambert, Grace Lambert, Gillian Larson, Christopher Lay, Oriana Leckert, Phoebe Lee, Rich Levy, Emily Lindsey, Joan Lucius, Howe Lye-Starks, James MacDonald, Ivory Madison, Julie Maloney, Colette Marie, Edward Mafoud, Teresa Mahoney, Sienna Malik, Joseph Marcincuk, Rebecca Margulies, Rebecca Martinez, Sheila McCormick, Matthew McCullough, David McDevitt, Sean McGoey, Jon McGregor, Colleen Mcguire, Rose McMahill, Buck McWilliams, Rosalie Miletich, Victoria Millard, Michael Miller, Tammy Miller, Jaina Mōan, Concepción Moreno, Robert Mosby, Maria Newman, William Nichols, Maggie Norcross-Devin, Ron Nurwisah, John Oliver, Katie O'Neill, Stephanie Orozco, Debbra Palmer, David Palmquist, Eileen Parks, Emma Pattison, Scott Paxton, David Pepe, Alison Pereto, Adam & Janeane Perry, Brendan Peterson, Eric Peterson, Jennifer Pietrzak, Christine Pirrone, Tim Porcelli, Luke Pyzik, Roberto Quesada, Mark & Pat Radtke, Ferose Rasheed, Christine Ratto, Channing Redford, Cindy Reid, Derrick Reider, Milo Riggs, Forrest Rike, Simon Robertson, Charlotte Robinson, Beverly Rogers, Xavier Romo, Sarah Rupard, Jo Russ, Rocco Russo, Amanda Rzicznek, Sequential Artists Workshop, Julie Sabey, Sonja Saltman, Jillian Sandell, Gemma Clarke Sands, Julie Schmidt, Brad Schnurr, Miriam Shearing, Seana Shiffrin, Meghan Sitar, Jack Smiles, Audrey Smith, Matthew Smith, Trouper Snow, Claire Sokolich, Arnault Souques, Brandi Spaethe, Lorna Spencer, Christina Stark, Laurie Stone, Melissa Strilecki, Patrick Sutton, Linda Tibbits, Chelsea Tiffany, Mary Ting, Kristy Totten, Francesca Varagnolo, Anthony Vick, Joy Vincent Villanueva, Elizabeth Wallman, Adam Warner, Jared Weigley, Darren Weller, Jon B. Wellinghoff, Jacqueline Welsh, Joanna Wendel, Kevin Westell, James Wetzel, Madison Whatley, J S White, Chloe Wieland, Diane Wiener, Janice Williams, Stacy Willis, Annie Winerip, Craig Winslow, Philip Wolf, Teresa Wong, Michael Woo, Courtney Wright, Lincoln Wright, Jane Yates, Jennifer Young, Ivan Zinn

CONTRIBUTORS

Jon Aye is an illustrator, cartoonist, and educator based in the UK. He has contributed illustrations and comics to a number of anthologies and magazines and has self-published several comics and zines.

Soni Brown is a Jamaican writer based in Las Vegas. She is currently writing essays about the Black immigrant experience while her polydactyl cat, Priscilla Purrsley, sleeps on her lap.

Jennifer Chang is the author of *The History of Anonymity* and *Some Say the Lark*, which won the 2018 William Carlos Williams Award. She cochairs the advisory board of Kundiman, teaches at George Washington University, and lives in Washington, DC.

Anelise Chen is working on a book about clams. She teaches writing at Columbia University.

Franny Choi's most recent book, *Soft Science* (Alice James Books), won the Elgin Award for Science Fiction Poetry. She teaches at Williams College and is currently at work on an essay collection about race, feminism, and robots.

Carolyn Forché is an American poet, translator, and memoirist. Her books of poetry are *Blue Hour*, *The Angel of History*, *The Country between Us*, *Gathering the Tribes*, and *In the Lateness of the World*. Her memoir, *What You Have Heard Is True*, was published by Penguin Press in 2019. In 2013, Forché received the Academy of American Poets Fellowship, given for distinguished poetic achievement. In 2017, she became one of the first two poets to receive the Windham-Campbell Prize. She is a University Professor at Georgetown University. She lives in Maryland with her husband, photographer Harry Mattison.

Ricardo Frasso Jaramillo is a writer of nonfiction and poetry from Philadelphia. His work has been published in *The New York Times*, *The Rumpus*, *Salon*, and other places. He is a 2021 Periplus Fellow and a former Fulbright Fellow at la Universidad Nacional Autónoma de México. He currently works in the wellness center of a public high school for immigrant youth in Oakland, California.

Elizabeth Greenspan is a writer based in Philadelphia. She writes mostly about cities, politics, and design. Her work has appeared in *The New Yorker*, *Architect*, *Bloomberg Businessweek*, *The New Republic*, and *Places Journal*, among other publications. She teaches urban studies and creative writing at the University of Pennsylvania and is the author of *Battle for Ground Zero: Inside the Political Struggle to Rebuild the World Trade Center*.

Sophie Haigney writes about books, visual art, and technology for publications including *The New York Times Magazine*, *The New Yorker*, and *The Baffler*.

Micha Huigen is an illustrator from the Netherlands with an immersive style and a recognizable use of color. His illustrations are composed to make the viewer feel as if they could wander around in them and discover things hidden in corners and crevices. He makes personal as well as commissioned works, including editorial illustrations and designs for album covers, gig posters, and T-shirts.

Kameelah Janan Rasheed is a learner from East Palo Alto, California, currently based in Brooklyn, New York. Her art has been exhibited nationally and internationally. She is the author of two artist's books: *An Alphabetical Accumulation of Approximate Observations* (Endless Editions, 2019) and *No New Theories* (Printed Matter, 2019). She is a 2021 Guggenheim Fellow in Fine Arts.

Stephen Kearse is a reporter, critic, and author.

Keith Leonard is the author of the poetry collection *Ramshackle Ode* (Houghton Mifflin Harcourt, 2016). He lives in Columbus, Ohio.

Xavier Lissillour is a freelance illustrator from France who studied fine arts and applied arts. He works primarily for newspapers such as *Le Monde*, *Le Temps*, and *Libération*.

Melissa Locker is a writer and music podcast impresario in the making. She lives on the internet and runs on coffee. You can follow her at @woolyknickers but not in real life.

CONTRIBUTORS

Kathy MacLeod is a cartoonist and illustrator based in Berlin. She is currently working on her first graphic novel.

Jordan Taliha McDonald is an essayist, critic, cultural worker, and (sometimes) poet from Seat Pleasant, Maryland. Her work has appeared in *Vulture*, *The Offing*, *Artsy*, *Africa Is a Country*, *Blacks Rule*, *Hayden's Ferry Review*, and other publications. She is a graduate student in Black literature, among other things, at Harvard University. She allegedly holds a certificate in "pen game, writing, and form" from the Onika Maraj School of Barb Studies.

John Menick is a writer and artist living in New York City.

Shruti Ravindran is a writer and producer presently based in Brooklyn, New York.

Jude Stewart has written about culture for *The Atlantic*, *Slate*, *Cabinet*, *Design Observer*, *Gastronomica*, and *The Art of Eating*, among other publications. She is the author of: *ROY G. BIV: An Exceedingly Surprising Book about Color* and *Patternalia: An Unconventional History of Polka Dots, Stripes, Plaid, Camouflage, and Other Graphic Patterns*. Her latest book, *Revelations in Air: A Guidebook to Smell*, from which the microessays in this issue were adapted, will be published by Penguin Books in October 2021.

Fernando Valverde has been voted the most relevant Spanish-language poet born since 1970 by a group of two hundred representatives from universities around the world. His books have been translated into several languages and published in Europe and the United States. He has received some of the most significant awards for Spanish-language poetry, among them the Federico García Lorca Award, the Emilio Alarcos Poetry Prize, and the Antonio Machado International Literature Prize. He was nominated for a Latin Grammy in 2014 for his collaboration on a work of fusion between poetry and flamenco. He is a distinguished visiting professor at the University of Virginia.

Teresa Wong is author of the graphic memoir *Dear Scarlet: The Story of My Postpartum Depression*. Her comics have appeared in *The Rumpus* and *Event*. She is the 2021–22 Canadian Writer-in-Residence at the University of Calgary.

Jesse Zhang is an illustrator born, raised, and still happily living in Brooklyn, New York. She creates in a tiny studio with her cat, Margot. She works in watercolor, inks, and digitally. Her work often features surreal figures and landscapes with touches of mystery and whimsy.

OUR NEXT ISSUE IS ABOUT ATTENTION

Don't miss our special themed issue, out this December, and featuring, among other things:

HAFIZAH GETER ON GASLIGHTING

ROSS SIMONINI ON GENERALISM

LAUREN MICHELE JACKSON ON RHETORICAL DEFLECTION

Plus interviews with:

BLACK THOUGHT

SHANNON FINNEGAN and BOJANA COKLYAT

PERCIVAL EVERETT

MATTHEW JEON

And new comics from GINA WYNBRANDT and AMY KURZWEIL

---

500 MG OF EXTRA-STRENGTH NONFICTION

THE BELIEVER IS A NONPROFIT MAGAZINE PUBLISHED BY THE BEVERLY ROGERS, CAROL C. HARTER BLACK MOUNTAIN INSTITUTE AT THE UNIVERSITY OF NEVADA, LAS VEGAS. BMI BRINGS WRITERS AND THE LITERARY IMAGINATION INTO THE HEART OF PUBLIC LIFE THROUGH LIVE EXPERIENCES, FELLOWSHIPS, AND INNOVATIVE MEDIA. HEARTFELT THANKS TO ALL THE FRIENDS, BOARD MEMBERS, AND DONORS WHOSE TALENTS, GENEROSITY, AND SUPPORT MAKE OUR WORK POSSIBLE. THIS PROJECT IS SUPPORTED IN PART BY THE NATIONAL ENDOWMENT FOR THE ARTS. FIND BMI ONLINE TO LEARN HOW YOU CAN LEND YOUR SUPPORT TO WRITERS, EDITORS, AND READERS EVERYWHERE.